WHO DO I THINK I AM?

In Memory of

James White (1913–2003)
Director of the National Gallery of Ireland, 1964–80

&

Terence de Vere White (1912–94)
A Governor & Guardian of the National Gallery of
Ireland, 1955–90

WHO DO I THINK I AM?

A Memoir

HOMAN POTTERTON

MERRION
PRESS

First published in 2017 by
Merrion Press
10 George's Street
Newbridge
Co. Kildare
Ireland
www.merrionpress.ie

© 2017, Homan Potterton

9781785371509 (Cloth)
9781785371479 (Kindle)
9781785371486 (Epub)
9781785371493 (PDF)

British Library Cataloguing in Publication Data
An entry can be found on request

Library of Congress Cataloging in Publication Data
An entry can be found on request

Design by Sin É Design
Typeset in Minion 11.5pt

Jacket front: Andrew Festing (b. 1941), *Portrait of Homan Potterton in the director's office of the National Gallery of Ireland*, 1986. Exhibited at the Royal Society of Portrait Painters, London, 1987. Oil on canvas, 90 x 110 cm. (Author's Collection, © The Artist, 1986. Photo: Roy Hewson.)

Jacket back: Thomas Ryan, PRHA (b. 1929), cartoon: *Farewell, or The Going of Homan: a Tragedy*. Signed and dated: 'Thomas Ryan 9 June 1988'. The Governors and Guardians of the National Gallery lament the departure of their Director. The one female member of the Board is Ann Reihill. (Author's Collection.)

Contents

Prologue

'The National Gallery Restaurant' by Paul Durcan

One of the snags about the National Gallery Restaurant
Is that in order to gain access to it
One has to pass through the National Gallery.
I don't mind saying that at half past twelve in the day,
In my handmade pigskin brogues and my pinstripe double-vent,
I don't feel like being looked at by persons in pictures
Or, worse, having to wax eloquent to a client's wife
About why it is that St Joseph is a black man
In Poussin's picture of 'the Holy Family':
The historical fact is that St Joseph was a white man.
I'd prefer to converse about her BMW – or my BMW –
Or the pros and cons of open-plan in office-block architecture.
I clench the handle of my briefcase
Wishing to Jesus Christ that I could strangle Homan Potterton–
The new young dynamic whizz-kid Director.
Oh but he's a flash in the pan –
Otherwise he'd have the savvy to close the National Gallery
When the National Gallery Restaurant is open.
Who does Homan Potterton think he is – Homan Potterton?

From *The Berlin Wall Cafe* by Paul Durcan published by Harvill
Press. Reproduced by permission of The Random House Group Ltd.
©1995.

The poet Paul Durcan published this poem first in *Image* magazine and when I read it (having, to my shame, never heard of Paul) I was not very impressed. I was engaged at the time in trying to close, not the National Gallery, but the National Gallery restaurant. It, and its menus, dated from 1968 and very few of the people who lunched there – arriving in their BMWs and discussing office-block architecture – had the slightest interest in Poussin or indeed any other artist represented in the gallery. As to why St Joseph is a black man in Poussin's *Holy Family*, I had had very little time to consider such iconographical complexities since becoming director of the gallery a year or so previously.

But I was new, and I was young, and I am flattered that Paul described me as a 'dynamic whizz-kid'. But was I a 'flash in the pan'?

Yes, I am afraid I was. Paul was right. Many people thought it unseemly when I resigned after only eight years in office.

Mine was not the shortest-lived directorship: several of my predecessors – Hugh Lane among them[1]– served for an even shorter period. But, appointed in December 1979 at the age of thirty-three, I was the youngest.

The road I had taken from a childhood in County Meath and schooldays in Kilkenny and Dublin to the director's office in Merrion Square had, in retrospect, been quite straightforward and what one might expect of any museum director: I studied art history at university and then studied more of it at another university, got a job in a museum or two, published some art-historical articles and books, and before I knew it, I was a director.

I did, however, make a few detours and stops as I travelled – quite unintentionally, at some speed – along this route. Some people engaged my attention; particular events caused me to linger; certain places appealed to me more than others. It was those detours and stops – rather than my progress – which rendered my journey enjoyable and (to me) memorable.

As to what I found when I reached my destination, much of that was enjoyable – and certainly memorable – too, although some of it was not. But I had arrived far too soon; my journey had been too short.

And that, I think, was what made me just 'a flash in the pan'.
As to who I thought I was, the following pages may tell.

Endnotes

1. Lane was appointed in March 1914 and drowned from the Lusitania fourteen months
    later on 7 May 1915.

CHAPTER 1

'WHERE THERE'S GRASS, THERE'S NO BRAINS'

When I was at Mountjoy School in Dublin, I once did a most dreadful thing.

In applying for Trinity College, it was required to include with the application a confidential reference as to one's character and abilities. This was sealed in an envelope by the referee and sent in to the college by the candidate, together with the application form. My reference, as was normal, was supplied by the headmaster of Mountjoy, William Tate. Before sending it in, I opened it and read what he had written. This was not only disreputable of me but also a very big mistake. Mr Tate wrote, among other comments, 'He has a colourless personality and he is unlikely to contribute anything to the university.' The assessment came as something of a blow (and I have never forgotten it) and, since that time, I have never, ever read any document or letter that was specifically not intended for my eyes.

Mountjoy School (now Mount Temple Comprehensive) was, by the time I got there as a boarder in 1961, no longer in its heyday. Originally in Mountjoy Square, the school had moved to the Malahide Road in about 1950, when it acquired a large red-brick Gothicky mansion (designed by the Belfast architects Lanyon, Lynn & Lanyon in 1863) with acres of grounds that stretched down almost to the Clontarf seafront. A functional wing had been tacked on to the original building to accommodate the school. Mr Tate, who had been a fine headmaster in his time, was by 1961 old and near retirement, and he had long since given up on imposing any order or ethos on the school and the hundred-and-fifty or so boys who went there, among them a large contingent of day boys. Games were not compulsory (as they had been

in my previous school, Kilkenny College), and there were practically
no extra-curricular programmes, no music or other cultural activities,
no choir, no dramatics, possibly no library: I don't think that there was
even a Scout troop. There was a lax approach to exeats – so that
permission to go into Dublin for an afternoon was easily obtained –
and little or no emphasis on aspiration or achievement. Only one of the
masters made a positive impression on me. This was T.J. McElligott[1]
who taught French. Unfortunately, I did not make a positive impression
on him. In spite of that, when I was appointed director of the National
Gallery of Ireland in Dublin he wrote to me (31 December 1979):

> It was in 1963 or 1964 that one of my pupils sent me a card
> from Florence whither he had gone to see the treasures of
> that city. And, even though I did not see the pupil in the
> intervening years, I had followed his progress. This is
> simply to say how very glad I am that you have been
> selected for what will be a wonderfully satisfying position
> in which you can fulfil your own ambition in the service
> of the country.

The only master I did seem to impress, but for the wrong reasons, was
the teacher of Irish. This was a weird (to me) *Gaeilgeoir* called 'Puck'
Franklin, who was given to telling smutty jokes in class at which he
sniggered riotously himself, but which we found simply embarrassing.
When I would fail to answer correctly some question he would have
put to me *as Gaeilge*, he would in his nasal voice, and with a sneer, say
to the class in English: 'Eh! Where there's grass, there's no brains.' He
would then repeat it in Irish as (evidently) it is a known Irish expression.

As to my 'colourless personality', I think – in retrospect and on
reflection – I would have to take issue with Mr Tate. Among my
possessions, I have recently come across a small silver medal inscribed
M.S.D. Deb. Soc. 1963: no name. It meant nothing to me until I ran into
a boy who had also been at the school; he said he remembered me
taking to the stage in the vast (and crowded) Metropolitan Hall in
Abbey Street representing Mountjoy at a huge inter-schools debate, and
how he had been staggered that I had had such confidence. Then I
recalled that I did debate at Mountjoy. This memory led me to

remember giving a talk at Mountjoy (illustrated with musical excerpts on a record player) about Gilbert and Sullivan: I think I was trying to set up a music-appreciation group. I took up the study of the piano again (although very few boys learned music at Mountjoy) and, as I have the *Studies & Pieces* (dated 1962) for the Grade V Royal Irish Academy of Music examination, I must have reached that level and been able to play, among other pieces, the Presto from Haydn's *Sonata in D*. It has, for some reason, stuck in my memory that, one day when I was practising (the piano was in a small room next to the Tates' private quarters), Mrs Tate came in and, smiling, said to me, 'Ah! ... Brahms.'

In the summer holidays between my two years at Mountjoy, I organised myself to spend three months with a family in France (this was quite unusual at the time) and, on my return to school, I set up, with my friend Malcolm Benson (who had also spent time in France), a *cercle français*. We were the only two members, but we did contribute humorous 'Notes' (in French) to the school magazine. Occasionally, dances were held in the school. Invitations were printed and we would send these out to any girls we knew (or would like to know) in other schools. The Alexandra College and Hillcourt girls were often too snobby to accept, but Bertrand & Rutland dames (as we called them) were known to be very game, and they would come in droves. One school dance coincided with the making in Ireland of the film *Of Human Bondage* with Laurence Harvey and Kim Novak. I sent Kim Novak – 'c/o Ardmore Studios' – an invitation to the Mountjoy dance (with a covering note saying it was from me). She replied with a charming handwritten letter to say how much she would have liked to come to the dance with me but, unfortunately, could not do so on account of her filming schedule.

There was a boy called Nick Robinson in my class and he and I were friends. He was very brainy – much brainier than me – as well as being artistic (he was always drawing clever little sketches of people). He seemed more sophisticated than the rest of us (he had been to restaurants with his father) and he had an irreverent sense of humour that I found appealing. Rather as an affectation, he took the *Guardian* (and had it delivered) every day in order to do the crossword: this was all the more provocative as his father was at the time (I am fairly sure) on the board, if not the actual chairman, of *The Irish Times*. Nick once came up with the idea of writing a hoax letter to the *Guardian* – which they published. In it he wrote that he had recently spotted a rare bird – 'a black-backed ammeter' – in Ireland and 'he wondered if it could have been blown there, together with atomic fall-out, on winds from the South Atlantic, its usual nesting place'. We were studying physics at the time. An ammeter is an instrument for measuring electric current in amperes: although generally black, it is not a bird.

A few days later, there was published a letter in response. The correspondent, from somewhere in England – and obviously a meteorologist of sorts – pointed out that the prevailing winds at the time could not have blown either atomic fall-out or an ammeter to Ireland.

This was too hilarious for us to let it drop, and so I took up my pen. I wrote to the paper to say that 'although I had never seen a black-backed ammeter in Ireland, I had once between the wars' (in other words, before I was born) 'observed in the Yeats Country of Sligo a broad white-backed ammeter'. This letter was also published.

I think I might have been secretary of the Debating Society and Nick may have been chairman. I have come across a memorandum from him (written on the writing-paper of the Hotel Taft, New York) proposing topics for debates. 'Has the emancipation of women justified itself in practice?' and 'Is modern feminine fashion a thing of beauty?' As Mountjoy was an all-boys school, these were certainly novel proposals. But Nick may have thought of them for a debate with the girls from Alexandra College whom I once invited to a debate at Mountjoy: their secretary was Margaret Furlong and meeting her in this way at this time led to a lifelong friendship.

On leaving Mountjoy, Nick and I both became solicitors' apprentices in the same Dublin firm, Matheson, Ormsby and Prentice. As it turned out, I never progressed very far along the road to becoming a solicitor but Nick, while reading for an honours degree in Legal Science at Trinity College Dublin, stayed the course.

Endnotes

1. Apart from being a teacher, he wrote about education in Ireland in *The Irish Times* and elsewhere. Author of *Secondary Education in Ireland, 1870–1921* (1981).

CHAPTER 2
ESCAPE

I do not know where I got the idea, when I was at Mountjoy, that I would go to France for the summer. My father had died two years previously, when I was fourteen, and life at home was no longer the same for me and I wanted to take flight (which my father would never have allowed). I could only go to France if I could find a family who would host me. Some Irish Catholic schools had links (mainly through the religious orders) with schools abroad and, in that way, pupil exchanges could be arranged, but Protestant schools – and certainly not Mountjoy – had none of those contacts. Some girls went as au pairs to foreign families (although this was still fairly novel at the time) but boys did not have that option, as child minding was the principal requirement and, at that time, boys did not do that. I got the name (probably from the French embassy) of some exchange agency and, sifting through the many opportunities advertised, came up with a fairly short list of families who would accept a boy without wanting to send a French boy back in return. I wrote off, in my best French, to several and eventually arranged to go to a family with seven children under the age of thirteen who lived and farmed in the region known as Beauce, between Paris and Orleans. I had in previous years been to summer camps in Scotland and Wales but had never been to London or indeed anywhere else, nor had I ever travelled alone (except on the train from Dublin to Kilkenny). Nevertheless, I took the mailboat to Holyhead, the overnight train (without a 'couchette') to Euston, the Tube to Victoria, a train to Newhaven, the ferry to Dieppe, and a final train to St Lazare in Paris: a twenty-four-hour journey. Monsieur Chassine met me there with his car, whisked me up and down the Champs Elysées and then the journey of an hour or more to 'Semonville, par Janville, Eure et Loir'. I was fairly exhausted when I arrived, and all the more so as I found that – in spite of Mr McElligott's teaching – I could neither speak nor understand a word of French. A meal was produced which I could not eat – the peas, in the French way, were floating in water and the lettuce was covered in oil – and then to bed.

I had not arrived at a château. Nor, indeed, had I even arrived at a house. There was none. There was a large square yard encircled by old stone farm buildings, one group of which – all at ground level – had been made into a dwelling. It was temporary, as Monsieur Chassine was later to explain: he had plans for building a house in an area to the back, which had already been arranged as a garden. My bedroom was just a corner of the large room where the two older boys slept: it had been screened off with a wardrobe and other furniture.

The farm, which was large, was entirely arable, as is Beauce in its entirety. There was not an animal in sight. Nor were there any hedges, just flat acres of wheat, barley and maize as far as the eye could see. County Meath it was not. It had been Madame Chassine's childhood home. Monsieur Chassine, as I was to notice over the summer, was a very efficient farmer with a keen interest in being up to date, and his ambition in marrying Madame Chassine was matched by his ambition in all other aspects of his existence as well. It was that ambition which had brought me into their lives.

Although the children were all very young, Monsieur Chassine thought that they should be exposed to different worlds and experiences. As a means of achieving this, he came up with the idea of having a foreigner come and live with them. Madame Chassine (as I was to discover much later) was opposed to this and only eventually agreed, on condition that 'the foreigner' would not be a girl. A door, thereby, was opened for me. I suffered a bout of homesickness after about ten days – it was all so very unfamiliar – but I soon got over that. There were no plans as to what I was expected to do except, in a general way, to keep an eye on the children. (I was neither paying nor being paid for my stay.) Every afternoon, I cycled with four or five of the older ones to the public swimming pool two miles away in Janville. There the children were safe, as there was a lifeguard on duty, but in the case of any minor mishaps or fallings-out, I would intervene and attempt to make things better. In the mornings, I might dead-head the geraniums or the roses, prune the vines in the garden (having been shown how to do so), feed the rabbits which were kept in a hutch in the yard, pick the vegetables and the fruit (Madame Chassine preserved both), collect the eggs and do other simple chores, but I never had any sense that I was being made to work, because I was not. Soon, on my own initiative, I might help in the house as well – setting and clearing the table, perhaps hanging out the washing or emptying the dishwasher, a novelty in itself as I had never seen one before. As the youngest of eight myself, used to helping out and mucking in at home, none of this was any bother to me, and I enjoyed it. They spoke no English, so I was obliged to speak French as best I could from the moment I arrived. The children soon learned, amidst their laughter, to understand me and imitate me. Madame Chassine, it seemed, found that she enjoyed trying to chat to me as she went about preparing meals (as it turned out, she was a fabulous cook) and after dinner in the evenings, Monsieur Chassine would invite me into his study to listen to a record of some classical music (he was educating himself as well as his children), talk to him as best I could and, on occasion, share a glass of whisky. When I wrote and told my mother about this, she replied very promptly and very severely: 'On no account should you ever touch whisky. It has been the ruination of many a good man before now and it could be your ruin too if you are not careful.'

Monsieur Chassine had a hobby: he had an aeroplane and was skilled also at gliding (*vol à voile*). I remember him returning one Sunday evening flushed with excitement: he had managed to glide all the way from Orléans (where he kept his plane) to Lyon, a distance of about 500 kilometres. He never took me up in his glider (thank goodness) but he did fly me in his two-seater plane, and we circled over Beauce and swept low over the farm, from where Madame Chassine and the children waved at us. I had never been in an aeroplane before, not even a commercial one, so the flight was very thrilling, but my insides jangled about a bit too much for my liking and I was relieved when we came back to earth.

If all of this sounds like a wonderful experience for a sixteen-year-old, that is because it was wonderful. And then there was the icing on the cake. Many Sundays, Monsieur Chassine would load all the family and me into the car and we would go off visiting sights: I remember Chartres Cathedral, the châteaux at Blois, Chambord and Cheverny in particular, but there were several more. These visits, organised for my benefit I am sure – as Monsieur Chassine could see that I loved everything I saw – must have been an agony for the children, who were all so very young. But they were being brought up very strictly and they had to behave. The climax came in August with a full day at the Château of Versailles, culminating in a magnificent *son et lumière* as night descended. This was out of this world for someone who had never even seen a firework before: the fountains – illuminated and playing to the music of the court of Louis XIV, the sound effects of horses and carriages clip-clopping through the woods, ballerinas as swans appearing to rise out of the *Bassin de Neptune*, regiments of seventeenth-century soldiers marching, the commentary spoken in beautiful French, and then the fireworks themselves. I was knocked sideways by the magnificence and beauty of it all. It was a day and evening that I have never forgotten: Sunday 5 August 1962.

How can I be so specific about the date? As we sat in our seats waiting for the spectacle to begin, there was a definite murmur among the audience. People seemed troubled by something; strangers leaned over to talk to one other; anyone with a newspaper was persuaded to share it. And in all those newspapers were photographs of Marilyn Monroe: she had killed herself (apparently) at her home in Los Angeles just hours previously.

Further excitement (as far as I was concerned) was occasioned by where we were seated. There was nothing special about our seats (except that they were good), and that made it all the more remarkable that seated two rows directly in front of us were Ike and Mamie Eisenhower. He had ended his term as president of the United States only the previous year and yet here he was – the former Supreme Commander of the Allied Forces in Europe, the man who had liberated France from the Nazis less than twenty years previously – quietly seated with his wife as members of the public at a very public spectacle, and without any entourage while the French audience, instead of applauding him or acknowledging him in any way, simply ignored him.

I have distant (very distant) French relations through my paternal great-great-grandfather. This was Sigismund Rentzsch (1776–1843), a

German watchmaker who in about 1809 settled in London, where, based in St James's, he became quite well known. He invented and patented a number of novel movements for clocks and watches and was patronised by the Court: a receipt (dated 1840) survives in the sum of nine pounds, four shillings and sixpence for repairs to the clocks and watches of Her Late Royal Highness Princess Augusta (daughter of George III). Sigismund Rentzsch had five children by his first (German) wife and eleven by his second, Mary Ransom, whom he married in London. One of these eleven, Rosina (1835–1909), somehow found her way to Ireland (possibly as a governess), where she met, in the area of Edenderry, an Edward Homan (1825–1909). They subsequently married, and their daughter, Charlotte (1866–1955) – my grandmother – married Thomas Potterton of Ardkill, Carbury in 1892. Rosina's eldest sister, Augusta, married a Frenchman, Dr Scipion Gas of Lyon, and it is from this marriage that my French relations – at least the ones I have met – are descended. They are called 'Allibert'.

When my Aunt Polly[1] – Charlotte's daughter – who was frantically keen on the family tree, heard that I was going to France, she became insistent that I would look up 'the cousins'. She immediately wrote off to an elderly Nelly Allibert, who lived in a suburb of Paris, and said that I would be coming to stay. It would have been a great inconvenience I am sure for Nelly to have a strange sixteen-year-old boy in her house, but she was the soul of kindness and arranged, after a few days, that I would go to her daughter, Nane, who lived on the rue d'Amsterdam with her husband. It was from there that I had the experience of a lifetime. After a good Sunday lunch, when other cousins were invited, one of them – Odette de Lestanville – who was about thirty and had done a course at the Louvre, took me to the museum. Looking at the pictures, she explained the different periods, told me about the artists, uncovered the stories in the pictures, and pointed to comparisons with other paintings and sculptures. She was a gentle guide who made everything fascinating and nothing in any way forbidding. By the end of the visit, I was hooked and, since that day, whenever I enter the Louvre I think of that afternoon. Forty years on, a few years ago, I looked up Odette and wrote to her. I told her how magic her company had been for me all those decades ago. She wrote back, but seemed to have no clear recollection of me[2]; but I have never forgotten her.

During those few days in Paris, assiduously sightseeing on my own, I had further opportunities to extend my education. As I was taking in the wonderful view from the esplanade of the Palais de Chaillot, a man came along and engaged me in conversation. After a few preliminaries, he offered to take me to the Folies Bergère and suggested a rendezvous the following day. But even though I was only sixteen, I had the sense to realise that he probably had 'folies' of an entirely different order in mind, and that the Louvre with Odette had been a much safer option. And so, intrigued though I was, I politely said, '*Merci beaucoup, monsieur, mais non.*'

I managed to stay with the Chassines for almost three months, from the day school broke up in June to when term started in early September. On my way back from France, I stopped in London where Aunt Polly had arranged for me to stay with another Rentzsch cousin, Laurie Rentzsch and his wife, Phyl, a very stylish (to me) couple who lived at Harrow-on-the-Hill. Their children Terry and Pamela were adults by this time and had left home. As a young man, Laurie had spent holidays in Ireland with his Irish cousins (my uncles and aunts) and he made me very welcome. Eventually, I got home, but although my French was fluent, it was very poor grammatically and my accent was atrociously anglophone. But my sensibilities had been opened to so much more than the French language during those three months and, within me, I was changed.

As a child, I had always felt 'like a fish out of water' at Rathcormick. Appropriately, on account of my name, I had inherited the Homan genes of my father and his mother, my grandmother, Charlotte Homan, whereas my five older brothers all took after our mother. As a result, although we all got on well together, I had little in common with them. But the experience of France, of seeing Blois, Chartres, Versailles and much more, led me to see that I had not been 'out of water' at all. I had merely been swimming in the wrong pond. And from that time on, as far as I was concerned, it was: County Meath . . . goodbye.

Endnotes

1. My father's sister Polly (also Mary or Mollie) Campion.
2. However, following Odette's death in December 2016, her son Henri wrote to me to say that his mother had remembered me.

CHAPTER 3

THE COLLEGE OF THE HOLY AND UNDIVIDED

After another year at Mountjoy, and getting some sort of results in the Leaving Certificate, I went up to Trinity in October 1963. I was too young – I had been seventeen the previous May – and Mr Tate's assessment that 'He is unlikely to contribute anything to the university' proved in time to be both justified and accurate. In the absence of any career guidance (I don't think such a thing existed in those days), I made a mess of deciding what to read and ended up with an impossible workload and studying some subjects – among them the law – in which I had no interest at all. In addition, I was a solicitor's apprentice, which involved working in a law office at the same time as studying. I am at a loss to explain how my choices came about, but I was doing a pass law degree, which involved in the first two years three separate subjects: contract, property and torts; I was simultaneously doing a pass arts degree, which also involved three separate subjects, in my case (in the first two years) economics, French and English. Had I fixed on doing an honours degree in legal science or English, my life would have been very much simpler. The first thing to go was the solicitor's apprenticeship: I just stopped going in to Matheson, Ormsby and Prentice. (They didn't seem to mind.) Next went the law studies: without owning up to the fact (either to my mother or to my brother Elliott, who was paying my fees), I just dropped out of the courses. At the end of my senior freshman year, I failed French: I could speak it, but too colloquially; I did not write it well; and I was felled by some of the literature. I liked Racine's *Phèdre* (I felt sorry for Hippolyte) and I could handle Maupassant, but the poets, Lamartine, Baudelaire and Verlaine defeated me. Even in English, I am not poetic.

But then a glimmer of light appeared at the end of the tunnel.

It was 1965 and word spread that, in a temporary lecture theatre in the basement of the New Library (the Berkeley), the most engaging lectures were being delivered on Monday and Thursday afternoons at five o'clock. The subject was the history of art and the lecturer, recently enticed to the college from the Ulster Museum, was a formidable, elegant, entertaining, mildly eccentric, knowledgeable enthusiast, a lady approaching her fortieth year, with a voice (and the diction to go with it) that was quite simply electrifying. She was called Anne Crookshank.[1] I sneaked into the back for one lecture. A slide of Titian's great *Assumption of the Virgin* from the Church of the Frari in Venice was on the screen. 'And here we have the Virgin Mary,' intoned Miss Crookshank, speaking mainly through her nose, 'making her way to heaven, clearly under her own steam'.

This is for me, I thought, as I sat there in the dark and I immediately decided to join her course.

It was her second year of teaching when I joined and I was, therefore among her earliest pupils. The course, which she taught single-handedly with only occasional support from a guest lecturer, covered the history of Western Art from the Early Greeks to the present day. It could have been called 'From the Kouros to Kinetic' and Anne travelled with ease and fully in command from one century to another, from one country to another. The way she pronounced Malevich and Goncharova still rings in my ears and I recall writing an essay on Masaccio's frescoes in the Brancacci Chapel in Florence and comparing them with another fresco cycle, (I can't remember which: perhaps Piero della Francescca in Arezzo.)

The course was taught over the two sophister years of the general studies degree: students dropped a subject after their freshmen years and replaced it with Anne. But dropping a subject was quite different to failing one, and I was not allowed to exchange my failed French for art history: I had to repeat my senior freshman year and somehow pass three subjects (I replaced French with history) and then moved to history of art. Doing that meant that my undergraduate studies took five, rather than the customary four years. But, at least – and at last – I was on the right track and, of the three subjects I was now taking for a general studies degree – history of art, English and economics – two of them were perfect for me, and I loved them.

Anne made an enormous impression on me, as she did on everyone who encountered her. Her lectures were not filled with dry facts and her slides very often appeared on the screen back to front. The result was that one looked up the facts in the library afterwards (and remembered them); and for years afterwards, one would come across pictures in museums that looked familiar but yet were not quite right. It caused one to look all the harder before realising that, unlike Anne's slides, they were the right way round. She had huge enthusiasm, which she expressed with a dry humour, thereby removing all sense of awe that one might have about a work of art. She led one into the subject.

'What is the principal difference between the two versions of Leonardo's *Virgin of the Rocks*?' she would ask in a seminar. Passing around a book of Leonardo illustrations, she would then wait, exasperated, until someone eventually noticed that in the Louvre painting the angel is pointing.

She made one long to travel, to see the actual works about which she was so eloquent. Having whetted our appetites by her exposition of Giotto's frescoes in the Upper Church of San Francesco at Assisi, she warned us that 'on no account must we go there on a Sunday as the town is simply overrun by charabancs of Italian sailors'. She knew well that everyone – men and women – would, as a result of her warning, make a point of going to Assisi only on a Sunday. I was too timid to get to know her, except in the formal way that a seminar demanded, and it was only after I had sat my finals that I felt she noticed me. Before the results came out, she hailed me in Front Square one day. 'Marvellous,' she said, 'you need have no worries. You answered wonderfully well.'

I do not think I had 'a colourless personality' when I went up to Trinity. But I certainly developed one when I was there. The college in those days could be a very intimidating place, socially rather than academically, and social life certainly took precedence over academic engagement. There were some 3,000 students and, of these, about 30 per cent were English, a significant proportion were from Northern Ireland, and the rest were Southern Irish Protestants like myself. Catholics required a dispensation from the Archbishop of Dublin, which was not easily obtained, to attend this College of the Holy and Undivided Trinity as it was deemed to be a Protestant university. Of the English 30 per cent, it was said (and the evidence seemed – to me at

14

least – to support it) that they were mainly minor-public-school people who were too dim to be accepted by Oxford or Cambridge and too snobby to have gone anywhere else, other than Trinity. Lest this assessment seems harsh, it is confirmed by one of their number, Peter Hinchcliffe, who came up to Trinity in 1957 and became, ultimately, British High Commissioner in Zambia. He has written:

> I had much in common with many others of my Junior Freshman class, including my English public-school background, with its uniform of tweed sports jacket and cavalry twill trousers, loud voice, braying vowels and regulation thick skin. Many of us seemed brashly insensitive to our novel existence in a foreign land. And, like so many of this generation of students from across the water, I had failed to find an Oxbridge college that felt it would benefit from my attendance.[2]

This English contingent dominated the university. They established themselves as an elite: they had, after all, been trained to do so – no matter where they found themselves on the globe – at their English public schools. Most Irish undergraduates found them intimidating, and their snobbery – as a general rule, they did not know, and did not want to know, the Irish students – was so alien to the Irish temperament that we did not know how to deal with it. One of their number, contemporary with me, Mirabel Walker, has written (in *Trinity Tales*) 'one of the odd things about being in Ireland at Trinity was that I made very few Irish friends there'. These English seemed to run The Hist (the College Historical Society) and The Phil (the Philosophical Society), Players, the Boat Club, *Trinity News*, the magazine *TCD Miscellany*, and much else, while we Irish retreated into our colourless shells. But, as revealed by Jeremy Lewis (in his amusing memoir *Playing for Time*), the public-school types also had their inner insecurities, but they disguised their uncertainties better than we Irish managed to do. On going to Ireland for the first time, he 'wasn't altogether sure whether Dublin was in the North or the Republic': he wasn't alone among the English undergraduates in that. For some time, he knew 'none of my Irish fellow-students, nor was I to do so until some terms later' (when he met the poet Derek Mahon, (who comes from Northern Ireland). Writing wittily, he divides the undergraduate population into 'English public-school boys, green-blazered Ulstermen, and the Catholic Irish – a third of the total – Orangemen, undesirable aliens from over the water and several Nigerians': Evidently he did not even know that Irish Protestants like myself existed (unless he thought of us as Orangemen, which we, decidedly, were not) and that it was we who made up about 'a third of the total'.

I joined the Hist and made my maiden speech, but the experience so terrified me that I never spoke there again: I, who only a year or so previously had addressed – without a hint of nervousness – an audience of hundreds in the Metropolitan Hall. I am writing about my own perceptions but, with exceptions, I think many other Irish students felt the same. Several that I knew, finding themselves, like myself, studying the wrong subject, dropped out. Their decision to do so was, I feel sure, as much influenced by the atmosphere in Trinity as it was by their academic failure. For whatever reason, I decided within myself that I would stay the course. I wanted a degree and I was not going to be beaten. I told myself (and I still think of this): if I survive the social intimidation of Trinity, nothing or no one will ever intimidate me socially again.

Having had digs with a wonderfully eccentric Miss Fleming (Helen) on Leinster Road, Rathmines, in my first years (where I shared with, among others, Malcolm Benson and Charles Smyth), I took rooms in my sophister years: first in New Square, where I shared with an unusual friend, Reggie Fairfax-Crone. Reggie was English and older than most undergraduates, having already studied elsewhere before coming up to Trinity, and was, improbably, studying engineering. He was very clever, widely read, and with a penchant for arcane information about all sorts of different subjects; and for some reason, he found me an appreciative audience.

'"Wherefore have ye left your sheep"' he reprimanded me, 'did not mean "Where have you left your sheep" but "For what reason have you left them."'

'And does the same apply to "Wherefore art thou, Romeo?"' I asked.
'Of course,' he said.

Although we have remained lifelong friends (when he married

Carmel I was asked to be godfather to one of his daughters), sharing rooms with him was rather a trial, and the following year I found a single set in the Graduates Memorial Building. Reggie had a seductively appealing younger sister, Penny, who would sometimes visit from England, and she and I embarked upon a sometimes-reckless romance. Exceedingly attractive in looks and personality (so much so that my mother deemed her 'dangerous'), she was very clever, culturally stimulating, socially enervating, and tremendous fun. Maddeningly unreliable at times, she came to exert considerable influence on me, giving me a confidence that I had lacked, drawing me out of myself, and in time introducing me to a wider world, and – by her example – pointing my life in all the right directions. Charm, a dubious commodity in my mother's opinion, was as her second name and she had it in bucketfuls. She spoke with an English accent that sounded a little too posh for Trim, pronouncing the word 'Aga' as 'aahGaah' when we called it 'the Agga'. Penny and I are friends to this day and I am also godfather to one of her sons.

Endnotes

1. (1927–2016). Lecturer (at this time) and later professor of the History of Art in Trinity and previously keeper of Art at the Ulster Museum. Author (with the Knight of Glin) of *The Painters of Ireland 1660–1920* and many other publications. Obituary by Robert O'Byrne, Apollo, October 2016.
2. *Trinity Tales: Trinity College Dublin in the Sixties* (2009). See also Anne Leonard, *Portrait of an Era: Trinity College, Dublin in the 1960s*; and Jeremy Lewis, *Playing for Time* (1987).

CHAPTER 4
FRIENDSHIPS AND FOREIGN PARTS

General studies had an advantage over honours degrees in that the end-of-year exams took place in June, and one was then free for four months until the start of the Michaelmas term in late October. I would go to London immediately term ended in June, and find myself a job (or jobs) and a place to live. I would work, and save money, for about two months and then take off for another two months hitchhiking in France, Italy, Spain and, one year, Morocco. (I had read *Brideshead Revisited*.) My mother had her concerns about this and wrote to me, 'Poste Restante, Tangier' (12 September 1968), to tell me that my Aunt Polly had come to lunch: 'She was quite worried about you getting lifts to Morocco, said there are queer people in the world. I hope you are all right staying there – be careful, as we read so much about Dope dens etc. I know you have sense.'

It was news to me that my mother was given to reading about dope dens, but her anxieties in respect of my welfare were ill-founded. On my arrival in Morocco, I am sorry to say that the 'Dope dens' of Tangier eluded me. But, during these summers away from Trinity, and from Ireland, I did have a host of other experiences that enriched my life greatly. They, and the people I encountered, meld in my memory now and the chronology is hazy. One year, I got a job doing accounts (yes, accounts) in the *Daily Mirror* offices in Holborn; but the accounts I did were not for the *Daily Mirror* but for one of their weekly publications, a tabloid called *Reveille*. It was one of the first mainstream publications to feature photographs of glamour models – it may have been banned in Ireland on that account – but it also covered, in a saucy way, the worlds of pop and royalty. This was an office job, nine to five, but at six o'clock I would make my way to a pub nearby, where I worked as a barman until closing time at eleven o'clock. Another year, I went into Claridge's Hotel and asked for a job, and was taken on to work in the Still Room. The hours were seven in the morning until three in the afternoon. I made Melba toast from seven till ten, crafted butter pats from ten till twelve, and brewed coffee from noon till three. I had the afternoon off and then returned at six for a second job (until eleven at night) on one of the floors. There, I was on duty in the pantry where room-service meals were put together: they came up in a lift from the kitchens and I would set up the trolleys for the waiters to take to the rooms. I never did any waiting myself and never met any of the guests. A manager took a shine to me – I think he felt that, from his point of view, I might have more to offer than Melba toast – and over the weeks that I was there he made suggestions that I should think of a career in hotel management: he could help me get a traineeship in Claridge's if I was so inclined. I wrote and told my mother about this and she replied (on 15 August 1966): 'You were very lucky to get a job in that good Hotel. The idea of doing "Hotel Management"? A degree in Law would be less worry and more secure.' Another of my jobs was in some sort of small family-run printing firm. I can't recall what I did there but when I was leaving, the owner tried to persuade me to stay on. 'You could have a career here,' he said, pointing out that he and his wife had no children to take on the business. But I was not tempted.

One year I rented a room in Barkston Gardens, off the Earl's Court Road, with a sinister landlord who lived with his wife on the ground floor and always emerged into the hall to see who was entering or leaving. If I was five minutes late in paying the rent, they would send their bruiser of a son up to bang on my door and threaten me with eviction if I did not produce the cash there and then. Much superior was the accommodation I found (through friends) another year. This was in a council flat in Streatham with a 'Mrs Hutt' (as I shall call her). She was posh but, having fallen on hard times (hence the council flat), took various cooking jobs here and there. She had mislaid her husband and, much to her own embarrassment (and the embarrassment of everyone else), had taken an Irish navvy as a live-in lover. Her eldest son, who was in the RAF and modelled himself on the actor Leslie Phillips, did not live with her but appeared from time to time. But her second son, who was mildly mentally handicapped, did, and so did her daughter, a happy blonde twenty-something who came and went as she pleased, always with a friend or more in tow. I was happy squeezed into this 'ménage' although, as I was working from early morning till late at night, I was only really there on Sundays, when Mrs Hutt would cook a fabulous Sunday lunch, which we ate on our knees at five o'clock in the afternoon (having spent lunchtime in the pub down the road).

A young Australian artist whom I met, Michael Garady, lived with his friend in Rutland Mews off Exhibition Road. Once, when I was stuck for accommodation, he invited me there for a couple of weeks (his friend being away). Michael, who was handsome in a masculine way, with tousled blond curly hair and, in manner, tentative and fey, was having some success in London with his painting and was working towards an exhibition: 'I have to finish many paintings to let the Grosvenor Gallery choose in September for the November exhibition. Unfortunately they take a long time to dry and I will need to have them finished,' he wrote to me (on 9 August 1966). His sister, Saxon, who had never been to Europe before, was about to arrive from Australia: she would be accompanied by a girlfriend, who I think was called Diana. They arrived, Saxon a rollicking, large, good-looking blonde and Diana, petite and more mysterious. They immediately bought a Jaguar car and drove around London in whichever gear they managed to find: accustomed only to automatic transmission, they did not know, until I showed them, that you had to change gear. Without meaning to be, they were both in their own way completely and bombastically outrageous, and they had not been very long in London before they found themselves – on account of a mishap in an antique shop – in Marylebone Magistrates Court. Michael was offered the loan of a flat in Paris (84 Boulevard Rochechouart – my mother wrote to me there) and a plan was made for Saxon and Diana to drive over to stay with him, bringing me with them. And that is what happened.

On the trip over, when I mentioned that I hoped to go to Morocco, they thought that a wonderful idea and immediately offered to drive me there. They had no notion where any place was but, in the event, they returned to London in their Jaguar and I set off for Morocco on my own. A year later, Michael being away, his friend Peter Feuchtwanger invited me to stay in Rutland Mews until I found some place of my own. Peter was German, and a classical pianist and composer. He was obsessively devoted to the memory of the great Romanian pianist Clara Haskill (d.1960), and had composed a work for violin and sitar for Yehudi Menuhin and Ravi Shankar. At the time I was staying with him he was composing the music for a ballet to be staged at Covent Garden and, by way of preparation, had been allocated complimentary seats for every ballet performance. This meant ballet two or three nights a week; and on several nights, he took me with him: a car collected us and we sat in the stalls. I saw Monica Mason, Anthony Dowell and Antoinette Sibley in new ballets by Kenneth MacMillan but alas, I did not see Fonteyn and Nureyev. But the real treat came after the performances. Peter, taking me with him, went backstage to chat with the dancers in their dressing rooms, as they removed all those bandages from their exhausted feet. At Trinity, I hardly dared enter the doors of the Players Theatre, much less talk to any of the student-actors; but backstage at Covent Garden with Peter I managed to take it in my stride. A year or so after I wrote this memory, I came upon Peter's obituary in the *Daily Telegraph* (28 June 2016). He had recently died aged 85. He was described as 'the go-to teacher for many of the world's leading concert pianists, among them Shura Cherkassky, Martha Argerich, and David Helfgott; but he himself had given up performing when he was only 20'. With sadness, and regret that I had not revived my friendship with him in my adult life, I read with some surprise 'he is survived by his partner, the artist, Michael Garady'.

After about two months of working long hours, I would set off on my travels with the money I had saved. Hitchhiking was quite normal in those days before motorways, and some well-publicised incidents – murder, mainly – made it less attractive. Youth hostels were popular. Students from all over Europe criss-crossed France, Spain and Italy, eating sparsely, dossing down and making friendships along the way. I never encountered drugs or even excessive drinking, and my most threatening experiences (at least that I remember) involved a short-haired young woman in a Renault Dauphine who gave me a lift near Besançon, and a plump baker doing his deliveries in a van among the hills above Nice. Using the French verb *profiter*, they both immediately made it clear that, as they had never met an Irishman before, they would very much like to 'profit' by meeting one then.

I would generally stay for a week or so in Paris – finding a cheap hotel in the hinterland of St Michel – and then set off. The first year, my goal was Switzerland, where a friend from school and Trinity, Walter Lewis, was working in an hotel. I hitchhiked there, seeing the Romanesque Abbey church at Vézelay and the Well of Moses at Dijon – as well as getting sunstroke by the lake in Lausanne – on the way. Walter's boss gave him very little time off, so I did not stay long, and then hitchhiked down to Milan. I don't recall going to see Leonardo's *Last Supper* but I do remember a Jehovah's Witness who tried to interest me as I lingered in front of the Duomo. I got to Florence, which I was determined to do. A postcard to my mother: 'At last, I got here. It is absolutely beautiful & mad hot. I have got rid of the friend, thank goodness' (presumably someone I had been hitch-hiking with) 'and am thoroughly enjoying it all now. The youth hostel here is like a mansion, with beautiful ceilings and frescoes.' My Aunt Isa[1] had told me about Michelangelo's *David*: she had been reading *The Agony and the Ecstasy*, the biography of Michelangelo by Irving Stone, and she made her description of the carving of the David so vivid that I absolutely had to see it.

I hitchhiked back by way of Pisa – 'eating lots of spaghetti & enjoying myself', according to a postcard to my mother (1 August 1963) – and the French Riviera, in Nice sleeping in an abandoned car that I found somewhere to the east of the port, and then it was back to Paris, staying for a few days with the Chassines on the way.

The following year, I went directly to Nice. I sent my mother a postcard from Vichy:

> I am hitchhiking to Nice. I got one lift last night to here – 150 miles and very good. I arrived at 12 midnight having left Paris at 5.30. Altogether about 250 miles. This is a spa town like Bath only not as beautiful. My address in Nice is c/o Cooks, 5 Promenade des Anglais.

In Paris I had made friends with a very droll Swedish student of psychology who was touring by car with his uncle; but, in a very Swedish way, the uncle was three years younger than the nephew, Lars. This is a friendship that has lasted to this day, almost fifty years. Lars and I still keep in contact and over the decades he has visited me many times and in many places, and I have stayed with him on several occasions in Stockholm. Lars Fimmerstad became a noted humorous columnist on the leading Swedish newspaper, *Svenska Dagbladet*. Two years after meeting, we decided to combine our student summer travels and met in Rome. We stayed there for about two or three weeks, ravenously visiting every museum and church, studying the stones in the Forum and on the Appian Way, eating frugally, going to *Aïda* at the Baths of Caracalla, and generally having a lot of fun.

Of the relatively few of my letters which my mother saved, I have one or two from this time. 'We went to the opera one night in the open air,' I wrote (29 July 1967). 'It was just fantastic. Absolutely huge, with almost a thousand people on stage at any one time. They also had carriages drawn by four white horses. In another scene, there were camels. It really was a marvellous night.'

Lars is someone who sees humour in almost any situation, interpreting things with the eye of a psychologist – and a Swedish psychologist at that – so that events which on the surface appear dull become immediately entertaining. He deploys a similar approach with people. To my young Irish eyes and ears – he speaks with a perfect Oxford accent, with only occasional lapses of grammar and syntax – he often seemed totally absurd but that – as a general rule – made him very amusing company indeed. I wrote to my mother (19 July 1967): 'Lars, the Swede, is getting a bit on my nerves – but then who wouldn't? He tends to be a bit old-fashioned and refuses to sit beside people on the buses. Another thing, he wants to talk all the time, and I get fed up of that.' After Rome, we hitchhiked to Naples, saw the sights and visited Pompeii, and then took the overnight ferry – sleeping on the deck – to Palermo in Sicily, where we stayed, mainly in the seaside town of Cefalù but also in Taormina.

'It really is one of the most beautiful places I've ever been in,' I informed my mother (27 July 1967). 'Yesterday we saw smoke coming out of Etna. The village is high up, built into a cliff, and you get a bus down the cliff to the sea – which is very, very clear and deep. We will probably stay here until early next week and then go back to Rome. We have seen a tremendous amount.'

From Sicily, we went back to Rome. A postcard (dated 2 August 1967) of the Temple of Aesculapius in the Borghese Gardens to my mother: 'Returned here yesterday from Sicily, where we really had a terrific time. I am going to Florence on Friday just to see a friend.' This was a handsome upper-class young Florentine, Carlo Olivieri, who lived with his mother on the Lungarno and whose father was an admiral in the Italian navy. I had met him in France two years previously and the friendship continued – mainly through correspondence – for a number of years but we have, unfortunately, long since lost touch.

Carlo, I recall, introduced me to the novels, in French, of Julien Green but I found them too difficult and his recommendation that I read Andre Gide's *Les Faux Monnayeurs* (also in French) struck more of a chord with me.

The year I went to Morocco, and in the absence of Saxon and Diana driving me there, I hitch-hiked through France, crossed the Pyrenees, and then travelled down the east coast of Spain to Algeciras, where I took the ferry to what I thought would be Tangier but turned out to be Ceuta, the Spanish enclave on the north coast of Africa. From there, it was a bus the fifty or so kilometres to Tangier, where I found a room in a seedy hotel in the medina. I stayed for a week or so and then took a bus down to Fez and on to Meknès. I had an introduction (through Carlo Olivieri) to an American living in Rabat, and I went and stayed with him for a few days. This was the nearest I came to witnessing the decadent expatriate Morocco that was so notorious. There was an 'atmosphere' in the American's house: Arab boys seemed to come and go as they pleased and make themselves very much at home. I neither saw nor experienced anything but I was uneasy. (I was only 20 at the time.) I wanted to move on.

As I could not face hitch-hiking all the way back to Paris, I telegraphed my friend Speer Ogle in Dublin and asked him to lend me the train fare and wire it to me in Rabat, which he did; and so I got to Paris, but I was still without a sou in my pocket. I was not in the least concerned as it was in my head (someone must have told me so) that, if stranded abroad, all one had to do was to go to one's embassy and demand to be repatriated. So, cleaning myself up as best I could, I made my way to the Irish Embassy on the Avenue Foch. There I was seen by a young diplomat who quickly disabused me of the notion that I might be sent home to Ireland free of charge. But seeing perhaps a look of panic on my face, he delved into his trouser pocket and pulled out a wad of notes. Peeling a few of them away, he handed them to me. 'I'm not supposed to do this and please don't mention that I did so,' he said, 'but I myself (not the Embassy) can lend you some Francs and you can send them back to me when you get home. Would that help?' In my mind, I can still see the way he took out the notes and handed them to me but I have no clear memory of who he was. Inexplicably, however, the name Campbell comes into my mind, and with some investigation, I find that a John Campbell was a junior diplomat in the Paris Embassy in the 1960s (he married a French wife in 1964). Ten years my senior (it transpires), it must have been he who helped me. If it was he, his subsequent career took him as Ambassador to China, to Portugal and to Germany, worthy rewards in my view for a man who had made a kindly gesture towards a foolish 20-year-old.

Eventually, I got home. And then it was back to the dull days of Trinity, a very small circle of friends[2] and not a lot of fun.

There was only one of my Trinity summers when I did not get away. When my plans for doing so were already well advanced, my mother wrote to me (18 May 1965):

> Elliott and Maud were here last night. You know, Elliott is quite concerned about you and says that you are not looking well at all. He told me he offered you £7 a week to go and stay in Rathcormick for five or six weeks and drive a tractor for him. He doesn't mind about driving the tractor, but he feels if you had that definite job it would keep you out in the air and would do you a lot of good. Maud also said she'd see you had good meals and try to build you up a bit. I think you ought to do this and not bother about France for this year. Elliott does not mind your going to France, but he thinks it is really foolish and you come back jaded. I wish you would do this, it is for your good and when Elliott was interested enough in you to suggest this, I think you should agree with him. As I say, don't think he wants you just for the sake of driving the tractor, he doesn't. It is your health he is concerned with and I think you would be wise to accept his proposal with thanks, rather than go against him. He does feel a certain responsibility for you and when you don't ever take his advice, he can't help losing interest in you. I hope you will do as I ask you. You are very young and with a little

guidance from Elliott you would do better and I know he
will always help you if you co-operate.

I did as my mother asked me, put travel out of my mind, and went to
stay and work in Rathcormick for a couple of months. I worked the
hours the labourers on the farm did and had them for company during
the day; and I learned to be adept at manoeuvring the tractor and
anything that might be attached to it. I brought in the hay and then I cut
the silage and brought that in too. When the wheat and barley were being
harvested, I followed the combine-harvester on my tractor and decanted
the grain when the bin was full. I baled the straw and brought that into
the barn. All of this did 'keep me out in the air', although whether it 'did
me a lot of good' I am not so sure. In my own mind, a day discovering
Fontainebleau or a morning admiring the frescoes of Mantegna in the
Camera degli Sposi in Mantua might have been better for me; and the
foreign students I could have met in such places would no doubt have
been more interesting than the company I had in the farmyard. But the
summer was by no means all torture. The children – all six of them –
were entertaining, Maud was kind and good company, and I got to know
(for the first time in my life) my brother Elliott: sixteen years my senior,
he was fair-minded, reasonable and very practical, and worked ruthlessly
hard at his estate-agency business. It was good of him to give me the
opportunity (and to pay me well) and it was done with good intentions.
None of this, however, shook me in my resolve that my life would take
me along a path that was as far removed from the farming world of
Rathcormick as I could possibly reach.

It wasn't Rathcormick itself. My childhood there had been very happy
and I was proud of the fact that my family had lived in the place for
hundreds of years: my great (five times) grandfather first leased the farm
on 28 July 1710 and we had been in continuous occupation ever since.

But animals and the dirt and discomfort of the outdoors and the
constant hard and heavy labour lacked all appeal for me and I knew it.

Endnotes

1. My father's sister, Mrs William Tyrrell of Coolcor, Carbury.
2. Of the friends I did make, several were ex-Alexandra College girls: Margaret Furlong,
   Meriel Hayes and Deirdre Sheppard. Elizabeth Strong from Edinburgh, but with family
   roots in Co. Meath, also came into my life at this time.

CHAPTER 5
ENCOUNTERS

When I was at Trinity, I met the King of Saxony. Except that the King of Saxony I thought I met was not the king at all. He was, rather, His Royal Highness Prinz Ernst Heinrich Ferdinand Franz Joseph Otto Maria Melchiades of Saxony, the youngest son of the last King of Saxony, Frederick August III, by his wife the Archduchess Louise of Austria, Princess of Tuscany.

I did not meet Prinz Ernst in the august precincts of Trinity College, which would not have been improbable; instead, I was introduced to him in the much more unlikely setting of Trim Livestock Market, the cattle sales-yard established by my late father in 1957 and managed in my Trinity days by my brothers Elliott and Raymond.

While a student, I was supported, and my fees paid, by Elliott through the family auctioneering business. In the winter and spring vacations, Elliott would offer me the opportunity of working as the auctioneer's clerk in the cattle market and would pay me a daily wage. I was grateful for this but, at the same time, I hated the cattle market just as I hated everything about farming. But my mother would be insistent: 'When he is good enough to offer you the work, you should show willing and go and do it,' she would say and, on the mornings of the market, she would get me out of bed early and dispatch me off to the sales-yard.

The auction took place in a large covered building with an arena – the ring – in the centre, through which the cattle were paraded. It was encircled by tiered seats for clients, and on one side was the auctioneer's box. This was something like an enclosed balcony overlooking the ring, with access from a door at the back of the box. The auctioneer – Elliott – was seated to one side; his clerk – me – to the other. Between the raised platforms on which we sat was a narrow gap where vendors would stand at a lower level and identify their cattle in the ring by peering through a tiny slit: they could see the proceedings but, most importantly, they could not be seen by potential purchasers. When standing there, their heads would be roughly level with my feet. As clerk, it was my job to write in a register – as the various lots came through the ring – the lot number, the name of the vendor, the breed of cattle being sold, their gender and number, and the price achieved. As the auction moved very fast, this had to be done at speed and with absolute accuracy. I was soon able to identify the various breeds – Aberdeen Angus, Shorthorn or Hereford Crossbreed – and I only rarely made an error in counting the number of cattle in a lot. The difficulty arose in getting the name of the vendor. As they stood below me squinting through the slit, I could only see the tops of their heads and, not knowing them, would have to ask them 'What is the name, please?' Understandably, vendors were very preoccupied and anxious as they watched their livelihood being sold within a space of minutes, and it was very difficult to get them to answer me. 'What is the name, please?' I would repeat, and repeat again. Elliott, trying to concentrate on conducting the auction, would become irritated by my ineffective politeness and would snap at me: 'He's Paudge O'Toole' or 'That's Larkin, he's here often enough for you to know him by now.'

On one day, the man who came into the box and took his stand peeping through the slit was ruddy-faced and wearing a tattered gaberdine, Wellington boots, and a much-soiled brown brimmed hat. He was as nervous as every other vendor.

'What is the name, please?' I said.

And then I said it again, and again.

In the meantime, Elliott's patience was being sorely tested. Eventually, and without interrupting the bidding, he shouted across at me: 'That's the King of Saxony.'

The way he said it, one would have thought that royalty passed through the box every other day.

I wrote down 'K of Saxony. 8 Hereford Cross bullocks' in the register.

Prinz Ernst (b. 1896) had been brought up in Dresden at the Court of Saxony. He joined the army in the First World War and took part in the Battle of the Somme. In 1918 his father was forced to abdicate when

Saxony became a Free State. The Prinz opposed the Nazis and, on witnessing the bombing of Dresden in 1945, he fled the city (having buried crates of the family's treasures in a forest) to escape the advance of the Red Army. His first wife (and mother of his three sons) died in 1941 and he then married an aristocratic actress, Virginia Dulon, in 1947. That year they moved to Ireland, where he purchased a farm of about 300 acres, Coolamber, near Delvin, County Westmeath. There he lived until his death (on a visit to Germany) in 1971. The Princess Virginia stayed on in Ireland for the next thirty years and died at Coolamber in 2002.

From my art history studies, I knew vaguely that the Electors of Saxony (forebears of the kings) had assembled fabulous art collections which are housed in various museums in Dresden. Any general book on the history of art includes reproductions of such famous Dresden masterpieces as Raphael's *Sistine Madonna*, Giorgione's *Sleeping Venus*, Rembrandt's *Ganymede* and Vermeer's *Procuress*. I also knew that the Italian painter Bernardo Bellotto had been invited by the Elector of the day to come to Dresden and paint (famous) views of the city. I would very much have liked to have talked to Prinz Ernst about all of this but, unfortunately, my duties in the auctioneer's box precluded me from doing so and I was never to encounter him again.

A more satisfactory encounter – and one that led to a deep, lifelong friendship – took place in Trinity itself. One of the very few societies I joined and took part in was the Arts Society. I cannot recall now what the society actually did but they must – on at one least occasion – have put on an exhibition, because I was sitting at a table outside an exhibition soliciting custom when along came a dapper gentleman in his late thirties, balding but handsome and with large brown eyes, a very punctilious manner, a wry, witty expression, and a precision about his speech that was quite singular. He started to talk to me. He was not connected to the university but soon declared his cultural credentials: he had a great interest in pictures, which is why he had sought out the student exhibition, had lived in Rome for many years, and was now working with the Irish Arts Council. In addition he volunteered that he had been to school at St Columba's and had once been secretary to an MP in the House of Commons (Sir Lance Mallalieu). He asked me about myself, told me how wonderful it must be to be in Trinity, asked me if I painted and, if so, could he see my work. (I didn't paint.) He suggested that perhaps I might like to meet for a drink sometime, and asked how he might contact me. 'A note to my rooms in Number Nine,' I said. On departing, he handed me his card. Engraved and discreet, 'Mr Speer Ogle', it read, above the address of the Kildare Street Club.

And that was how I met someone who was to have an enormous influence on my life, becoming a very dear friend and remaining so to the end of his days.

Up to this, I think the only person I had met whose style I would want to emulate had been my Aunt Polly, a clergyman's widow. But although, from school and university, I had often visited her at her home in Claremont Villas, Glenageary, I was not overly close to her. As she had (with little money) always 'collected', her house was wonderful, falling down with lovely things: a wall lined with pewter plates, Percy French watercolours, Dublin delft, ruby glass, needlework-covered chairs, and much more. She was also interested in 'antiquities' – and people – and spent a lot of time ferreting about: for example, she interviewed, and wrote about, the last poplin-makers in Dublin, the Elliotts.[1] But Aunt Polly was merely a drop at the bottom of a glass compared to the influence that Speer was to have upon me.

He rented a flat (which he had done for many years) on the second floor of a house in Upper Fitzwilliam Street. This was small: there was a sitting room, a bedroom, a cramped corridor that was the kitchen, in which there was a Baby Belling cooker on a cupboard, and a bathroom. The place was chock-a-block: pictures, vitrines of china, a bronze of the equestrian *Marcus Aurelius* on the floor, part of a *pietra dura* cabinet under a table, an armchair decked with a fur throw. Speer told me this was made from the pouches of kangaroos and had come from Australia. In a corner to the right of the chimney there was a portrait (unlit) of a seated gentleman, half-length in profile, wearing a crimson silk dressing gown. It was Speer by Harry Robertson Craig and had been exhibited at the RHA in 1955.

'Terence de Vere White reviewed the exhibition in *The Irish Times*,' Speer told me, 'and said I looked like *Whistler's Mother*.' (I looked up Whistler's famous portrait of his old mother, seated in profile, three-quarter length, against a blank wall when I went to the library the next day.)

Speer did not tell me at that time what Lennox Robinson, in reviewing the RHA exhibition in the *Irish Independent*, had written about his portrait:

> Robertson Craig has portraits of two attractive young men, whose acquaintance I should like to make. One of them is, extraordinarily, called Speer Ogle. I can hardly believe this; it is surely a name invented by Henry James; it is a character out of *The Turn of the Screw*, he is Miss Jessel's half-brother, yet he does not look a bit evil.

Speer's pictures were lit by placing lamps beneath them, rather than using picture lights; a divan was home to a tiger skin with the head intact. The divan was also littered with loose engravings, mainly of Rome.

'They are not Piranesi,' said Speer (I looked him up later in the library too), 'they are only Domenico de' Rossi.'

He saw me looking at a bronze statuette of a young man almost hidden by gin and whiskey bottles on a small table. 'That's Antinous,' he said. 'He and Hadrian were rather close. But it's only a nineteenth-century tourist bronze from the museum in Naples.' (I wasn't sure what all that meant.)

I admired the modest glass chandelier hanging from the ceiling in the centre of the room. 'Oh! But it's just from Woolworths,' he said. 'It's plastic.'

He reached up and flicked the drops with his fingernail. 'See! It doesn't tinkle.'

It was a lesson I was later to absorb: junk can have style and, if mixed with beautiful things, can appear beautiful too. Looking together at a dark oil painting of a lake by moonlight surrounded by trees, Speer said, 'I've never liked the boat on the lake. I think it takes away from the composition. I once took the picture to Old Gorry the restorer and asked him to sink it, but he couldn't.'

The Story of San Michele by Axel Munthe was open by an armchair. 'I've read it millions of times,' said Speer. 'San Michele is on Capri near the villa of the Emperor Tiberius. It's a beautiful spot.'

He said 'Tiberius' in such a way that I was encouraged to find out more in the library.

He told me that, through Terence de Vere White,[2] with whom he was friendly, he had met Compton Mackenzie, and he urged me to read Mackenzie's novel, *Sinister Street*. At a later stage he gave me a present of a paperback *Giovanni's Room* by James Baldwin.

There was a small crucifix, with an ivory figure of Christ on a malachite cross, hanging in a corner. It looked very nice there but, nevertheless – little Protestant that I was and knowing that Speer was also Protestant – it caused me some worry, as did the framed photograph of Pope John XXIII on the mantelpiece. But, in time, Speer revealed that he had met Pope John on several occasions.

'It was at the time of the Rome Olympics,' he said. 'I had a job meeting athletes and dignitaries at the airport in my car and taking them to wherever they wanted to go. One or two of them had an audience with the pope, and I went with them.'

All the furniture looked lovely to me and Speer explained that he had inherited it from his grandmother and great-aunt, who together had brought him up.

'My father farmed in County Carlow and was devoted to my mother,' he told me. 'But when I was born and my mother brought me home as a baby to Kilcomney – that was the name of our place – my father told her to take me away again, as he had wanted a daughter. And so I was left with my grandmother and great-aunt in Kenilworth Square and brought up by them. I hardly knew my mother or father at all.'

This story of his background, both heartless and affecting, was as good as anything that I was reading at Trinity in the novels of Walter Scott. Early on, he told me about his younger friend Henry, a Scot who worked in the British Foreign Office, and to whom he was devoted (and would remain so for the next fifty or more years).

Over the ensuing years, the notes requesting assignations which Speer left for me at my rooms became more frequent and our friendship – which was always Platonic – deepened. He prided himself on being able to produce a full dinner of roast pheasant and all the trimmings on the Baby Belling (with no fridge) and I was sometimes treated to this. He had beautiful antique silver, old Waterford glass and lovely china, and would somehow manage to set a table (or the corner of a table) in the crowded sitting room. But mainly he would take me out to eat. Although he sometimes talked of Jammet's, he never took me there, and a favourite, when it came to posh, was the Beaufield Mews. This was a restaurant arranged in a converted stable with a large antique shop – with a superb stock of beautiful things – above. We would look at the antiques – it did not seem like he was teaching me, but he was – and then we would dine. But more usually we went, later at night after the library in Trinity had closed, to a much more modest Indian restaurant on Leeson Street called the Golden Orient. We always ate the same thing: pakoras, followed by beef curry with poppadoms, followed by lychees and accompanied by a carafe of white wine. It was hardly gourmet. Speer liked his curry very hot and derived enormous amusement from getting the friendly waitress to say the word 'vindaloo' in her (very) Dublin accent.

'It can't be hot enough for me,' he would insist when ordering.

'Shur you mean a *vindaloo*,' the waitress would reply over our suppressed giggles.

But Speer would want to hear it again.

'No, I mean even hotter,' he would say in his precise manner.

'I'll ask the chef,' the waitress would say, 'but a *vindaloo* is as hot as you get round here.'

Sometimes, on Sundays, we would go to lunch in a small (and to me horrid) hotel he knew in Dun Laoghaire: they had a dog there that he liked, and he was passionate about dogs. Then we would walk over Killiney Hill. More lavish Sunday expeditions involved the Downshire Arms in Blessington and a walk at the Sugarloaf. He took me to the Sunday evening promenade concerts with the Radio Eireann Symphony Orchestra conducted by Tibor Paul in the Gaiety, and he introduced me to a Christmas *Messiah* with Our Lady's Choral Society in the National Stadium. When Nelson's Pillar was blown up, he heard it on the early news and dashed down to O'Connell Street and retrieved a piece of the sculptured stone rope which had been part of the Nelson statue: he gave me a fragment.

He taught me a lot of nonsense too, which makes me laugh when I think of it today. One does not carry an umbrella in the country; no brown shoes after six o'clock; and there was something about it not being done to look out of an open window that I never fully understood and I did on occasion peek out the windows of 13 Upper Fitzwilliam Street when he was not looking. He called an apple tart an apple cake and pronounced the word 'recipe' as 'receep' (as did my elderly Aunt Isa). He struck terror into me by telling me how one must eat an oyster, warning me with frightening detail that if one ever ate an oyster that was 'off', one would never be able to eat an oyster again. He then explained the procedure for getting the oyster from the shell to one's mouth and then the vital moment, allowing it to linger for a split second on the back of the tongue, when one could establish if it was 'off'.

'If you are in any doubt, you must spit it out immediately,' he said, 'even if it goes on the floor.' It was years before I was actually able to enjoy eating oysters.

He had many deliberately old-fashioned affectations, chief among them being a veneration of Queen Elizabeth and Winston Churchill; by the same token, he maintained that Ireland had become little more than a hotbed of treachery and 'Republicanism'. The destruction of Nelson's Pillar was really the last straw. Although they were voiced in apparent deadly earnest, he was very amusing in enunciating his views, but I am glad to say that I knew not to take them seriously, and I did not absorb them.

I have perhaps made him sound effete, an aesthete in the manner of Evelyn Waugh's Anthony Blanche, but he was not that in the least (and he affected to be horrified by such characters). In fact, he was not really like anyone else at all. Above all, he was enormous fun.

I was very lucky to have met him and even luckier that he took me up; and our friendship over sixty years is one of the most treasured memories from of my life.[3]

Endnotes

1. Mary Campion, 'An Old Dublin Industry – Poplin', *Dublin Historical Record,* vol. 19 (1963).

2. Irish novelist, biographer, and lawyer (1912–94). Literary Editor of *The Irish Times,* 1961–77. One-time trustee of the National Library, the Chester Beatty Library, a director of the Gate Theatre, member of the Arts Council and the Irish Academy of Letters. Professor of Literature at the RHA. Married, as his second wife, to the biographer Victoria Glendinning. Obituary by Maeve Binchy, *The Independent,* 18 June 1994.

3. Speer died in his 90th year in Rome, where he had lived for more than fifty years, on 10 December 2016 (after this account was written) and is buried, with his grandmother and great-aunt, in Mount Jerome, Dublin. Henry predeceased him by about two years.

CHAPTER 6
TIMES PAST

A few years ago, I was driving down through France, alone, and daydreaming behind the wheel as kilometre after kilometre of motorway rolled by. Suddenly I saw a sign indicating a road off to the right. 'Janville', it said. I swerved off without thinking.

'This is where I was all those years ago,' I said to myself, 'my first time ever in France. How many years could it be?'

I calculated about forty.

I had kept up with the Chassines for a few years after my stay with them. I would write to them and I would go and visit, for a week or so, on my hitch-hiking holidays in France. I was always welcome but gradually contact was lost and it was decades since I had even sent them a Christmas card. But on this day, as I looked for the road to Semonville, I suddenly got cold feet. What was I doing? They might have forgotten me. They are probably dead. Pascal (the eldest boy) could be living there now, and with a horrid wife who would not welcome me. I tried to work out what age the parents would now be if they were still alive, and then I realised that I had no clue what age they had been when I had stayed with them. I drove cautiously, trying to remember the way, and then I recognised the exterior wall of the yard (with its postbox) running along the road. There was a car in front of me. It turned into the yard. Somewhat embarrassed, I hesitated and then followed. An attractive woman, in her fifties perhaps, neat and clean, had stepped out of the car and was holding a bag of shopping in each hand. 'Too young to be Madame Chassine,' I thought, 'but too old to be Pascal's wife either.' I was puzzled as I got out of the car and went over to her.

'Madame Chassine?' I said, knowing that that would cover the possibility of her being either Madame Chassine or her daughter-in-law.

She too was puzzled.

"*Oui?*' she replied.

And then I saw that, young-looking though she was, it was indeed my Madame Chassine.

'Do you recognise me?' I asked.

She looked me up and down.

'*Non. Pas du tout.*'

The French can only pronounce my name 'o-MAN', with no 'H' and the emphasis on the second syllable, and that was what the Chassines called me.

'*Je suis o-MAN*,' I said.

She let out a little shriek, dropped the shopping bags to the ground, and put her hands up to her mouth. We both stood there, silent, for a moment and then she ran over and hugged me. It was very emotional for us both and it took a few minutes for us to recover.

'François will be thrilled to see you,' she said. 'Come in, come in. We have often talked about you over the years and the children have never forgotten you. None of them are here any more. They all have careers. It's just François and me.'

I picked up the bags of shopping and went with her: through what had been the house when I was there and out to the garden. The house that Monsieur Chassine was planning in my time had been built but, of course, it was no longer new. We went into a lovely big kitchen. Madame Chassine was giddy with chatter, remembering those years long ago, as she put away the shopping.

'François should be back soon,' she said, glancing at the clock and looking at me again and again. When he arrived, he was puzzled by the stranger with his wife.

'Do you not know who it is?' she said to him.

And then we had the 'o-MAN' and the emotion all over again.

She quickly prepared a lovely lunch and we talked away. None of the boys had wanted to farm and all had other careers. Nor did any of them live nearby. Pascal was married here; Jean-Michel was working there; Veronique was someplace else; Marie-Silvie had three children; Françoise had four; Denis had never married. Thomas (who had been a delicate little toddler when I was there) had died young. There had been another baby after my time. It dawned on me that they were all now men and women of practically the same age as myself: I had only been six years older than Pascal. I asked what age the parents had been when I was there. Madame Chassine had been in her late twenties, he in his early thirties. I told them how the months I had spent with them had changed my life. They could not comprehend this.

'How?' they asked.

'Everything,' I said.

After lunch François took me on a tour. There was much that was the same but a great deal that had been changed. Trees that had been saplings when I was there, were huge. A swimming pool had been installed (it was now almost empty and green); a hard tennis court had been built (it was now overgrown with weeds); the paling round a paddock, where horses had obviously been galloped, had fallen into disrepair. But in the yard everything was pristine and the evidence was that Monsieur Chassine was still the efficient farmer he was when I was there. He explained to me that for years he had worked with the government in the scientific development of certain crops. We went into the old house, now abandoned, and I saw the corner of the room that had been my bedroom.

Back in the kitchen, Micheline (as I was now calling her) told me that, when François was seventy a year or so previously, the children had put together a video of old film clips for him. Would I like to see it? I recalled that François had always been filming with a cine-camera when I was there. She brought me into the sitting room, darkened the room, put on the video and left me there to watch it.

All the children were in the film. That was the day they were all going to the wedding, I recalled. There's Mémère, the old granny, coming for Sunday lunch, Pascal showing off, Thomas in tears. And then . . . o-MAN. There I was, aged sixteen, pushing the children on the *balançoire*, loading them up on their bicycles, behind the wheel of the old 2CV, carrying a dead rabbit by its ears. I have hardly ever seen photographs of myself from those years, and never a film. I was overcome.

I left them late in the afternoon and continued on my journey. I had been very moved by the visit, haunted, almost traumatised, and I remained so for several days. It was the images of the empty swimming pool and the weed-covered tennis court that stayed with me. Neither the pool nor the court had been there in my time. They had been installed later, had been enjoyed for years by a young family growing up, and were now abandoned: a generation, a whole lifetime, had come and gone in the decades since I, as a sixteen-year-old, had been so happy there.

My life – well, about five decades of it – had come and gone too.

But what I saw on that video had been the beginning.

CHAPTER 7
A PROPER JOB

I have a recurring dream in which I am about to sit university finals. In the dream, I have not revised and am convinced that I am going to fail, and I haven't a clue what I want to do in life or where to go. As a result, I decide to stay on at university. On the assumption that this must be a dream that other people have as well, and wondering what it can mean, I looked it up.

Oh dear! It's all to do with my realising through my experience of later life that, basically, I made a mess of my university years. 'Most dreams taking us back to earlier school experiences have to do with a nagging recollection of not having done all that we might have at that time.' Sadly, I cannot argue with that. For one reason or another, I did not take advantage of all that Trinity had to offer. I did not enjoy my time there; I do not have nice memories of the place; I did not make many friends; in fact, the only saving grace was my introduction to the world of art history by means of the stupendous teaching of Anne Crookshank.

When I did graduate, although I knew I wanted more than Anne had managed to impart in two years, I was not at all sure about a future career. It was by no means clear in those days – at least it was not clear to me – that one could make a career in art history, and so I considered other options. The Hong Kong & Shanghai Bank (which was not then the HSBC that it is today) was a popular choice for graduates wanting to work abroad (and that included me); the world of advertising attracted arts graduates who sought something creative and I did apply to a firm called Benton & Bowles in Knightsbridge but the experience of the interview convinced me that advertising was not for me. Because of my working in Claridge's, hotel management strayed into my mind, although it soon strayed out again. I felt I was too Irish to even think of Sotheby's or Christie's. But if I really wanted to learn more than Anne had taught me, then I could: there was the Courtauld Institute in London, and I could do another art history degree there.

It was all too confusing and, to solve my dilemma, I decided I needed a year abroad to think. I would go to Germany. I had never been there, and did not know a word of German; it would be a new experience. I enrolled in a language school in Cologne for three months in the autumn and found accommodation (through the school) with a widow and her unpleasant adult son. I wrote to my mother (on 6 October 1968):

> I have meals with the family. She is very rough, and a war widow. The son, who is about thirty, speaks good English and thinks he knows just about everything. All the time it is how great the Germans are, etc, etc. I just told him the other night what everyone thought about the Germans, and that shut him up.

When I came home in December (for my Trinity Commencements), I went to see Anne Crookshank and asked her about the Courtauld.

'By all means apply,' she said, 'and I'll give you a good reference. It's fiercely competitive but my pupil Margaret Mitchell got in last year.'

But although Anne and I were still very much teacher and pupil at this stage, she had observed something of my character over the two years of my sitting at the back of her seminar room.

'But there are other options,' she said. 'Have you thought of Edinburgh, which has a very good reputation under David Talbot Rice? Or the University of East Anglia: that's a new department? They might suit you better than the more hothouse atmosphere of the Courtauld.'

The way she said 'hothouse' alerted me.

'And Edinburgh would be a friendlier environment than London can be,' she added.

After Christmas, I returned to Germany but this time I went to Munich. There was a reason for my choice: Penny was there. But our nine months in the city is a story that must – in the interests of discretion – wait to be told in full another day. Sufficient to say that we had a fabulous time. I taught English at the Berlitz School and we travelled a lot, to Salzburg, to Prague, and we drove to Greece. Penny was very musical and had a beautiful singing voice. Her rendering to her own accompaniment on the piano of Schubert's *Die Forelle* with beautiful German diction could and did (on one occasion) bring tears to the eyes of even a German. We went very often – gaining a substantial discount on last-minute tickets with our student-cards – to the best of opera and to wonderful concerts. Afterwards, walking through the night streets in the snow, Penny would burst into loud song, paraphrasing musically much of what we had just heard. My pocket diary from the time records that we heard Daniel Barenboim, Hans Hotter, David and Igor Oistrakh, Michelangelo Benedetti (drunk at the keyboard, as I recall), Rita Streich, Birgit Nilsson, Otto Klemperer, Herman Prey and Dietrich Fischer-Dieskau in the concert hall, and, at the opera, a complete Ring Cycle, *Arabella, The Sicilian Vespers, Tristan, Rosenkavalier, Faust, Orpheo, The Marriage of Figaro, Rigoletto, Madame Butterfly* and *Die Freischütz*. Penny remembers a conductor dropping dead on the podium during a performance at the opera but I have no recollection of that.

I bought an ancient Volkswagen Beetle convertible, and we toured the castles of King Ludwig, and learned a lot about Bavarian Rococo. We lived in the student quarter of Schwabing, near the English Garden. I learned very little German. My only regret is that I did not learn to ski. The snow lasts in Munich until well into March, and skiing is possible almost on one's doorstep; but, foolishly, I did not take it up.

I soon found employment. 'Now I have got all sorts of good news for you,' I wrote to my mother (1 February 1969).

'The most important thing is that I have landed the most marvellous job. I got it through one of the schools I applied to teach in. It is giving an intensive course in English to two ladies. The director of the school, who is awfully nice and has given me all sorts of help, tells me that they are both immensely rich and also very snobby.[1] This is just a sudden sort of whim that they have got, that they want to learn English, and is an excuse to spend some of their husbands' money. I have to teach them from 9 to 1, then go to lunch with them until 2 (talking English). I get an allowance to cover the cost of the lunch and get paid £12 10s per week. The unfortunate thing is that these women will, I am sure, get tired of English after about three weeks. 'No, I no longer teach the two ladies,' I informed my mother (on 5 March 1969). 'They have gone to France to buy clothes and won't be back for a while. Anyway, they had got fed up of the classes, as their English was nearly as good as mine.'

But my carefree Munich existence was not without some clouds. Reminding me that Elliott did feel a responsibility for me, my mother wrote to say he had said she should 'take me home'. I replied (7 April 1969):

> Elliott is talking nonsense telling you to take me home and I am glad that you and Alice have the good sense to see that. I just want you to see and remember that I am, and always have been, completely different in temperament to any of the others, so to try and make me lead the same sort of lives they do, would be absolute madness, and were I to come home and work in Dublin, which is what Elliott wants, I would be very, very unhappy. You must know that I am not wasting my time here or anywhere else, and you may rest assured that I will turn out alright, so don't worry.

The paragraph which followed contained the sort of news that could only have worried my mother more and added fuel to Elliott's fire:

> I went to High Mass with this family that I have got to know. There was one Cardinal and four bishops – all very colourful. There was an enormous crowd of people, all waiting to get communion from the old Cardinal. Ordinary old bloke he was too: just as bad as they are at home.

But all the time, I knew that this happy, carefree and very irresponsible life had to end and that I must not stay on in Munich for more than a year or I might be trapped, with no qualifications and no career, in an expatriate existence for life. Furthermore, Penny and I had influenced each other too much and we had become too alike to make a success of any longer-term partnership and, with sadness, we both knew it. I applied to the Courtauld and to Edinburgh University, and I was interviewed for a place on their courses by both. The interview at the

Courtauld was in February or March. My friend Peter Feuchtwanger wrote to me (on 24 January 1969): 'Was pleased to receive your letter this morning and to learn that you are planning to come to London for the interview. When will it be? I shall write to Prof Gombrich[2] the moment you have a definite date. I hope you will stay with me.'

My Courtauld interview, by Anthony Blunt[3] and one of his lecturers (I don't recall who), was one of the cruellest experiences I ever endured, and I have never forgotten it. Blunt started the interview by telling me that they did not normally accept someone with my background but that they had had one of Anne Crookshank's pupils the previous year and 'she had done rather well'. As an art history qualification was offered by very few universities at this time, I must have been relatively rare among applicants in that I already had a degree in the subject. So, if that was not an acceptable background, I did not know what could have been. In stating in my application (as one was asked to do) the two fields of study that interested me, I had plumped for 'seventeenth- and eighteenth-century painting and architecture' and 'German Expressionist painting'.

When we were seated around a table, Sir Anthony opened the interview. 'Perhaps we could show you some photographs,' he said, glancing towards his colleague, 'and ask you to identify them.'

The colleague passed a small black-and-white photograph across the table. In most cases, German Expressionist painters are recognised by their colour, although there are some artists – Kandinsky, Klee and Franz Marc, with his horses, for example – that are more obvious by their style. A small black-and-white photograph is by no means the easiest means of identifying an artist of this school. As I tentatively assessed the photographs, Sir Anthony – noisily drawing in his breath through his teeth – made me aware of how little I knew. But at the same time, I got some artists right. Wearily, Sir A moved the interview on to the eighteenth century, and more photographs were produced. Throwing one across at me (and this I recall as though it were yesterday), he said, 'You won't recognise this, but look at the photograph and let us hear your reasoning.' As it happened, I did recognise the image (I don't know how).

'It's the Double Cube Room at Wilton,' I said. 'Inigo Jones, about 1650.'

The interview was soon over. I was very shocked by the experience and, not surprisingly, I was turned down.

Within five years I was an assistant keeper at the London National Gallery, having beaten several of Blunt's graduates in the selection process for the post. Naturally, I met Sir Anthony at events in the gallery and I would also meet him socially, in particular at the house of my friend John Kenworthy-Browne. I always wanted to tell Blunt that he had once interviewed me, and I wanted to tell him how uncalled for it had been to treat any young person the way he had treated me. But I never had the nerve to do so. When, a few years later, he was unmasked as the despicable traitor he was, there was no one who was more pleased than me. Turned down by Sir Anthony, my path was directed towards Edinburgh, where I was interviewed for a place on the post-graduate course by Professor Talbot Rice. David Talbot Rice was a distinguished scholar of Byzantine art and a gentleman and his interviewing technique was in marked contrast to Sir Anthony's cruelty. I was accepted by him and that, as it turned out, was a fortunate and very happy turn of events.

As Elliott's generosity in funding my education had (understandably) come to an end with my graduation from Trinity, I had to find the means of supporting myself through two years' study in Edinburgh. An odd little legacy from Old Elliott Potterton (see *Rathcormick*), which had accumulated since his death in 1929, was in my name and, now that I was over twenty-one, it became available to me. I used it, and I also looked for whatever grants I might find. A Carnegie Trust in Scotland gave bursaries to anyone of Scottish descent who wanted to study in Scotland and, when my mother told me that her grandmother was Scots (which was true), I successfully applied. I also obtained funds from the Arts Council in Ireland: Mervyn Wall[4] the novelist, who was secretary of the Council, told me many years later that he had looked at my application sympathetically as he knew of me through Speer Ogle. Then there was the Purser–Griffith Scholarship and Prize. This was based upon an exam that was set in alternate years by Trinity and University College Dublin (UCD). From Edinburgh I enrolled for the exam – which was to be held in UCD that year – but my application was met by the History of Art Department in UCD, then under the formidable Françoise Henry,[5] with extreme resistance. Although I had given details of my birth and education in Ireland, including a degree from Trinity it was not enough to confirm that I was Irish and, therefore, eligible to sit the exam. A copy of my passport and an affidavit – yes, an affidavit – from a solicitor was demanded to confirm my Irish credentials. The exam consisted of two papers: one, a general history of European painting, and another on a special subject chosen by candidates in advance. I selected 'Eighteenth-century British Portrait Painting'. On the day of the exam, when the special subject paper was put in front of me, I saw immediately that the questions were not confined to British painting but ranged over the full canvas of European portraiture. I answered the required number of questions as best I could, but I did write a letter of protest afterwards. I was informed that I had passed the exam but, if I wanted, I could re-sit the special paper. Passing the exam was no good to me: I needed the scholarship, or at very least the prize, and so I sat the exam again. I won the prize; the scholarship went to a diligent nun from UCD.

The fact of the matter was that Françoise Henry could not abide Anne Crookshank. Françoise was the grande dame of Irish art studies – albeit Celtic ones – and had been teaching at UCD since 1932. She had very little interest in post-Renaissance Irish art – which was Anne's field – and she resented Trinity setting up a history of art department. Matters were not helped by the fact that they were both very formidable and domineering women and both grazed the same field when, in actual fact, the Prairie would not have been extensive enough to contain them. It should be stated, though, that Anne had nothing but admiration for Françoise.

At Edinburgh, I chose to specialise in seventeenth- and eighteenth-century art and architecture, and my tutor was Alistair Rowan.[6] He was (and still is) a very good lecturer, although less electrifying than Anne. As a tutor he was exacting and, because there was only one other student, Neil Burton,[7] studying the same subject as me (the entire class of postgraduates numbered only about ten or twelve), Alistair gave us a lot of his time. Neil and I got on very well and I liked his lovely Oxford girlfriend, Andrea, very much. The course was a two-year one, culminating in exams and the submission of a 10,000-word thesis. When it came to choosing a topic for my thesis, it was Anne who suggested Irish sculpture and, specifically, Irish church monuments.

'They are there to be discovered,' she said, 'it's only a matter of getting into the churches and that's much easier than getting into private houses to look at pictures. But do prepare! You must go through the *Journals of the Association for the Preservation of the Memorials of the Dead in Ireland*. They are in the library here. They document some monuments but not the sculptors, of course. It's for you to identify the sculptors.'

And so I spent the Christmas and Easter vacations combing through these turgid journals (and other sources) and compiling lists of what I had to find. In the dishevelled Volkswagen Beetle – left-hand drive, convertible, with a tattered roof, and an uncertain temperament – that I had brought home from Munich, I had a merry time driving the length and breadth of Ireland that summer in pursuit of sculptors, and photographing and recording all that I found. I had many interesting encounters. Finding Helen Roe[8] and Nora O'Sullivan deep in the undergrowth of a churchyard in County Laois was one. Helen, who was a medievalist (and delightful), asked me what I was doing.

'Looking for eighteenth- and nineteenth-century monuments,' I explained.

'But those are not monuments,' she objected, 'they're modern.'

On a sunny Sunday afternoon, battling my way to see the sculptor Joseph Wilton's beautiful – but vandalised – Dawson monument at Dartrey County Monaghan, I came across the architect Jeremy Williams[9] encamped with a detachment of other enthusiasts in the stables at Dartrey, which they were supposedly restoring. It was my first time meeting Jeremy, who was to become a friend for life.

I found lots of monuments, far too many to incorporate coherently into a shortish thesis, and so I picked a single sculptor – an Englishman who had settled in Ireland in the early eighteenth century, William Kidwell – and I investigated him and wrote him up. Kidwell was hardly a 'name', in fact he wasn't a name at all and, as a sculptor, he was very minor indeed; but my thesis appealed to the external examiner, Professor John Steer. Depressed by the annual task of reading theses on the usual subjects, such as Robert Adam, Alexander Runciman, David Wilkie or Charles Rennie Mackintosh, Steer was taken by the nonsensical novelty of Kidwell and insisted on giving me a high mark. Alistair Rowan suggested I turn the thesis into a 'Shorter Notice' for the *Burlington Magazine* and he sent it to the editor, Benedict Nicolson, who published it. The dottiness of all of this did not stop there. Charles Brett[10] of the Ulster Architectural Heritage Society asked me to put together all my monuments in a dictionary format and he published my text under the auspices of his society in an ugly little typewritten book.

Finishing in Edinburgh, I was, like all new graduates, in the dire position of having to find a job. I applied for whatever was on offer in the provincial museums of England, but without success. Then one Sunday morning, Desmond Guinness – whom I did not know – telephoned me at home in Trim.

'It's Desmond, Desmond Guinness,' he said in his whispering voice. 'Is that Homan?' It was as though we were old friends. 'Miss Crookshank tells me that you have written the most marvellous thesis, and I so long to read it.'

He invited me to Leixlip that afternoon, asking me to bring my thesis with me and, at the end of about an hour's chat, he said that if I had no better offer, he could give me work at Leixlip for a month or two sorting photographs and Georgian Society files.

'Could I start tomorrow morning?'

I was delighted: it was a break, and I have never forgotten Desmond's kindness.

The couple of months I spent at Leixlip that summer were just wonderful. Desmond's wife Mariga was not there, although she appeared for a week or so, making her presence felt by the rustling of her petticoat under a long tartan skirt as she descended the stairs. Patricia McSweeney, an American, was Desmond's secretary: 'raven-haired Miss McSweeney' as she was referred to in a newspaper interview. She was the greatest of fun. We worked from an office upstairs, which Desmond also sometimes shared, and Patricia and I had many hilarious moments together. I was still quite timid and shy – and, frankly, in awe of the circumstances in which I found myself – but I was treated by Desmond rather in the manner of an eighteenth-century tutor in an aristocratic household. I was included in the dining room at lunch every day, with Desmond and whatever guests there were, and in that way I encountered a host of exotic (to me) individuals. His brother Jonathan; the legendary wealthy aesthete Rory Cameron[11] and his handsome boyfriend (and gardener), Gilbert; Desmond and Helen

Leslie; sundry rich (and confused by Leixlip) Americans; Mark Bence-Jones[12] and his wife, who asked for a glass of milk with her lunch rather than wine; and many more. I was invited to the Leixlip 'Dinner and Dancing' in Horse Show Week. It was all terrific. I observed and took things in: Desmond's sense of fun and style, his ease, his kindness and thoughtfulness, his lack of snobbery.

One afternoon, I was in Dublin and walking through Trinity when I was hailed by Anne Crookshank.

'You must go immediately and ring James White,'[13] she said. 'John Gilmartin[14] has got a good job in the Birmingham Museum and is leaving the National Gallery. I've told James that you are the man to take John's place.'

I did as I was bidden. James invited me to come to the gallery. We had a brief talk and he asked me when I could start. The post was a menial one, with a desk at the end of the library, but as Michael Wynne was James's only curatorial assistant, there would be lots of interesting work to do. I would be the 'temporary cataloguer'. When my mother rang my brother Elliott to boast that I had now got a proper job, he asked what sort of job.

'As a temporary cataloguer in the National Gallery,' she said proudly.

'Temporary?' said Elliott. 'The postman who brings the letters to Rathcormick has been temporary for thirty-five years.'

But my mother's satisfaction was undimmed. She had been indulgent of my migration from incipient solicitor to the unfamiliar territory of art historian and, although never without some strictures, she had always tolerated all my other nonsense as well – such as my enthusiasm for foreign travel.

'But I always knew you wouldn't let me down,' is what she said in reporting Elliott's reaction.

In the diary pages that follow, written at the time I worked under James White in the National Gallery, I seem to denigrate James. But this is a callow youth who is writing. Yes, there were things about James that could be denigrated: his lack of academic credentials, for a start. And his eye for a picture could sometimes be shaky. His writing on art tended towards the haphazard. But James had many other qualities that elevated him above the ordinary as a director and which accounted for his success. He was a superb communicator, both as a lecturer on art and in handling public relations. The gallery (and James) was always in the news. He could get on with people – from the man in the street to the highest in the land, be they politicians, business tycoons, foreign ambassadors or the old Anglo-Irish gentry. Had I been endowed with even a fraction of his political acumen, I would, in later years, have been a great deal more successful as director of the gallery than I ever was. James liked to be liked but did not bear grudges if he was not. Working under him could be something of a roller coaster, as some of my diary entries imply. He himself worked at speed; he got things done; all was possible; and he expected those who worked with him to be of the same frame of mind. Maddening he might have been on occasion, but he was also endearing, and by the time I left the gallery after just over two years, I was very fond of him. He too liked me (as later chapters here will show) and, after I went to London, he would sometimes look me up and ask me to dine with him and over dinner indulge his penchant for naughty chat. His wife, Aggie, was someone I came to admire greatly too. She was stylish and dignified, and always forthright in her views. James seemed to keep her in the background, but she was very sound and sensible and gave James a very contented family life.

James was the instigator in establishing at this time the Association of Irish Art Historians – a novel concept, as there were hardly any Irish art historians to speak of. His principal challenge was to get Françoise Henry to sit round a table with Anne Crookshank; and in this he eventually succeeded. Notwithstanding there being such a very small pool in which to fish, discussions as to who counted as an art historian were protracted. Were the scholars of early Irish art really art historians in the strict sense of the word? There were those who would want to be included – was it enough to have passed the Purser–Griffith exam? – but were not considered sufficiently academic; and there were those who were desirable as members, such as John Teahan[15] and Catriona MacLeod[16] in the National Museum, but would they join? No question mark hung over the eligibility of the tiny terrier that was Mrs Leask[17]: she would almost be accepted *honoris causa*. And what about architectural historians?

Eventually, things got under way, and I was made assistant honorary secretary. James came up with a project for members to update the Irish biographies in the multi-volume *Thieme-Becker Künsterlexikon*, and lists of suitable entries were solicited. As to whether Thieme-Becker wanted their Irish biographies updated, no one actually knew. But in the event, it did not matter one way or another, as nothing ever happened. I did not know Françoise Henry, but once or twice, following a meeting, she came to the gallery and, on finding me at my desk in the library, sat down opposite me. She was terrifically large (and was to become even larger) and I found her acutely fearsome. She would come to correct some details in the minutes that I had sent out. She did not do this in an unkind or bullying way but more to inculcate in me an appreciation that accuracy was important. It dawned on me after a couple of these sessions that she was actually trying to reach out and befriend me. But as I left the gallery before too long, it was a friendship that had no time to blossom. In spite of that, Françoise was to play a pivotal role at a later – and crucial – stage of my career.

It is difficult to imagine today, when art history is such a firmly established discipline being taught in colleges all over Ireland (and England), and when there are so many people doing research over a very broad spectrum, that in the 1960s the subject was new, with degree courses in Britain limited in the main to the Courtauld Institute, Edinburgh University and the University of East Anglia. Françoise had, from as early as 1934, been giving lectures on European painting in UCD when she was attached to the French Department and, from 1948, to the Department of Archeology. It was only in 1965 that she established the History of Art Department: that was the same year that Anne appeared in Trinity, setting up the Art History Department there. Insofar as post-Renaissance Irish art was concerned, very few people had engaged in research, and publishing outlets had been few. One must rummage through the pages of the *Capuchin Annual*, the *Father Mathew Record* and *Studies* to find what articles on Irish artists there were. There one will come across, among the very few, Máirin Allen (who, I think, was a pupil of Françoise) writing about Evie Hone and other Irish artists as early as the 1940s, and Con Curran (C.P. Curran),[18] Tom McGreevy[19] and Eithne Waldron[20] contributing slightly later. But from the late 1960s things began to change, and it was Anne, more than Françoise, who encouraged research on topics that would hardly have been considered worthy of study a decade earlier. Jeanne Sheehy[21] was the first of Anne's hens who was set to hatch, with an M.Litt thesis on

Walter Osborne, and others quickly followed: Michael Wynne[22] (Irish stained glass), John Hutchinson[23] (James Arthur O'Connor) and Julian Campbell[24] (Irish artists in early-twentieth-century France), to cite but three. The *Irish Georgian Society Bulletin* was an outlet for articles on (mainly) eighteenth-century art and architecture, *Studies* was still in circulation and, in the North, Charlie Brett was publishing madly under the auspices of the Ulster Architectural Heritage Society.

From the pages of my 1973 diary, it seems that those of us who were interested in Irish art research formed a very small clique: the names are few, and oft repeated. Anne, the Knight of Glin[25] Desmond Guinness, Maurice Craig, Eddie McParland[26] Jeanne Sheehy, Hugh Dixon,[27] Rolf Loeber,[28] Charlie Brett and myself. We were a small clique – and a very Trinity–Georgian Society clique at that. If there were others, in UCD or elsewhere, who were equally active, they mainly eluded us: Michael Wynne (researching Thomas Frye) and Hilary Pyle (Jack B. Yeats) in the National Gallery we knew about, and John Gilmartin had written about the Dublin sculptor Peter Turnerelli; John Turpin[29] was working on Daniel Maclise and John O'Grady[30] on Sarah Purser; but that was more or less it. The National Museum kept itself out of bounds, with virtually all of its eighteenth- and nineteenth-century collections unavailable, and it was only with the advent years later of Mairead Dunlevy[31] there that things (and the curators) became more accessible.

Being now in 'a proper job', I was faced with finding a place to live in Dublin. I saw no reason – except for the fact that I had no money – why I should not buy a house.

'I can borrow the money from the bank and take lodgers to pay it off', I said to my mother when she enquired as to how I intended to proceed.

'I see', she said.

But as I looked for houses, and she saw that I was serious, she offered to help me.

'There is no use in my leaving you money after my death', she said. 'You won't need it then. Besides, I don't intend dying for some years yet.'

She was in her late sixties at the time. I found a house – a beautiful house, 169 Rathgar Road – and bought it at auction for £11,000. My mother gave me £5,000 – 'That's your inheritance', she said, 'don't expect anything more' – and I got a loan from the bank for the balance. My meagre salary as a temporary cataloguer rendered me ineligible for a proper mortgage.

The house, in brick, was a typical Dublin house of its time (I suppose about 1840) and was, therefore, elegantly planned. Three storeys, with high steps leading up to the hall door, and two beautiful reception rooms linked by a double opening, the detailing of which was Greek Revival. There was a long back garden with a tumbledown mews at the end. Although not divided, it had been in three fairly simple flats, so there were basic kitchens and bathrooms on each floor.

'It's all ready for lodgers,' I said to my mother in my attempts to persuade her that it was an ideal buy.

I moved in the day I bought it, and then went out and bought seven beds: one for me and one for any guest I might have in the reception rooms, three for upstairs, and two for the basement. I put a placard in the upstairs window facing the road: 'Rooms to Rent', it read.

There then unfolded a most extraordinary set of circumstances.

Almost immediately, along came three young men. They inspected the upstairs flat, came down, asked what the rent was, and said they would take it. I enquired if any or all of them were gainfully employed.

'We're actors,' they said, with that assurance which actors have, and without actually assuring me that they were employed.

One of them spoke with an English accent, another was Northern Irish, and the third was American. None of this, by my reckoning, augured well, and I had the sense to realise that I would be taking a risk by letting them have the flat. I knew that actors kept very irregular hours and that they also led very irregular (and unconventional) lives, but I liked the look of this trio and felt that they would be more congenial to have upstairs than some more steady lodgers. I delved further.

'And are any of you actually acting at the moment?' I asked.

'Of course,' came the reply. 'We're in the Project.'

It was as though they were stating that they were members of the Royal Shakespeare Company.

The Project, which had only recently been set up, was (to me) a sort of louche arts centre which staged alternative theatre and alternative art exhibitions, poetry readings and the like. It never lasted very long in any one venue and, whenever it was in the news (which was often), it was on account of its irregular finances rather than its artistic programme. Still, very much against my better judgement, I offered them the flat and they moved in.

The three young men who by this means came to live upstairs were Alan Stanford, Gerard McSorley and the American, whose name escapes me.

'I'm not an actor,' he corrected me, 'I'm a playwright.'

'And have some of your plays been performed here?' I asked.

'Not yet, but I've several things in the pipeline.'

But Tennessee Williams he was not and (as I learned from Gerard many years later) his plays remained in the pipeline and he was destined for oblivion. But oblivion was not for Alan or Gerard. Alan Stanford remained in Ireland, and was to become one of the most celebrated actors in the land and a mainstay of the Gate Theatre; Gerard McSorley's career took him to the Abbey, where he too was a success. Decades later, when I was living in New York, he came to Broadway playing the priest in Brian Friel's *Dancing at Lughnasa*. He was no longer the cute little black-haired youth who had lived at Number 169 but stocky and greying. While in New York, he was lodging with my friend, the dress designer Mary O'Donnell, and through her I met him. I had them to a party at my flat and we talked of Rathgar Road. They had all loved being there, he said, and he remembered it well.

Next, I had to let the basement rooms. Along came another Englishman. Young, elegant, with well-groomed, long black hair, and a pink shirt.

'A bit fancy,' I thought.

But as it turned out he was not fancy at all. He liked the flat.

'And do you intend living here alone?' I asked. 'It's really meant for two.'

'Oh no!' he said. 'I'll be sharing it with a friend.'

'I would have to meet your friend before deciding,' I said.

The following evening there arrived on my doorstep a face that was vaguely familiar: a good-looking – in a sexy way – young man in jeans and a leather blouson. This was the potential flat-sharer.

'I know your face,' I said, 'but I can't think how.'

'I'm Jim Bartley,' he said with some diffidence. 'Perhaps you've seen me on Telefís.'

Indeed I had. He was Sean Nolan, the heart-throb in a long-running soap, *Tolka Row*.

'What is this?' I thought. 'All these actors. Am I to become, inadvertently, a theatrical landlord?'

The Englishman was a photographer, but no ordinary photographer: he was Mike Bunn, who was to make his career in Ireland and become its most celebrated and best-known fashion photographer.

And there I was, landlord to all these celebrities-in-waiting, paying my bank loan, and living a life of elegance in my own two rooms. But it came to an end before all that long when I moved to London, to take up a job in the National Gallery. I decanted my lodgers (all of whom had proved to be excellent tenants) and sold the house on my departure.

Endnotes

1. I recall that one of the ladies was a Frau Springer, married to one of the sons of the Axel Springer publishing empire.
2. Ernst Gombrich (1901–2001) the doyen of British art historians and hugely influential, he was a Professor at the Warburg Institute. A friend of Peter Feuchtwanger and a German Jewish emigre. Peter thought he might be able to help me get into the Courtauld.
3. (1907–83) Director of the Courtauld Institute, 1947–74; Surveyor of the King's (and later the Queen's) Pictures, 1945–72. Authority on the artist Poussin. Exposed in 1979 as a Soviet spy.
4. (z`z1908–97) He was Secretary of the Arts Council from 1957–75. His comic fantasy novels (published in the 1940s), *The Unfortunate Fursey* and *The Return of Fursey* are his best known.
5. (1902–82). Renowned scholar of Irish art in the early-Christian period. Born in France, she graduated from the Sorbonne and first came to Ireland in 1926 and was moved to focus on early Irish medieval sculpture as a subject of research. Appointed to the French Department of UCD in 1932, she later moved to the Department of Archaeology while teaching a course on the History of European Painting; and established the History of Art Department in 1965. She first published her *Irish Art* in 1940 and this was expanded to a three-volume *L'Art Irandais* in 1963. Subsequently published in English, it remains the standard text on early Irish Art.
6. Architectural historian, b.1938. Lecturer in Fine Art at the University of Edinburgh, later Professor of History of Art at UCD, Principal of Edinburgh College of Art, Professor of History of Art at University College Cork (UCC). Editor of *The Buildings of Ireland* series and author of the North-West Ulster volume.
7. Neil had read history at Oxford and has had a distinguished career as an architectural historian, first with the Council for Places of Worship, then with GLC Historic Buildings, next with English Heritage and, later, as Secretary of the Georgian Group. Now a private architectural historian.
8. An early woman graduate of Trinity College, she taught at Alexandra College and

became an authority on the art of Early Christian Ireland. The first woman President of the Royal Society of Antiquaries of Ireland.

9. Architect, artist, writer, conservationist and conversationalist, and polymath (1943–2015). Author *of Architecture in Ireland, 1837–1921* (1994). (d. 24 December 2015). Obituary by Charles Lysaght *Irish Independent*, 10 January 2016.

10. (1928–2005). Belfast solicitor, journalist, author and founder (and chairman) of the Ulster Architectural Heritage Society.

11. Decorator, socialite host, author (d.1985) and son of the scandalous Lady Kenmare. His villa, *La Fiorentina* at St Jean Cap Ferrat, was a mecca for the international beau monde.

12. (1930–2010). 'An elegant writer on architecture, Roman Catholicism, Ireland and the Raj with an admiration for the upper classes and grand houses.' Obituary, *Daily Telegraph*, 30 April 2010.

13. Lecturer in the history of art, appointed curator of the Dublin Municipal Gallery (now the Hugh Lane) in 1960 and director of the National Gallery of Ireland, 1964–80. My obituary of James, *Burlington Magazine* (September 2013).

14. Dr John Maiben Gilmartin, my predecessor as temporary cataloguer in the National Gallery of Ireland and later deputy keeper of art in the City Museum & Art Gallery, Birmingham. Subsequently, long-time art history lecturer in the College of Marketing and Design (later the Dublin Institute of Technology). President of the Friends of the National Collections of Ireland (FNCI).

15. Keeper of the Art and Industry Department of the National Museum of Ireland who wrote extensively on Irish furniture and decorative arts.

16. A curator at the National Museum of Ireland, she was a specialist on eighteenth- and nineteenth-century decorative arts. She published on Irish eighteenth-century glass and other topics.

17. Ada Longfield Leask (1899–1987), widow of Harold Leask, Inspector of National Monuments in Ireland and author of *Irish Churches & Monastic Buildings*. She was a graduate in law from Trinity who researched and published widely (long before many people were interested) on Irish decorative arts of the eighteenth century.

18. C.P. Curran (1880–1972) was a lawyer and historian of eighteenth-century Dublin architecture. Author of *Dublin Decorative Plasterwork* (1967).

19. Poet, friend in Paris of Samuel Beckett, and director of the National Gallery of Ireland, 1950–63.

20. Assistant to Tom McGreevy at the National Gallery and curator of the Dublin Municipal Gallery (the Hugh Lane), 1964–90.

21. (1939–99). Authority on Walter Osborne and the Celtic Revival in art, she was virtually the first of the modern generation of Irish art historians to study (at the beginning, largely under the aegis of Anne Crookshank) Irish art from the eighteenth to twentieth centuries. From an artistic (and slightly bohemian) background, she had studied something or other in Paris. Her Walter Osborne thesis was published in a book (1974) and further in the catalogue of the Osborne exhibition in the National Gallery (1983). Her book on *The Celtic Revival 1830–1930* (1980), although by her account only a general survey, is still regarded as a landmark of research. In the mid-1970s she took up a post as lecturer in the history of art in what became Oxford Brooks University, and remained there until her death.

22. (1937–2003). A curator at the National Gallery of Ireland, 1965–97. He was assistant director to James White. Deeply religious (he had studied for the priesthood in Rome

for six years), his degree was in archaeology from UCD. He later researched and published on Irish stained glass and Irish painting in the eighteenth century and was widely regarded as an authority. He suffered ill-health for much of his life.

23. Director of the Douglas Hyde Gallery, Trinity College, Dublin from 1991. Author of *James Arthur O'Connor* (1985).

24. b. 1949. Artist and art historian, and the leading authority on Irish artists of the late-nineteenth and early twentieth century. Author of *The Irish Impressionists* (1984). Lecturer in the National College of Art and, since 1986, tutor in art history at the Crawford College of Art.

25. Desmond FitzGerald (1937–2011), the twenty-ninth and last Knight of Glin. He worked in the furniture department of the Victoria & Albert Museum and returned to Ireland in the 1980s, when he became Christie's Irish representative. Later President of the Irish Georgian Society.

26. Graduate of UCD and Cambridge, he became a lecturer in the Trinity History of Art Department in 1973. Author of *James Gandon* (1985) and *Public Architecture in Ireland, 1680–1760* (2001).

27. An English architectural historian who came to Belfast in 1970 as a research assistant to Alistair Rowan on the *Buildings of Ireland* project. Later attached to the Institute of Irish Studies in Belfast and active in the Ulster Architectural Heritage Society. He published widely on Belfast architecture in the Victorian period. From the mid-1980s, National Trust curator for north-east England.

28. A Dutch psychiatrist, graduate of the Queen's University, Kingston, Ontario. He came to Ireland about this time (1973) and developed a serious interest in seventeenth-century Irish architecture and researched assiduously (and widely), resulting in his *Biographical Dictionary of Architects in Ireland, 1600–1720* (1981).

29. Later professor of the history of art at the National College of Art and Design. He has published extensively on the history of Irish sculpture, painting, design and art education.

30. Lecturer in the history of art in UCD, and authority on Sarah Purser.

31. (1941–2008). She joined the National Museum of Ireland (NMI) in 1970 and became a leading authority on Irish decorative arts, and Irish dress and costume in particular. Briefly Director of the Hunt Museum, she became Keeper of the NMI Art & Industry Division. Author of *Dress in Ireland* (1989). Obituary, *Irish Independent*, 23 March 2008.

CHAPTER 8
DUBLIN DIARY 1, 1973

I always keep a pocket-diary where I occasionally enter comments about places I have been or people I have met and I have referred to these diaries throughout these Memories. When I worked in an office, I naturally had an Appointments Diary and, in writing the chapter about my time as Director of the National Gallery, I have used those diaries as *aides-memoires*. But I have never actually written a diary except for about six months in 1973. At the time I was working in the National Gallery of Ireland and living on Rathgar Road in Dublin. It was a period when I was enjoying making friends in the Dublin art world and, in my first formal job, embarking on my own career.

9 January 1973: Today James White was all fussed as Father Barrett[1] wrote a rude letter saying he wanted to resign from the Association of Irish Art Historians (of which I am Secretary) because the meetings were never held at a time when he could attend. Also complaining that I had not notified him of the correct date of the meeting; which was a lie.

Lunch at Ted Smyth's.[2] Odd lunch of cheese and bread and stuff of which I got very little even though I was hungry. A lot of fresh young Third Secretaries from Foreign Affairs including quite a nice girl called Clare somebody.[3] Charles Lysaght,[4] of whom I had heard much also there and Brian McCarthy[5] whom I had only met once before. He works in Trinity Library and is v. unpopular in many quarters. He was pleasant to me though.

Tonight Phil McMaster and Bibi Plunkett called for about an hour. Both very difficult to talk to. I suspect because it is more Bohemian not to talk. She called my back room Rothschild Green – as it is almost the same colour as a Rothschild flat in London. She also said that Aggie Leslie,[6] who now lives with Maurice Craig,[7] claims to have been the first woman to appear nude on the London stage – and move. A good story at any rate. Aunt Polly rang to ask me what issue of *Country Life* my article had appeared in. Uncle Hubert[8] came to the Gallery with Godfrey and Cecil so I invited them to have tea.

10 January: Tonight Caroline and Andrew O'Connor who is a restorer in the Gallery invited me to dinner to meet his father, Patrick O'Connor,[9] as I am to research the grandfather, Andrew O'Connor the sculptor. PO'C has something of a scandalous reputation in Dublin and his name is not popular with everyone as he reputedly smuggled, or some such, Guardi pictures out of Bantry House at the time that he was Curator of the Municipal Gallery. I knew I would be in for some treats if I handled him properly. He is very charming and jolly – looking the part with a longish beard of grey and flowing hair. He is quite a raconteur but sometimes incredibly vulgar and uses atrocious language but for all that v. good company. He overestimates the importance of everything – including himself. A picture is always a £20 picture or else a Velázquez. And, supposedly, Benedict Nicolson[10] or Christopher Wright[11] have never published anything without PO'C seeing it first and giving his advice. He was divorced a month ago in Tunbridge Wells. I asked him if he had had to spend a night in a Brighton hotel with a chambermaid and a private detective at the keyhole, but he said he didn't bother with any of that nonsense. I think his wife was called Anne and she apparently knew all sorts of people and was beloved by a lot of homosexual young men including John Gielgud, whom I would hardly refer to as young.

PO'C talked about his appointment to the Municipal. Patrick Kavanagh the poet needed cash and decided to go for the job. PO'C coached him – 'there are thirty-nine Lane pictures, etc.' – for the interview. James White was also a candidate. But due to some trickery the first interview and appointment was cancelled. For the second interview, PO'C decided to go for the job himself as he needed cash too. Bodkin[12] was on the interviewing committee and others whom I can't remember. They asked him how many Lane Pictures there were: thirty-nine; name five of them, which PO'C did – the most obscure five. A

Dublin Corporation man asked 'what about Manet's *Concert aux Tuileries?*' PO'C explained, 'lovely picture, but not a Lane Picture'.[13] They asked him to read a passage in French which they suspected all good curators should be able to speak. PO'C of course was fluent having been brought up in France. Anyway, he got the job, hands down, and Patrick Kavanagh remained penniless. He spoke of Terence de Vere White. At one time PO'C had put forward a picture of some lady's 'ass' nude by Orpen for the Friends of the National Collections to buy at £200. TdeVW pointed out that the Municipal Gallery already had lots of Orpens and turned the picture down. Lady Bare-ass (in fact Lady Glenavy) promptly sold the picture to America at a fantastic sum.

He brought up the subject of the Guardi paintings himself. He was approached by the Bank of Ireland (the Bantry House Trustees) to buy the pictures which he did with advice as to fair prices, etc. from both Christie's and Sotheby's and London dealers. He sold the pictures (save three) through the London dealer David Carritt to 'a man called Merton'. Merton caught up with Mrs Shelswell White's son and between them they said to PO'C 'if you don't give us the other three for nothing, we'll ruin your career' which they did by a campaign of publicity and blackmail.[14]

While at the Municipal, he sought a meeting with Sir Phillip Hendy, then Director of the London National Gallery, and made an agreement that England could keep *all* of the Lane Pictures and he would select thirty-nine pictures from the London NG as a swap. This Hendy agreed to, and the Duke of Wellington, who was Chairman of the committee for the Lane Pictures, also agreed as he, the Duke, thought the Lane Pictures much too good for Ireland and that no Irishman could make a sensible choice. PO'C picked the cream from the London NG collection and came back to Dublin and proposed the exchange to Dublin Corporation who wouldn't agree to it saying that they wanted their Impressionist paintings. I said I felt that Dublin should never ever get even a glimpse of the Lane Pictures as their behaviour was at all times disgraceful and they didn't deserve them. He agreed with me. Lord Moyne[15] was always a great friend of his so when Desmond and Mariga Guinness, newly married, first came to Dublin pretending to be penniless, PO'C took them under his wing. DG didn't know what he wanted to do at this time. They travelled the country together and would put up at small country hotels. PO'C would order a room and a meal and D&M would come in and cadge food from him, supposedly having no money for food for themselves. Desmond would play some musical instrument on pavements and Mariga would pass round a hat. When their first child was born they called him Patrick after PO'C. All of this sounded very spurious to me. He spoke a lot about his father –which, after all, was why I was there. Andrew O'Connor (the sculptor) was divorced at an early age and this made his career v. difficult as he could never be commissioned for anything by the Catholic Church. This has never been known before and even young Andrew had never heard it of his grandfather. I gathered neither Andrew nor Patrick were very keen on Jessie.[16] She kept Andrew *père* isolated and never allowed him models. She is still alive and living in a nursing home in Dun Laoghaire.

11 January: Today was a meeting of the Association of Irish Art Historians of which I am Assistant Honorary Secretary. The Keeper of Art from the Ulster Museum, James Ford Smith – who is totally blind with a white cane – is Honorary Secretary. I do all the work. James F-S was there; Desmond Guinness; Anne Crookshank; Hilary Pyle; Helen Roe; and Mrs Leask, who complains all the time of not being able to hear, which is not surprising as she is talking all the time. A lot of nonsense was discussed and Michael Wynne was in the Chair. After the meeting I went to dinner with Jeanne Sheehy and Hugh Dixon. Hugh stayed the night. This morning I had a Christmas card from Speer Ogle in Rome, who hopes for 1973 to be peaceful, personally and publicly!

27 January: Burke's Club at Lisnabrooka, County Galway. Only Charles Benson[17] and David Butler[18] and me. Also Nesta Fitzgerald and a girl called Veronica Heywood.[19] Lisnabrooka is the most beautiful house – only built in 1912 – and standing quite isolated above Ballynahinch Lake. It rained all the weekend; but even so the views were stupendous and not another house in sight. Lisnabrooka now belongs to people called Reid who live in London and they rent it out for fishing. It is furnished in a very casual way.

5 February: This morning I had to go into Trinity to borrow some slides for a lecture I am to give tomorrow night in Coleraine. I had a chat with Anne Crookshank and gave her an offprint of my article in *Country Life* about Mrs Hamilton's memorial. Anne does not care for Ted Hickey,[20] who is Keeper of Art at the Ulster Museum, and was not kind about him. She told me that she likes John O'Grady very much now and has taken him to lunch. This evening I went round to see Mrs Leask at her invitation. She lives in a bed-sitter in Mespil flats. She showed me some of her offprints – articles written over many years – and also the most beautiful embroidered curtains dating from about 1720, which she bought for thirty shillings some years ago. She was in better form than usual and didn't rail at me as she normally does. Desmond Guinness once published in the *Georgian Society Bulletin* an article which stated that ceiling paintings which were in Mount Vernon (Cork) were by 'Des Gray' (*sic*) even though the pictures are documented in *Strickland* as being by Nathaniel Grogan. When Mrs Leask pulled him up on it, Mariga said, 'Oh we only said they were by Des Gray because that was the only name we could remember.' Mrs Leask was horrified, and that the Guinnesses couldn't spell the Peter De Gree name correctly either but only as Mrs Leask had pronounced it. Rolf Loeber had' phoned her and pretended that he had met her at Leixlip, which Mrs L says he had not, and he invited her to lunch. She did not go to lunch but took him to the RIA and introduced him. Carola Peck[21] told Mrs L that she wasn't sure about Rolf and nor did it seem, from her conversation, was Mrs L. I am sure that Rolf did meet her and that she has forgotten.

6 February: Today I went to Coleraine to lecture on behalf of James White at the New University of Ulster. James, in typical vague fashion, had just asked me last Friday saying, 'Oh, it is something to do with Britain entering the Common Market: you know, cross-influences between British and European art through the centuries.' I prepared a lecture which in fact illustrated more continental influences on Britain: the usual things –Reynolds's *Portrait of Commodore Keppel* and the *Apollo Belvedere*, and beautiful slides of the Stourhead landscape compared with paintings by Claude, etc. Off I set, only to arrive in Coleraine and find that the lecture was in fact supposed to be British influences on continental art. Not to worry. I took the train to Belfast and had lunch with Hugh Dixon and his girlfriend Maggie, who is a violinist. As I walked up from the station towards Queen's, a bomb had just exploded wrecking a clothes shop and two cars. I then took the train in the afternoon to Coleraine and stayed in a hotel. Before my lecture I had drinks with an artist, Gordon Woods[22] who was organising my trip; Professor Walter Allen[23] of the English Department and Roy Morell. All very nice. My lecture went well and F. J. Hurst, who used to be Librarian at Trinity when I was an undergraduate, came up and spoke to me. He introduced me to his wife and I think he said her name was Theresa and that she came from Clare. Then I went to dinner with Gordon Woods at his house – with his wife and Walter Allen. I had studied WA's books when I read English at Trinity. He told me he lived on gin; which seemed to be quite true. His wife and family stayed in London (very sensibly) and he commuted. He said over dinner that he didn't like homemade wines since he went to lunch with Edward Hyams[24] and EH had given him some beetroot wine which WA said tasted just like the vinegar from bottled beetroot. We talked of Northern Ireland (of course) and WA looked very bored. He was very gentle and very unassuming.

7 February: Today there was a one-day strike called by Protestant loyalists in protest against two people being interned. Of course there were no trains so I had to rent a car and drive back to Dublin: through Cookstown and Armagh with lunch in the Shirley Arms in Carrickmacross. I saw no sign of trouble on the way and only one armed soldier.

9 February: There was a meeting of the Board of Governors and Guardians of the National Gallery and James White presented his *Annual Report*. Typical JW effort with more prominence given to what good value the restaurant is than to the year's acquisitions. Four (?) original watercolours by James Malton being offered by the Earl of Mayo for £5,000 each. These were turned down as being too expensive. Also two paintings by Roderic O'Conor for above £3,000 each offered by Seán O'Criadain.[25] One of these was purchased, the other refused: again too expensive. I met Derek Hill[26] in the hall and Michael Wynne introduced us. He is an artist living in County Donegal. He said his most recent portrait was of Archbishop McQuaid[27] and that he had been engaged to paint Lord O'Neill.[28] He said he had found that McQuaid had a good sense of humour; but when the BBC had sent over a photographer to photo McQuaid alongside the portrait, McQuaid had refused saying that 'he was a page that had turned'. Michael, who of course is a frantic Catholic, agreed that McQuaid was so genial and kind, which I don't believe he can be.

10 February: Spent the day gardening and in the evening dinner at Charles Benson's. About thirty people there – good. Who was there? Richard Pine[29] and Melanie; Clare O'Reilly; Jeremy Williams, David Butler and Nesta Fitzgerald.

13 February: Tonight Rolf Loeber's lecture to the Irish Georgian Society on *The Rise and Fall of Caroline Architecture in Ireland.* Anne Crookshank proposed the vote of thanks and Desmond (Guinness) asked me to second it, which I did. Except that I had a marvellous quote from Lord Orrery which I remembered but foolishly forgot to quote. Jeanne Sheehy and I sat together. Michael Magann, Nora O'Sullivan and lots of others there. Some people mentioned that they had seen my article in the *IGS Bulletin* which was published yesterday. William Kidwell at last published. When I wrote it as my thesis in Edinburgh my greatest hope was that it would appear in the Bulletin: little did I expect that by the time it would, I would have already contributed to the *Burlington Magazine, Country Life* and *Apollo* as well. Today I had lunch with Jeanne and someone called Gifford Craven[30] or Lewis who is starting a small publishing firm and is to publish a series of monographs by Irish art historians. She asked me to contribute. So, with me on the *O'Connell Monument* and other titles by Jeanne, Eddie McParland and Roger Stalley,[31] I will be in good company.

17 February: Lunch at Consuelo[32] and Brian O'Connor's. Never been there before. Eight people: a solicitor and his wife, a barrister and his wife, two Cruess Callaghan cousins and Gabby Hogan. Very correct but very nice and I like Consuelo very much. I sat beside her at lunch and tried to prod her about Maurice Craig's stint at An Taisce of which she is a committee member. No go though. She did tell me that people often mistook her husband Brian for Lord Iveagh. Oh really . . . ?

21 February: Viewing day at Castlemartin, County Kildare for Lord Gowrie's[33] auction tomorrow. I went down this morning on behalf of the Gallery. Nothing of great interest and not a nice house at all. Tony O'Reilly has bought it – he is welcome to it.

Paddy Lynch[34] at dinner in the University Club tonight quoted George O'Brien[35] on W.B. Yeats: 'WBY I would have thought was a brilliant conversationalist, if I did not understand the use of the English language.'

26 February: Opening of the exhibition of Irish Cartoons of the Eighteenth Century in Trinity Library by R.B. MacDowell,[36] who did not speak as well as often. Nick and Mary Robinson[37] there, John Gilmartin, Professor Sydney Cole[38] and Veronica Morrow[39] Baron Randal Mac Donnell[40] sporting a green carnation and gazing longingly at a drunk young man on a settee: all to great effect.

28 February: I invited James and Aggie White, John Gilmartin and Ted Smyth to drinks at 169. James in bad mood all day, which is quite rare but mellowed in the evening. Ted told some story of a newly-appointed Minister whom people said should have been made Minister for Transport as he looked like a lorry-driver. Aggie pricked up at this and James warned Ted that he must never 'talk' in his career as people like Aggie are bound to repeat it. John Gilmartin on good form and talked of the importance in life of having an ideal to aspire to, in his case people like Eoin O'Mahony[41] and Anne Crookshank: what a mixture!

5 March: Yesterday announced in *The Times* two jobs for me: Research Assistant in the Scottish National Portrait Gallery, which I am too senior for but which pays better than the NGI. Also an Assistant Keeper which I am qualified for – but for which the minimum age is twenty-eight. I want more than anything to get an Assistant Keepership in one of the London galleries and wonder if I should 'step down' to Research Assistant in Scottish NPG as a stepping stone for the V&A or the Tate and thence to Director of the NGI at 35! Then today an advertisement for an Assistant Keepership in the Department of Paintings in the V&A. Exactly my job, and one for which I am qualified, and I want it more than anything. I will discuss it with James White, Michael Wynne and Anne Crookshank. I must get this job. There are responsibilities for the

Constable Collection. Unfortunately I had a very good enquiry from the V&A about our Constable landscape in the NGI, to which I have not yet replied. Tomorrow I will write and hope that that will help rather than hinder. The Knight of Glin will be in Dublin next week and I will use him if I can. I'll also apply for the senior Edinburgh job.

8 March: Press showing of my exhibition of NGI prints and paintings of Dublin, staged at the last minute but, by all accounts, well done. Bruce Arnold[42] was there being sceptical. Also Lionel Fleming[43] whom James White introduced me to, and Ned McGuire[44]. In the afternoon I had a chat with Anne Crookshank about the V&A job: very enthusiastic immediately but says we must not be optimistic. She will drop my name when in London next week and the Knight will help. In the evening Anne opened an exhibition of photographs of Irish sculptures at Number 3 Henrietta Street and spoke very well.

9 March: Hugh Dixon to stay. James White opened an exhibition of Micheál Mac Liammóir's stage designs in the King's Hospital. James talked on, as usual, about how long he had been a friend of Michael, etc., etc. and was not very coherent. Afterwards he introduced me to MMcL, who immediately started to talk to someone else in French. Hilton Edwards also there and gazing adoringly at MMcL all the way through the speeches. I am sure it is all a big act. Seán O'Criadain asked me and Hugh and Jeanne Sheehy back afterwards. I had to go and lecture to the ESB on what to see in the National Gallery. I was well inebriated and lectured absolute rubbish, at which they laughed heartily the whole way through. Then to Seán's, where I enjoyed myself immensely. Seán talks a lot and I am not sure one can believe all he says.

10 March: I assisted in a Victorian tour of Dublin with Hugh Dixon and Jeanne. In the evening drinks in Enniskerry on the invitation of John and Rubel Ross. John was sort of my master when I was a solicitor's apprentice in Matheson, Ormsby and Prentice, and collects English watercolours. Mrs Ross is lovely.

12 March: Dinner at Maurice Craig's. Anne Crookshank, the Knight of Glin, Hugh Dixon, Jeanne, the Loebers and me. Aggie Leslie cooked cannelloni and displayed her curves to advantage in a slinky long dress and no foundations. The Knight was perky and rude as usual; but entertaining. Wearing a purple polo neck which he pulled up to scratch himself quite freely at dinner: not an appetising sight. He also interrupts everyone. Maurice being more defenceless and less vain than usual. Jeanne was in love with him and wanted to marry him but Aggie jumped in first.

13 March: Andrew O'Connor lectures in the King's Hospital on the restoration of paintings. Afterwards, at a party in Andrew and Caroline's. Serge Philipson[45] is there being a perfect bore as usual. The Evie Hone window in KH was entirely invisible during the lecture as it was dark outside; but Patrick O'Connor said he had never seen Evie Hone looking better, as she had neither taste nor talent.

15 March: Eddie McParland lectures on *Thomas Ivory and the Blue Coat School*. It's very cold. Eddie lectures very well, of course, though a bit stagey on appearing brilliant.

18 March: Lunch at Rathcormick following morning service in Ballivor church. Bishop and Mrs Pike[46] there. He is very jolly and a former rugby player and she is very friendly and open. Ballivor church has been renovated by Elliott. This includes the cutting down of all the lovely old beech trees; and the removal of all the headstones, many of them our family. Elliott means well and the Bishop praises the 'improvements' in his sermon but I feel it is an absolute scandal and typical of the Church of Ireland.

21 March: Speer Ogle, back from Rome for his annual visit, telephoned and we had a drink in the Kildare Street Club. He is same as ever and we get on very well. At 8.00 a concert in the National Gallery organised by the German Cultural Institute. James White in America and Michael Wynne away so I am there, on duty as it were. I sit with Jeremy Williams, who nods so vigorously to the music that he falls asleep in spite of the fact that I am unable to have the hideous fluorescent lighting turned off during the music. Afterwards a reception at the Institute at which I know very few people but meet a nice German, the headmaster of St Killian's, the German school in Clonskeagh, Dublin. Called Rudiger Heinz, I learn. Very tall and blond, an archetypical German 'jugend' although not so 'jugendlich' any more. He hates Ireland and the Irish, which of course I am forced to defend.

22 March: I have lunch with the publisher from Mercier Press to whom I have sent the draft of our schools textbook on Irish art. He is very impressed by the book and wants to go ahead with it. Gill and Macmillan turned it down. I lay on all the stuff: Maurice Craig and Anne Crookshank will read the proofs and James White will write a foreword. He seems very enthusiastic and at the end of lunch all is settled. Jeanne Sheehy, who has written the book with me, hears afterwards indirectly that he is keen. Six o'clock and I invite Speer, Jeremy Williams, Seán O'Criadain, Jennifer Leslie and Christopher Ashe[47] to drinks at 169. Afterwards, dinner with Speer. Everyone complimentary about 169 including Speer, who had not seen it since the week I moved in. He complains that I don't water the plants. At dinner he suggests us making a trip together to Ethiopia or down the Nile (which Speer says should be 'up' the Nile); but of course that will never happen.

23 March: Father Cyril Barrett of Warwick University and Jeanne Sheehy to drinks at 169 and afterwards we go to dinner: not enjoyable.

24 March: Count Randal MacDonnell's investiture as a Knight of Malta 'by Honour and Devotion' in the Chapel Royal at Dublin Castle. Afterwards a reception in the Order's headquarters which is the vicarage of St Bartholomew's, Ballsbridge. Odd that. Not as impressive a ceremony as I had hoped. Aileen Galvin[48] is made a Dame and Lady Galvin an Order of Merit or something. At the reception I met a man called Harrington from Limerick whom I thought was Lord Harrington but he wasn't; and an American from Louisiana who was charming.

29 March: AGM of the Friends of the National Collections of Ireland in the National Gallery. I sit with Oliver Dowling[49] of the Arts Council. Lord Rosse[50] in the Chair – who is appalling and ineffectual, and treats the members as though he was their nanny in their nursery. I feel like proposing his resignation but of course I don't. Derrick Waldron-Lynch,[51] on my information (conveyed secretly to him), makes a to-do as CIE are selling pictures which the Arts Council had helped them to buy. Derek, who is standing for the Senate on a Trinity ticket and is not all that popular, makes everyone take notice of him. Willie Dillon[52] asks if anything has been done about the National Museum: Rosse waves his hands above his head and says it is all very much in the air at the moment. The Museum is a disgrace to the country. At the reception afterwards I speak with Caitríona MacLeod[53] who is a bit silly really and speaks with a voice that sounds English (but not posh); but Jeanne told me that it is actually a 'Wrath-meens' (Rathmines) accent. Consuelo is there looking lovely as usual. I introduced Mrs Leask to Seán O'Criadain.

3 April: Dinner at Veronica Morrow's at 129 Lower Baggot Street: an American from Paris is guest of honour. Prof and Mrs Robert Hewson – Roman Law at Trinity and living in Kentstown Rectory, County Meath. Mavis Arnold but not Bruce, Consuelo and Brian O'Connor. I sit between Mrs Hewson and Veronica. I immediately tell Mrs Hewson my story of the keys to Kentstown church being held by a Catholic woman opposite who drapes them in a rosary. I know this as I went to her when I wanted to get into the church to look for monuments. Mrs Hewson smiles awkwardly and tells me that, while her husband is a Protestant, she is a Roman Catholic. Change of conversation. I say that I felt sure that Protestant churches could be very well adapted for living in. He is quite shy but very easy company. She, though not intellectual, is what I imagine all Oxford dons' wives to be like. Mavis is lively and good company. Rosita Sweetman's book[54] on Irish personalities is discussed and I say that Rosita was clearly very young and riddled with an inferiority complex. Mavis does not like this. She says Bruce is in London to bid on two very important Ashford landscapes at Sotheby's tomorrow. (He bought them for £17,000.) Mavis, pretending to be naive, asks me if the Gallery will be bidding for the Ashfords. I reply that the Gallery simply doesn't bid at auctions. End of conversation.

5 April: James White asks me to speak at the Painting of the Month dinner in the Gallery as he is 'in mourning'. (His favourite uncle has died.) He selects the painting of *The Nativity* by Giroloma Troppa which, I suggest to him, might be too much of a Christmas subject. He says 'No, not really as it is after all nearly Easter which he knows is Christ's death but birth and death are both religious anyway so the choice of subject in fact suits well.' This is typical James White logic. I am photographed at the dinner by the *Evening Herald*, together with the man who played music.

Endnotes

1. Cyril Barrett (1925–2003). A convivial Jesuit priest, philosopher and art historian. Reader in Philosophy at the University of Warwick and authority on Wittgenstein. His book on OpArt was published in 1970. He wrote the catalogue of the important exhibition of *Irish Art in the 19th Century* held in Cork in 1971.
2. Auditor of The Hist (College Historical Society) in Trinity, 1971–72 and in 1973 a junior diplomat in the Department of Foreign Affairs. Later Chief Administrative Officer at H.J. Heinz and later with McGraw Hill. Married to the novelist, Mary Breastead. His sister, Anne, is married to my brother Raymond.
3. Clare O'Flaherty (1947–2004). Diplomat, served in Rome, Paris, Geneva and Washington and ultimately (2002) appointed Ambassador to Finland but did not take office owing to ill-health. Obituary, *The Irish Times*, 25 September 2004.
4. Lawyer, writer, obituarist and the biographer of Brendan Bracken.
5. Later used the name Robert and Dean of St Patrick's Cathedral, 1999–2012.
6. Agnes Bernelle (1923–99), actress and singer and former wife of Desmond Leslie. Her autobiography is *The Fun Palace* (1995). It had for long been the law that nudity was permitted on the stage if the nude did not move.
7. The doyen of Irish architectural historians (1919–2011), poet and intellectual. His *Dublin 1600–1800* remains unsurpassed.
8. My father's brother, Hubert Potterton of Ardkill, Carbury; Cecil and Godfrey, his sons.
9. Son of the sculptor, Andrew O'Connor, and Curator of the Dublin Municipal Gallery, 1955–60.
10. Eminent British art historian (1914–78) and long-time Editor of the *Burlington Magazine*.
11. British art historian (b.1945) and prolific author, specialist in seventeenth-century Dutch and French painting.
12. Thomas Bodkin (1887–1961), Irish lawyer and art historian. Director of the National Gallery of Ireland, 1927–35, and Director of the Barber Institute in Birmingham, 1935–52.
13. The Manet Concert is in fact a Lane Picture.
14. The story of the Bantry House paintings by Guardi has been told by Peter Murray in

Irish Arts Review (2014) and largely corroborates what PO'C said. Except that PO'C didn't mention that he was in partnership with other Dublin dealers (including Nevil Orgel) and that Mrs Shelswell White's son, Egerton, subsequently took a court case (against his mother) but involving the Bank of Ireland Trustees, Orgel and PO'C. As a result of the controversy, PO'C resigned as Curator of the Municipal Gallery in 1960.

15. Bryan Guinness (1905–92). Writer of novels, plays, poetry and memoir. On the board of the National Gallery of Ireland for thirty-five years. His first wife (the mother of his son Desmond) was Diana Mitford.

16. The sculptor's second wife; and his muse and model.

17. Later keeper of early printed books in Trinity Library.

18. A garrulous and amusing Dublin barrister (son of the Bishop of Connor) who subsequently died young. Later married to Nesta Fitzgerald ('not' the daughter of the Knight of Glin).

19. A young (then) English artist who came to live in Ireland in 1968 and has remained there. She taught in the Dún Laoghaire School of Art and works mainly in watercolour.

20. (1940–2005). Born in Wicklow and a graduate of UCD, he joined the Ulster Museum as a research assistant in 1970 and was appointed keeper of art two years later. He remained there for twenty years. Understated in his demeanour, the poet Michael Longley described him (accurately) as 'a rumpled man about town, a tousled dandy'.

21. Wife of Julian Peck, they lived in a state of magnificence at Rathbeale Hall, Swords and later moved to Prehen, Derry. Her book, *Mariga (Guinness) and her Friends* was published in 1995.

22. Northern Irish painter and sculptor (b.1938). For long Director of Art & Design Education at the University of Ulster.

23. Literary critic and novelist (1911–95). Author of the classic study, *The English Novel* (1951). From 1967, Professor of English Studies at the University of Ulster.

24. English author of *Irish Gardens* (1967) and many other titles.

25. A published poet (under the name Jack Creedon) he had lived in America for a number of years and had returned to Ireland about 1970 where he became an astute picture dealer using the Irish version of his name. The paintings of Roderic O'Conor were his early speciality. Later in life he created (with Peter Lamb) a celebrated garden at Ballinacarriga, Co. Cork.

26. (1916–2000). English portrait and landscape painter resident in County Donegal. See further Chapter 7.

27. John Charles McQuaid (1895–1973), Catholic Archbishop of Dublin, 1940–72. He is renowned for the excessive influence he had over all Irish Governments and his ban on Catholics attending Trinity College.

28. Terence, Baron O'Neill of the Maine (1914–90). He succeeded Brookborough as (Ulster Unionist) Prime Minister of Northern Ireland and initiated far-reaching reforms, among them a rapprochement with the Republic. In an historic act, he met with Seán

Lemass in Dublin in 1965 and was, in 1972, appointed a Governor and Guardian of the National Gallery of Ireland.

29. An Englishman (b.1949) who came to Trinity and remained in Ireland where he worked as Concerts Manager in RTÉ. An author, music and literary critic and authority on the work of Lawrence Durrell. He married Melanie Chance.

30. She wasn't called Gifford Craven. She is Gifford Lewis and her partner in a small publishing enterprise was Clare Craven. She is the author of books on Somerville & Ross, the Yeats Sisters, and Eva Gore-Booth.

31. Lecturer (and later Professor) in the History of Art Department in Trinity. Author of *The Cistercian Monasteries of Ireland* (1987) and *Early Medieval Architecture* (1999).

32. *Née* Cruess Callaghan. An environmentalist active in An Taisce and a Board member of the Beit Foundation. Author of a memoir, *Consuelo Remembers* (2002). She and her solicitor husband, Brian, led a bustling social life (*Irish Independent,* 7 January 2007).

33. Grey Ruthven, Second Earl of Gowrie (b.1939). Born in Ireland. Chairman of Sotheby's and of the Arts Council of England and (1983–85) UK Minister for the Arts.

34. Professor of Political Economy at UCD (d.2001) and regarded as one of the most respected and influential social and economic thinkers in the Ireland of his time.

35. Politician, economist and academic. Paddy Lynch's predecessor as Professor at UCD. Died 1973.

36. Professor of History and a legendary Junior Dean at Trinity. Notorious throughout his long life (1913–2011) for his eccentricities, conversation and wit.

37. *Née* Bourke (b.1944), President of Ireland, 1990–97. She married my friend from Mountjoy School, Nick Robinson, in 1970.

38. of Trinity

39. A graduate of, and librarian in, Trinity.

40. A colourful and sometimes controversial character who had come to Trinity as an undergraduate and has lingered in the Irish diaspora ever since. Author of *The Lost Houses of Ireland* (2002).

41. A Dublin 'character' (1905–70), referred to as 'The Pope O'Mahony' since his days at Clongowes. A great talker, dishevelled in appearance with a distinctive white beard, who trained as a barrister but preferred genealogy.

42. English writer (b.1936) living in Ireland and active as a political journalist, art critic and dealer, and one-time owner of the Neptune Gallery in Dublin. Author of biographies of Orpen, Yeats and Derek Hill.

43. Distinguished journalist on *The Irish Times*. His autobiography is *Head or Harp* (1965).

44. Senator Edward McGuire (1901–92), a long-time board member and Chairman of the National Gallery of Ireland. A noted art collector, owner of Brown Thomas, and one of the fathers of artistic appreciation in modern Ireland.

45. A German exile who came to Ireland in the 1930s and established a hat factory in the West. He collected some fine Old Masters and was a long-time Board member of the

National Gallery. Tired of him always pestering me, I once asked him bluntly which of his pictures he intended to bequeath to the Gallery and he told me none, as he had to leave them all to his daughter.

46. Robert Bonsall Pike (1905–73), Bishop of Meath 1959–73.

47. Working in the Neptune Gallery at this time, later established the Wellesley Ashe Gallery in South Frederick Street, dealing in Irish watercolours and drawings.

48. Daughter of Sir John Galvin (b.1902), an Australian–American millionaire who owned Loughlinstown House in Dublin and had racing interests in Ireland in the 1960s and 1970s.

49. Visual arts officer at the Arts Council. Later established the Oliver Dowling Gallery in Dublin, dealing in contemporary Irish art.

50. 6th Earl of Rosse (1906–79) of Birr Castle. Chancellor of the University of Dublin (Trinity) and long-time chairman of the Friends of the National Collections and many other organisations.

51. Medical GP in Athboy, d. 2003.

52. An antiques dealer with a shop in Dublin, Hibernian Antiques. Active in Georgian conservation and one of the first to restore a house in North Great George's Street.

53. A curator at the National Museum of Ireland, she was a specialist on nineteenth- and nineteenth-century decorative arts. She published on Irish eighteenth-century glass and other topics.

54. 'On Our Knees' (1972). Profiles of a cross-section of Irish people. Rosita Sweetman (b. 1948) was a founder member of the Irish Women's Liberation Movement. Her novel, 'Fathers Come First', was published in 1974.

CHAPTER 9
DUBLIN DIARY 2, 1973

5 April: Lunch today at Speer's invitation in the Kildare Street Club with Lord and Lady Wicklow[1] and Rosie Talbot.[2] I meet the Wicklows for the first time. She is absolutely charming and talked all through lunch. He is devoted to her and was quite happy to let her talk. She expresses great concern over the situation in Northern Ireland and seems deeply interested.

There is talk about Evelyn Waugh's Diaries, which are currently being published in the *Observer*. Billy Wicklow is mentioned in last Sunday's extract but nothing too damning, so they said. Rosie told Speer that Billy Wicklow only met Waugh once.[3] It was rather a posh day as, before lunch, we met the Marquess and Marchioness of Sligo (!) in the drawing-room. Rosie can be rather stiff. She said to me (opening gambit) 'I believe you are related to Harold Clarke' – I say 'well, not quite.'[4]

6 April: *Sleuth* at the Olympia with David & Hilda, Raymond & Anne,[5] who afterwards come to me for smoked salmon. T.P. McKenna and Donal Donnelly in the play: quite good.

14 April: Lunch with Speer and Diane Tomlinson[6] and Evanna McGilligan[7] in the Kildare Street Club. Evanna very friendly. The NGI has bought J-L David's *Death of Patroclus* for £250,000. James White's second-most-expensive purchase, having paid the same for the *Avignon Annunciation*. The *David* is a superb painting and very important, and definitely James's best purchase.

15 April: Speer and I are to go to Blessington for lunch. Speer arrives at 169 and has just seen the death in the papers of Lord Talbot de Malahide.[8] I am shocked. Milo, on an Hellenic cruise with Hugh Cobbe,[9] dies off Athens in his sleep. Milo and I had an embryonic friendship. I had been entertained at Malahide, and Milo had come to dinner once at 169. He was only 60. Speer and I go to Dun Laoghaire and I leave Speer to visit Rosie Talbot alone.

16 April: The rumour, spread by *The Irish Times*, is that Malahide Castle has been left to the Nation. This is untrue – but discussions between Milo and the government had taken place but nothing was finalised. I lunch with Flann O'Brien's brother – an O'Nuallain from the Department of Education – and Caoimhín Ó Marcaigh[10] to discuss the textbook on Irish art which I've written with Jeanne Sheehy and Peter Harbison and which is to be published by the Mercier Press. O'Nuallain, by whom I am not impressed, informs me that I must draw the students' attention to the fact that eighteenth-century Irish art was foreign and not indigenous to Ireland but merely a social-climbing art! I haven't the slightest intention of writing any such thing.

18 April: My monograph on the O'Connell Monument completed after a week's hectic work and given to Gifford & Craven the publisher.

21 April: Lunch with Willie and Anne Dillon in North Great George's Street. Mariga Guinness and children, plus party, there. Conor Griffin[11] and Lady Kelly.[12] She is the widow of the British Ambassador to Moscow: French, charming and slightly mad. She and I get on well and then she turns to Anne Dillon and – in French – asked Anne about me. Dinner with Rolf and Magda Loeber at Castletown: two Dutch friends of theirs and Anne Crookshank. Anne monopolises the conversation as usual and talks at length about what a good family she is from, and who she is connected with, and how Desmond Guinness hates to be told that her ancestors would not have spoken to his! In the course of the conversation, I say that Maurice Craig was not a success working for An Taisce. I feel this annoys Anne slightly.

25 April: I lunch with Speer in the Kildare Street Club. Speer is full of the dramas at Malahide and is staying on in Ireland for some time as Rosie has asked him to go through Milo's papers. Speer is planning the memorial services in St Paul's, Knightsbridge and in St Patrick's Cathedral. He wants to have *God Save the Queen* in St Pat's, which Rosie, sensibly, objects to. The British Ambassador is to be met at the door and escorted to the Vice-Regal pew. Speer wants to put the Taoiseach (or his rep) in the pew behind. Going up Kildare Street we meet Lady Kelly, whom Speer has never met. She recognises me and then Speer, as she has seen him with Rosie at Milo's funeral. She has lunched with Rosie and is overpowering about how Rosie is 'not yet quite right'. Speer sees a particularly gawkish-looking Garda outside the Dáil and wants to go over and ask him the way to the National Gallery just to see his reaction. I stop him doing any such thing.

28 April: I fly to Glasgow for a week's holiday in Scotland. Met at the airport by my friend Michael Gee with whom I am to stay. Visit Pollock House Museum where we have lunch and then drive to Lochgilphead and Michael's lovely cottage on the lake. The scenery is stunning on the drive and, when in Scotland, I always fail to see why so many people rave about Ireland.

4 May: I meet up with Michael in Glasgow and we go to see Scottish Opera's *Coronation of Poppea,* which is directed by Anthony Besch whom I met at the Wexford Opera. The opera is wonderful. On Wednesday, we went to Inveraray Castle and I was disappointed: it turns its back on the splendid site.

7 May: I return to the Gallery and find a letter from Bevis Hillier,[13] who is the new Editor of the *Connoisseur,* waiting for me. He accepts my article on the artist Charles Exshaw: so that means that I now have contributed articles to all the major British art journals – the *Burlington, Apollo* and *Country Life* – at which I am very satisfied. There is also a letter, with a lot of information, about Andrew O'Connor from the girl doing research for me in America. I am summoned for six o'clock in Anne Crookshank's rooms for a meeting to inaugurate an Irish Victorian Society. Jeremy Williams convenes the meeting and then, typically, is not there! Just Anne, the Loebers, Maurice Craig and Jeanne Sheehy. Nothing much is decided. I walk across College Park afterwards with Maurice Craig who admires the Museum Building and remarks that it is so akin to Coleshill![14] A very Maurice remark and Maurice at his affected best. He then says that the chimneys on the eaves are so seventeenth-century. I drop names like Belton[15] etc., just to show that I do know something. I admire the new gardening in the College which is being laid out by Lanning Roper[16] but MC not a bit interested in this. He drives away in his beaten-up Volkswagen.

8 May: I write a short article for *The Irish Times* on the David Allan[17] exhibition, which I saw in Scotland. I am sending it to Terence de Vere White. I tell James White that Scotland is very envious of his purchase of the 'David'. James again tells me how unpopular the purchase is in Dublin which is untrue as the Irish public are simply not sufficiently interested one way or the other. He says it will rate as the most important purchase of his career as Director, which I feel is quite true. I show the Bulgarian Minister for Trade and his delegation around the Gallery in the afternoon.

9 May: My twenty-seventh birthday. I receive no cards and feel sad at getting older and beginning to notice how young policemen are, etc. In the past week I have started to put on weight at an alarming rate which is the first time I have put on weight since I was fourteen. I think it is because I have been taking vitamin pills for the past three weeks, which I will certainly stop doing now. In the evening Burke's Club at the University Club. Willie Dillon, Francis and Christopher Ashe, Charles Benson. Willie in fine form and Charles proposes the motion 'That the State does not owe the artist a living or, alternatively, that people such as Mr Potterton and his kind are parasites on Society!' I am very amused.

19 May: I was invited to the Trinity Ball last night by an American girl, Rose Whitehill. I dance till five and get home shortly after six. Very trying. This morning I get up at 10.30 to go to Milo Talbot's memorial service in St Patrick's. I sit with Michael Wynne. The service is short and not very impressive. No address and the 'Trumpet Voluntary' as a recessional, which I didn't find all that appropriate. Rosie looks very well: entirely in black. She alone leads the mourners. The British, French and Australian ambassadors and Speer looking smart: the only man to carry a silk top hat (I bet it was Milo's). I sign the 'Present' sheet but do not speak to Rosie as I feel she has enough to cope with. I have applied for a job as Deputy Keeper of Prints and Drawings in the City Museum and Art Gallery, Birmingham. I would be equivalent to John Gilmartin there. I don't expect I shall get it; but interesting to see what happens. Baron Randal MacDonnell gave an elaborate lunch party in the Hibernian Hotel at 12 noon. Most people are still in ball dress from last night and look very weary. Micheál Mac Liammóir and Hilton are there and Randal dances attendance.

22 May: I take Speer to lunch at the University Club. He is still staying with Rosie alternatively at Malahide and at her home in Dun Laoghaire. He is in gossiping mood. He says that (according to Rosie) Brendan Oxmantown[18] (Lord Rosse's son) is better known as Michael but prefers to be called Brendan in Ireland and he has a really lovely wife. Next, Rex Beaumont[19] who is a great friend of Rosie's and whom Speer does not like. I say I would love to meet him. Recently Rex came to see Rosie, and Speer was delegated to meet his train from Mullingar at Westland Row: Speer went into the station and, when he introduced himself to Sexy Rexy (as he is called), Rex said 'How did you recognise me?' Speer was very tickled as Rex, of course, stood out like a sore thumb among fellow passengers from Mullingar. Speer says that Rex is looking for someone to live with as he had a young man from Bord na Móna, but the young man has now left. In the evening a cocktail party given by Francis and Christopher Ashe: lots of young people there and very enjoyable. Jennifer Leslie, Ros Hill,[20] Veronica Aliaga Kelly,[21] Simon McCormick,[22] etc. I go to dinner in Pheasantry afterwards with Veronica Heywood.

24 May: Dinner at Castletown to discuss the *Biographical Dictionary of Irish Architects*. I give Jeanne Sheehy a lift and arrive to find most people assembled on the steps: Desmond Guinness, Hugh Dixon, Eddie McParland, Charlie Brett[23] (whom I had never met before) and Rolf and Magda Loeber, who are our hosts. Anne Crookshank arrives immediately after Jeanne and me. Eddie is not wearing his sandals and I remark how disappointed I am. Charlie Brett introduces himself and we soon adjourn inside as the midges start to devour us. Talk is general and Anne is asked about her new house. The builders are still with her but must be finished by the time John Cornforth[24] arrives to stay at the end of the month. John couldn't bear them in the house. Desmond suggests that, on the contrary, he might like them. I suggest to Anne that she should perhaps retain them for a day just in case John liked them. Desmond says that Eleanor Wicklow (née Butler) inherited from her architect father papers that he was preparing on a dictionary of Irish architects, which were in fact the papers that belonged to Strickland[25] which are mentioned in the Preface to his artists *Dictionary*. She brought them into Hodges Figgis one day to have them valued and left them there. When she went to get them back, they had given them to someone who would appear to have been Con Curran.[26] When she went to get them from Curran, he told her that they had been burned. Anne volunteered that Con Curran had a mistress with whom he lived. Maurice had been in touch with some old man called Jones who has done research for a *Dictionary of Architects* but who is about to die. Maurice wrote him a cautious letter which he read to the meeting. Anne said it is a masterly letter to which Desmond added, 'that is why Maurice read it'. Maurice is vanity personified and is wearing bald suede shoes with turned-up soles, white socks, and half-mast trousers, and two pullovers. He looks generally dishevelled. He smokes his cigarette by holding it between his little and fourth fingers. After the meeting we go to Leixlip where Desmond has been giving a dinner party at the same time that he was at Castletown. Brian de Breffny,[27] Brendan Oxmantown and his wife, and some other people of varying decorative qualities. Eddie and I play table tennis and Brian de B talks at length about the smaller Irish country house.

26 May: I lead a tour of Victorian Dublin for An Taisce starting at the Mansion House, through Dawson and Kildare Streets, and finishing in the Museum Building in TCD.

28 May: Drinks with Patrick O'Connor to discuss my proposed catalogue of an English private collection of paintings (with which he is involved) about which I am not very certain. I am wary of what I am expected to write as I am not sure I believe all that O'Connor says. He has a landscape of the Lake of Killarney by Jonathan Fisher for £5,000: dull enough painting but exciting as it is the painting (supposedly) for the engraving. It is thought to be expensive.

30 May: Today is the Presidential election: Tom O'Higgins and Erskine Childers are the candidates and, of course, I vote for the Protestant Childers who is elected. O'Higgins's grandfather signed the death warrant for Childers's father. Dinner at Malahide Castle in the evening. Rosie entertaining there for the first time and I am among her first guests. I am bidden because Speer is staying with her. I give the Widow Fay[28] – Lilian, widow of Ambassador Bill – a lift and we are just four at dinner. Speer has warned me that Lilian will throw hysterics if I ever allow her to talk about her 'dear, departed Bill'. She longs to talk of him all the time but I manage to steer her clear. We have not met before but discover on the way to Malahide that we were both there before the last time Milo entertained a large party but Lilian and I had not met as there were quite a few others. Lilian tells Rosie that we had already met at Malahide; and Rosie, I sense, is not all that pleased as she does not like her friends to overlap with Milo's. After dinner Speer takes me on a tour of the Castle. Milo's apartments quite nicely furnished but a bedroom that is just spartan. E.M.Forster short stories on a shelf, 'a present from Tony Scotland'.[29] Rosie is nice to me and I leave Lilian home again. She is surprised that Rosie has been left Malahide. She says the Talbots are too shy by half and that Milo only used to let his hair down whenever he stayed with the Fays in embassies abroad; but that otherwise he was far too stiff.

1 June: Anne Crookshank, Rolf Loeber and I tour Dublin churches in the afternoon in search of seventeenth-century monuments. Anne is worried as she doesn't know where Mr Childers will go to church as the Chapel Royal in the Castle has been made RC. I suggest that he may simply go to Castleknock. In the evening, opening of a Deborah Brown[30] exhibition at the David Hendricks Gallery. I talk with DB (whom I had met with Anne C when visiting Osterley Park as a member of the public in September last). She is shy and understated. Objects in fibreglass are her art and look well in the sunshine. Charles Merrill[31] is also there looking fish-like as usual. James White and David Hendricks[32] both want to buy the same piece. Some have barbed wire with fibreglass which James suggests some critics will say is the influence of events in the North.

2 June: Drinks at Cobbe's in Newbridge by invitation of Mary Cobbe.[33] I have never been there before. I give Ros Hill a lift. Seán Galvin[34] there as well and one or two other people. We are not allowed comment on how lovely the house is as Uncle Tommy[35] does not like it. I ask Mrs Cobbe if they ever think of opening the house to the public and she says 'no' but that Alec has great ideas about that and opening the stables too. She says she hopes she is no longer there when that happens. She shows us the red drawing-room which is magnificent but only lit by lamps as the windows are shuttered. Afterwards we go and look at the stables and Uncle Tommy's pheasants. We were to have played croquet but the lawnmower is out of order and the lawn had not been cut. Seán Galvin, Ros Hill, Mary and I go to dinner afterwards.

4 June: Rosie Talbot is staying at Glin for the weekend and Speer is at Malahide. I need sand for my garden so I come out to get it from the beach at Malahide and collect Speer to hold the bag. We go for a walk in the Castle gardens, which I have never seen before and which Speer says he does not care for. He says they are too scientific and not enough atmosphere. The weather is beautiful and Speer wants to sit on the grass. This would be unheard of at Malahide as Milo would never even have taken tea in the garden. I leave Speer back to Dun Laoghaire to which Rosie has now returned. She presses me to come in and see her Fernley. She shows me the other pictures as well and is very charming.

18 June: Opening of the Sydney Nolan exhibition at the RDS. Irish Society at its highest and Lord Kenneth Clark speaks. The exhibition is opened by the Taoiseach, Liam Cosgrave, who speaks well by virtue of the fact that he speaks only for a short time. Kenneth Clark talks for ages and everyone gets very bored and they begin to chatter in a noisy crescendo. In the end, someone shouts at him to 'sit down and shut up' to which he replies that 'no, he won't, not until he has explained the paintings'. I talk to Mrs Leask, Lilian Fay, Seán Galvin and Harold Clarke. Afterwards dinner at Seán O'Criadain's where Anne Crookshank is with John Steer[36] her external examiner from St Andrews. He is very charming and examined me when I was at Edinburgh. Seán has produced more Roderic O'Conors.

22 June: Opening at David Hendricks Gallery of Kathleen Cooke exhibition – quite attractive. Afterwards dinner at Roger Stalley's. Only them, me and Jeanne Sheehy. Lots of gossip.

23 June: Dinner at Seán O'Criadain's. He and Peter Lamb have been swimming at Killiney. Jennie Leslie, Jeanne Sheehy, Vivian Ganly and Ciaran MacGonigal[37] whom I have not been introduced to before. He is a terrific gossip and knows every bit of information about everyone from De Valera down. He is also very amusing but pretends that he knows rather more than I think he does. Yet more Roderic O'Conors.

24 June: Drinks at Rosie Talbot's in Dun Laoghaire. Rosie discusses with me how to move her Fernley back to Malahide. Charles Lysaght arrives late as he has been to Boland's Mill to see De Valera perform his last public act as President.

28 June: Opening of the Royal Hibernian Academy Annual Exhibition: another Irish bun fight. President Childers's first visit as President to the National Gallery. He arrives with Mrs Childers who has taken too much sun in the garden of the Áras and looks very pink: the Aide-de-Camp chews gum. The Childers made a royal progress *en cercle*. He can actually see the pictures unlike the nearly-blind Dev who never could but always came nevertheless. A superb portrait by Eddie McGuire[38] of *Professor Jessop* from Trinity and some fine David Hones.[39] Seán O'Criadain buys a large painting by Maurice McGonigle who is President of the Academy. I buy a Robertson Craig[40] for £100.

30 June: I go to Mass in the Chapel Royal of the Castle for the Knights of Malta and afterwards a reception at their headquarters, the former (C of I) Vicarage on Clyde Road in Ballsbridge.

3 July: Andrew Ganly[41] invites me to come and view his Edward Smyth[42] riverine heads in walnut. I am not at all sure that they are Edward Smyth. I get one glass of Cinzano. Having left his wife, he is living with Derek Noble Johnston in a house they have bought together: Derek is not there. He shows me the house and, in his bedroom, a portrait of him over the mantle. I foolishly ask who the artist is and realise at the same time that it must be by his wife Bridget. He says, 'Oh! A member of my family.' I think he looks like a riverine head himself and he never stops talking.

10 July: Burke's Club at Willie Dillon's: splendid evening. David Cabot[43] very charming and good-looking. Willie in the Chair and Janet Moody[44] a guest with something of a social conscience who believes she should object to everything about the supposedly elite Burke's Club. Seán Galvin thinks I have been rude about his suit, which I have not. I entertain Professor William A. Gerdts[45] to lunch. I tell him I long to go to New York and he says he will see what he can do about getting a visiting fellowship for me.

29 October: It is almost four months since I have written in this diary during which time quite a lot of water has flowed under the bridge. The most important change has been that I have been appointed an Assistant Keeper at the London National Gallery; but have not yet taken up duty. I have been on holiday in Paris and have spent some time in Edinburgh. I have published an article in *The Arts in Ireland* on Harriet Hosmer's *Sleeping Faun* in Iveagh House, Dublin; and other articles have been accepted for *Country Life* and *Apollo*. My school book is nearly finished and I hope that it sells well and that the children are never as bored by it as I am now. My monograph on the O'Connell Monument has been published and, of the four titles in the series, mine got the best reviews in *The Irish Times* and the *Independent*.

I applied for the job in the National Gallery quite pessimistically as (a) I had never got an interview before and (b) I felt that the job was not at all my field and that I knew next to nothing about Old Master pictures and I have no languages worth talking about and am fairly incapable of learning any. James White, Anne Crookshank, Michael Wynne and Alistair Rowan are my referees. I give both James and

Michael as James takes no care with a reference at all and writes a lot of gush that I don't think anyone believes. So I give Michael in the hope that he will write something intelligible and believable. Also, I am sure that Michael will give me a good reference. Michael is away on holiday and my letter of invitation to interview arrives in the same post as letters to referees. I have not said anything about the job application to James and expect him to at least say that he is surprised that I am getting an interview. I go up to see him and he talks about something else. As I am leaving the room when his secretary comes in, he says quite casually, 'By the way, I have filled up those forms for you for the Tate (*sic*) and sent them off. I forged Michael's signature on his as he won't be back and they said they were urgent.' I am absolutely dumbfounded at his irresponsibility particularly as I know that Michael will be horrified. James never mentions the job again to me until the day that I am leaving for the interview and I ask him for tips. He is surprised that it is the National Gallery and not the Tate.

I go to my interview in London on 16 October and stay with a friend in Oxford. Four people in the room when I go in who turn out to be Professor Frances Haskell from Oxford, Michael Levey the Director of the National Gallery, Cecil Gould the Deputy Director and a woman from the Civil Service. Frances Haskell first talks to me and asks me about Cipriani.[46] He is kind and open and, in retrospect, very nice. Gould, whom I have heard is horrid, asks me if anything influenced me while I lived in Munich such as Early German painting. As I know nothing about Early German painting, I say 'no' but what did influence me were Bavarian Rococo churches. The ball was back in Gould's court and I hoped he didn't know anything about Bavarian rococo. He didn't.[47] Game to Potterton. Michael Levey said he had read my Kidwell article in the *Georgian Society Bulletin*. He said it was fine but what relation did it bear to what they wanted me to do? None at all, I thought, and so did he, but neither of us said it. The Civil Service woman asked why I had gone to Edinburgh University and she meant by that (I knew) why had I not gone to the Courtauld Institute. As I had thought out the answer to that one beforehand, I wasn't going to waste a good answer because she didn't say what she meant. So I replied that I had never met anyone who had liked the Courtauld so I applied to Edinburgh. This indeed was true and I didn't have to say what was also true, that the

Courtauld had turned me down. Levey and Haskell both laughed at this answer.[48] But, in spite of all these smart answers, I felt the interview had gone very badly and that I had appeared very stupid. So I was very surprised when I got the job. James White and Anne C are very pleased. But Michael Wynne and I are both worried at James's lie of a reference. While it is a very good story, it is one that can never be told. How to get a job in the London National Gallery? Get two references from James White for a job in the Tate.

November: Michael Wynne has written James White a most formal letter about the business of my reference. Addressed to 'Dear Director', it says he has consulted his spiritual adviser and in the letter he asks James never to forge his signature again, etc. James is very upset and wants to get on the next plane to London and go and see Michael Levey to tell him about the whole thing. He also wants to bring it up at a meeting of the Board of Governors and Guardians. I am upset as I do not want to have Michael's letter on the files of the Gallery as it could appear in time that I had cooked up the whole affair and that my career is based on a lie.

The next day, James discusses it with Terence de Vere White who is a solicitor. Terence, as Vice Chairman of the Board, tells James that he is to destroy Michael's letter and that he, Terence, will be answerable if there are ever any repercussions. Terence says that Michael is just putting his own guilty conscience onto James and that it is a typical thing for a failed priest to do. He says that he was never sure about Michael anyway and that never again could he support him. James says that he feels the same and that he could never recommend Michael as next Director. What a to-do!

7 December: I get my MA at Trinity for which I pay the princely sum of twenty pounds. Last night I am invited to the Commencements Dinner in the College (all the lovely silver on display) and sit beside Eddie McParland and opposite the Agent, Colonel Walshe. He is awful and seems to be a complete Philistine. He has already been responsible for pulling the wonderful Edwardian baths out of the Bath House and now he talks to Eddie and me about the merits of pulling the pews out of the College Chapel to make it more modern. Eddie and I are very firm with him.

16 December: Lunch with Professor Robert Hewson and his wife and daughter in their temporary home in Kentstown Rectory. He is exceptionally genial. We discuss Trinity and various things. He is on the Trinity committee, which decides on recipients of honorary degrees and he gaffed at lunch by saying that he had proposed Desmond Guinness for an honorary degree but that everyone opposed it mainly on account of Desmond's personal life. Hewson had put forward, rightly in my view, that DG had done a lot for Ireland and that he was still young unlike most of the people who get honorary degrees. McConnell, the Provost, told Hewson afterwards that he couldn't stand the colour of Desmond's eyes on a man. So that is why DG will not get an honorary degree.[49]

Endnotes

1. The 8th (and last) Earl of Wicklow (1902–78). His wife, Eleanor Butler, whom he married in 1959, was an architect and one-time Senator. A convert to Roman Catholicism, he wrote some books on religious topics and an autobiography, *Fireside Fusilier* (1958).

2. The Hon Rose Talbot (1915–2009). Sister of Lord Talbot de Malahide, with whom she lived at Malahide Castle, Dublin, for much of her life but later moved to Dun Laoghaire. On her brother's death in 1973, she inherited the castle, which she sold up, and took up residence on the Talbot estate at Malahide, Tasmania. Acting as a volunteer with the Samaritans, it is said that, when telephone callers said to her that they were about to commit suicide, she would tell them that 'it would be extremely irresponsible' to do so.

3. This can't be true, as Waugh wrote an introduction to Lord Wicklow's 1958 memoir, *Fireside Fusilier*.

4. Later chairman of Eason's. He restored (with his partner, Iain MacLachlann) a house in North Great George's Street and, later in life, created a noted garden in County Wicklow. His sister, Maud, was married to my brother, Elliott.

5. My brothers and sisters-in-law.

6. (1923–2015). Long-time assistant in the David Hendricks Gallery.

7. Daughter of Patrick McGilligan (1889–1979), lawyer and enormously influential Fine Gael politician. Evanna lived with her parents on Lansdowne Road and worked for many years in the Canadian Embassy.

8. 7th Baron Talbot of Malahide and 4th Baron Talbot de Malahide (1912–73). Diplomat and British ambassador to Laos, 1954–56. Botanist, he enhanced the gardens at Malahide very considerably and sponsored the publication of the multi-volume *Endemic Flora of Tasmania*.

9. Of Newbridge, Donabate. A foundation scholar in Classics (and senior to me by about two years) at Trinity. Ultimately head of music collections at the British Library. He edited the Letters of Ralph Vaughan Williams.

10. (1933–2014). Writer, editor and publisher, with, successively, the Educational Company of Ireland, the Mercier Press and An Gúm. A very active promoter of the Irish language, he was one-time manager of the Irish-language theatre An Damer. Obituary, *The Irish Times*, 19 April 2014.

11. Active as a volunteer with the Georgian Society and later a lawyer. He died young.

12. Widow of Sir David Kelly (d.1959). Marie-Noëlle was French and (according to her obituary in *The Times,* 24 February 1994), 'one of the *"grandes dames"* of British diplomacy who presided with great panache over embassies in Berne, Buenos Aires and Ankara' and wrote her autobiography, *Dawn to Dusk* (1960).

13. English art historian, author and journalist, b.1940.

14. A destroyed late-seventeenth-century house by the architect Roger Pratt in Warwickshire.

15. A house of the same date as Coleshill in Lincolnshire. It '*doesn't*' look like the Museum Building in the least.

16. (1912–83). A distinguished American landscape designer active and much sought after in England.

17. Scottish portrait and genre painter, 1744–96.

18. Later 7th Earl of Rosse (b.1936). He worked for the United Nations for many years before returning to Birr on the death of his father in 1979. Married to Alison, a talented watercolourist.

19. (1914–88). Born in England, he met Colonel Charles Howard-Bury (1881–1963), a mountaineer and politician, of Charleville, Tullamore and Belvedere, Mullingar, in the 1940s and became his life-companion, ultimately inheriting Belvedere, which he sold to Westmeath County Council in 1982. He published a volume of poetry, '*Me, Myself and I*', in 1973.

20. A student at Trinity and niece of Anne Crookshank.

21. Probably a Trinity student at this time; later a research assistant to Alistair Rowan on *The Buildings of Ireland.*

22. Dublin solicitor.

23. (1928–2005). Belfast solicitor, journalist, author and founder (and chairman) of the Ulster Architectural Heritage Society.

24. (1937–2004). Architectural historian with a particular interest in the English country house. Architectural editor of *Country Life*, 1967–77.

25. Walter Strickland (1850–1928), registrar in the National Gallery of Ireland and author of '*A Dictionary of Irish Artists*' *(1913).*

26. C.P. Curran (1880–1972) was a lawyer and historian of eighteenth-century Dublin architecture. Author of *Dublin Decorative Plasterwork* (1967).

27. Styling himself Baron de Breffny (a fictitious title), he came to live in Ireland with his Finnish-born wife, Ulli, at this time and subsequently bought and restored Castletown Cox in County Tipperary. He wrote several books on Irish houses and castles and established (with Ann Reihill) *Irish Arts Review*. Born 1931, died 1989.

28. Born Connolly, she had been married to the lawyer-ambassador William P. Fay, who had been Irish ambassador in Paris and later Washington. The couple had no children. Lilian took her role of ambassador's wife very seriously and brought style and glamour to the embassies over which she presided. WPF dropped dead while '*en poste*' in Washington and Lilian never fully recovered.

29. Handsome music presenter (b.1945) with a mellifluous voice on the BBC Third Programme. Milo had met him in Tasmania and was much smitten with him.

30. Northern Irish sculptor (b. 1927) known for her pioneering use of fibreglass.

31. American editor of *The Arts in Ireland*. Probably in his thirties in 1973, he had appeared in Dublin a year or two previously with an elderly Princess Evangeline Zalstem-Zaleski (b.1897), who was said to be his aunt. In actual fact he was her lover and they were very much feted in the Irish art world. They would marry in 1975, after they left Dublin. The princess had money (she was a Johnson, of Johnson & Johnson) and they took a house in Rathgar and set up this very handsome magazine of Irish art with Charles as the editor. Sadly, the publication did not last long and the couple departed Ireland after a very few years. The princess had earlier been married to the conductor Leopold Stokowski. Her title came from her second husband, a nobleman of Russian descent. Obituary in the *New York Times*, 18 June 1990.

32. Jamaican-born, he came to study at Trinity and stayed in Dublin for life (d. 1983). He opened his Ritchie Hendricks Gallery at 3 St Stephen's Green in 1956, later the Hendricks (at No 119). He had a very keen 'eye' and his gallery was of enormous importance for contemporary Irish art in the 1960s and 1970s. He and the collector Gordon Lambert were, extremely discreetly, life partners and it was largely David's eye and influence which informed Gordon's collecting.

33. Younger sister of Hugh and Alec Cobbe. She may have been a student at Trinity at this time.

34. Son of Sir John Galvin.

35. Thomas Cobbe (d.1985), the bachelor uncle of Hugh, Alec and Mary and owner of Newbridge.

36. (1928–2012). Professor of the history of art at St Andrew's and later Birkbeck College.

37. Son of the painter Maurice MacGonigal, arts commentator, journalist and broadcaster, later Director of the RHA Gallagher Gallery, the Hunt Museum and a board member of the Arts Council, the National Gallery and the Temple Bar Cultural Trust.

38. Irish portrait painter (1932–86). One of Ireland's most internationally known and distinguished artists. He won many awards and is represented in many public collections.

39. Irish portrait and landscape painter (b.1928). Later president of the Royal Hibernian Academy.

40. Harry Robertson Craig (1916–84), Irish (but born in Scotland) landscape and portrait artist. The partner of the painter Patrick Hennessy.

41. A dentist by profession and an Hellenophile by inclination and appearance. His wife Brigid Ganly was an artist of note.

42. Irish sculptor (1749–1812). He carved the stone heads representing the rivers of Ireland (hence riverine heads) on the Custom House in Dublin.

43. Natural History Professor at Trinity.

44. A contemporary of mine at Trinity, daughter of Professor T.W. Moody.

45. The distinguished author of numerous books on American art, he taught at the Graduate Center of City University, New York.

46. I had published an article, 'G.B. Cipriani at Lansdowne House', in *Apollo* (October 1972).

47. I was very wrong about that: he did know a great deal about it.

48. Both Francis Haskell and Michael Levey disliked the Courtauld Institute and would have done anything rather than appoint someone who had studied there. This was in my favour but it meant that candidates much better qualified than me such as Timothy Clifford and Christopher Wright – both of whom had applied for the post and had expertise in Old Master paintings – were overlooked. Michael probably also thought that I might be easier to work with, and to mould, than either Tim or Christopher.

49. DG was, quite rightly, awarded an honorary Doctorate of Laws by Trinity in 1980.

CHAPTER 10

ARRIVAL

I wrote a diary note for my first day at the National Gallery in London (22 January 1974).

> I go in at 10.15 and ask to see Cecil Gould[1] as arranged. He is charming and shows me round, to coffee, and eventually to Michael Levey who welcomes me most profusely to the Gallery and asks me if my office is alright, etc. Cecil invites me to go to lunch with him at the Reform Club together with Christopher Brown who is also an Assistant Keeper. At lunch, Cecil is out to impress with a lot of irreverent gossip: 'Ellis Waterhouse[2] was the first professional art historian in Britain as opposed to Kenneth Clark[3] who was the last amateur'; 'Wittkower's[4] English was always very bad and one suspected his German was even worse', etc., etc. Martin Davies (the previous Director) was very unpopular in the Gallery and evidently he and Cecil did not speak. Also (according to CG) MD was generally regarded as not knowing anything. Philip Hendy[5] (the Director before Davies) had an inferiority complex because of his lack of scholarship but felt that he compensated for it by having a good eye; but the truth was that he had no eye either. Cecil complains that his life work, books on Correggio and Leonardo, are both to appear simultaneously. Hearing all this, I think 'gosh!' while Christopher Brown accepts the offer of a brandy (which I decline) and puffs away on an outsize cigar. Back in the

Gallery, Michael Levey prances about (yes, prances). His office has been painted a pale lilac colour with his shirt matching. No pictures on the walls and a green carpet. His suit is Carnaby Street and he has high heels. I think 'gosh!' There are no lights anywhere on account of the power crisis[6] and all appears very gloomy.

I am lodging with a friend in Putney and, as I am going home on the Tube in the evening, I reflect: 'Well, this is it. I've arrived.'

I have looked up several of Michael Levey's obituaries (he died aged eighty-one in December 2008) and they all make him sound completely ordinary but the fact of the matter is Michael Levey was not at all ordinary. Charming, kind, considerate, very clever, intellectual, practical, efficient, talented, alternative yet conformist, socially adept but also gauche – all those things; but definitely not ordinary; on the contrary, he was, in almost every way, extraordinary.

He would, I am sure, be pleased that I am stating this. He himself said (in middle life), 'I don't want to be respectable. I'd really rather be dissolute and sexy than respectable, which is why I dress up.'[7] But actually, Michael was respectable and his yearning to be dissolute remained for all his life just that: a yearning, a toe in the water. His marriage, to the writer Brigid Brophy, was made to sound (by themselves in newspaper interviews) 'dissolute'; but it was Brigid and her lover, the poet Maureen Duffy, who were dissolute, while Michael was left (I feel sure) on the sidelines.

He was not, however, on the sidelines as an art historian: far from it. He was not on the sidelines as a museum administrator: far from it. He was not on the sidelines as a very stylish literary writer: far from it. He was tremendously talented in all those fields. He had a very good 'eye' when it came to assessing a painting – and made terrific acquisitions, and lots of them, for the National Gallery.

But having a good 'eye' and having 'taste' are two quite different things; and – when it came to things other than paintings – Michael had very little taste. Nor did he really have 'style'. His daughter has described the flat on the Old Brompton Road where they lived: 'a life-size statue of Antinous in one corner. An ebonised credenza displayed lucid chunks of coloured minerals. Four stylish spinning modern chairs from Peter Jones, high-backed scoops of avocado . . . on a dense black carpet and a chi-chi side table, an asymmetric slab of alabaster – dyed a strong turquoise.'[8]

This was Michael's taste.

Michael claimed he 'liked to dress up', but his sense of dress and his clothes were a disaster. He was very tall and naturally very slim but, in his late forties when I went to work in the gallery, his body was no longer that of a twenty-year-old; and his style of dress emphasised the fact. It was a sort of 'Mod' style (but 'Mod', I thought, went out in the Sixties). He shopped mainly in Take Six on the King's Road, which was a 'hip' shop at the time. The shirts, sometimes flowered but sometimes plain with very high white collars, were tight-fitting; the kipper tie – flowered – was knotted large; the suits – also tight-fitting – had elevated pointed shoulders and, yes, a slight flare to the trousers. And then the shoes: they were chunky with high wedge heels and perhaps in more than one colour. They did not look like leather. One newspaper article said (kindly) that 'he looked more like the proprietor of a Carnaby Street boutique than Director of one of the world's leading museums'. No he didn't. The proprietor of a Carnaby Street boutique would have looked good: Michael, as a general rule, did not.[9]

Being 'modern', he had almost no feeling for 'period': I remember one of the marble doorcases that are such a feature of the vestibule in the National Gallery being torn out (with his approval) to be replaced by a blank wall at the top of the formal stairs. I have read (the *Telegraph*) that he 'brought a fresh sense of style to the way the gallery displayed its collections, ordering bolder colour schemes'. That is not how I remember it. I only recall beautiful damask wall-hangings being taken down (I grabbed some of them to have curtains made which I have to this day) and replaced by a plain synthetic fabric in taupe or beige.

Being resolutely 'socialist' in his opinions – but full of contradictions – he disapproved of the usual things: country houses, their owners, and their collections; the gentlemen's clubs of Pall Mall; titles and royalty; private schools, probably (although his daughter, I'm fairly sure, went – like her mother – to St Paul's); private wealth; even the Royal Opera House in Covent Garden. And yet, when offered the knighthood that was his due, he accepted it although (as I recall) he had frequently mentioned the pleasure he would take in writing the letter turning it down. In earlier years, he had catalogued some of the Queen's pictures and had accepted membership of the Victorian Order for his pains. The rich did not appeal to him and he did not cultivate them: I do not remember ever seeing a Maecenas at the dull little gatherings that marked the opening of exhibitions in the gallery and nor do I remember much mention of the word 'sponsorship'. The high-rolling benefactors – the Sainsburys and J. Paul Getty II – came along in 1985, the year that Jacob Rothschild became chairman. Michael dispersed his own wealth – his salary – by lunching lavishly with an invitee every day in the best of restaurants, ordering wines that were often *grand cru*, and encouraging his guests to select the most expensive dishes. He, after a lot of faux agonising, would select only an omelette. (He was vegetarian.) In actual fact, he may have lunched like this every day because he was hungry: Brigid did not cook and nor, apparently, did Michael.

The marriage to Brigid Brophy was unconventional, or so they said themselves to any newspaper which would report the fact[10]. Marriage was 'an immoral social institution we ought never to have subscribed to', said Brigid, and Michael was 'the feminine principle in their marriage': he got 'more pleasure out of pleasure than anyone she had ever known'. Brigid herself 'would feel free to go off if she felt sexually excited about someone else'; Michael was less likely to do that: 'sexual frisson' for him could come 'from a painting'. This sort of talk no doubt sounded daring (and shocking) to Michael and Brigid – which is why they voiced it publicly – but the sixties had come and gone and it can't have sounded daring (or shocking) to many other people: I was about as conventional as one could find and I certainly was not shocked. In particular, because I was fairly certain that they lived very humdrum lives in their flat on the Old Brompton Road. According to their daughter,

> the drawing room, as they insisted on calling it, was suitable for visitors . . . painted terracotta with an ornate white cornice . . . a creamy marble mantelpiece with a huge gold mirror above it . . . The rest of the shadowy flat was more a private literary den lined with books and dotted

with ornaments: my parents collected nothing in particular, indeed scoffed at anyone who did, but they readily accumulated all manner of things they liked.

Kate Levey mentions 'visitors' but I was always under the impression that Michael and Brigid did not mix much socially at all. They certainly avoided 'public' events like gallery openings, and when they did go out – to the opera, a concert or the theatre – they would be paralysed by 'shyness' if they ran into anyone they knew. I once met them at Sadler's Wells and was sitting near them but Michael ignored me. But the following morning in the gallery, he made a point of being effusive in asking me what I had thought of the performance and had I enjoyed it, etc. In my seven years working in the gallery, I recall Brigid making an appearance only once, when she was persuaded (by the chairman of the trustees) to come to an opening and, even then, her shy discomfort was obvious as she scowled her way through the evening looking desperately miserable. She did not even come on the occasion when the Queen opened the Northern Extension. Brigid's novelette, *The Finishing Touch*, is about a girls' finishing school in the south of France run by a lesbian couple, one of whom – Antonia Mount – is (as admitted by Brigid) modelled on Anthony Blunt; but, as Michael did not care for Blunt, I am at a loss to know how Brigid could have known him sufficiently to create such a pen-portrait. I cannot imagine for one minute that they ever invited him into their 'drawing room'.

Brigid was many things. Like Michael, she was an atheist, a vegetarian and a socialist. She was also a feminist, a pacifist and a humanist – and bisexual. She was a polemicist, an activist and a campaigner: for Public Lending Rights, for animal rights (she was anti-vivisection) and many other causes. 'Her outspokenness, coupled with her public persona, which came across as strident and abrasive (while in reality she was shy and retiring) cemented the general perception of her as an opinionated, mischievous *enfant terrible*.'[11] According to her agent, Giles Gordon,[12] 'this deeply shy, courteous woman [was the author of] seven idiosyncratic novels [which] never sold particularly well', as well as biographies, essays, criticism and short stories. But 'Brigid was above all an Intellectual . . . ever the Aristotelian logician', according to Gordon, and to others 'the acknowledged high priestess of the British intelligentsia'. 'Uncompromisingly intellectual' was the general view. At the same time, the one thing that most people know about Brigid Brophy is that she was sent down from Oxford – for conduct unspecified – at the age of nineteen and that that was the end of her formal education. Her expulsion resulted, by her own account, in 'a consequent sense of nudity which I have never quite overcome'.[13]

Michael and Brigid both thought of themselves as Irish. Brigid actually once wrote an essay, 'Am I an Irishwoman?'[14] (I could have told her that she took herself far too seriously to be even remotely Irish.) Her father, John Brophy (1899–1965), a prolific writer of novels mainly set in the army, was born in Liverpool of Irish descent but referred to himself as Irish, and Brigid was given to going to Ireland, where nevertheless 'she felt a foreigner; but I feel a foreigner in England too'. On one occasion, taking Maureen Duffy with her to visit her 'ancestral roots' – the village of Ballybrophy in County Laois – they contacted Anne Crookshank (who was a sort of friend) to seek some recommendations: Anne's only recommendation, which she expressed with her customary forthrightness, was that they should avoid Ballybrophy altogether, as it was nothing but a few shacks thrown together 'and quite in the back of beyond'. Brigid's identification with Ireland did bring out some humour. 'Travelling Aer-cunniLingus, you meet a rare kind of fellatio' is a well-known, Brigid witticism and, setting out with Michael for the Wexford Opera Festival, she expected that Mozart's La Finta Giardiniera would be 'billed as 'La Feinta Giaoirdieniaraigh' or some such.'

Michael's Irishness was also fairly nebulous. His great-grandfather, Richard Michael O'Shaughnessy (1811–99), had been the conductor of the Theatre Royal Orchestra in Dublin for sixty years and, according to Grove's Dictionary, was 'a prolific composer of pantomines'. There are different versions as to why he changed his name to Levey: he took the name of his violin teacher because London audiences could not pronounce 'O'Shaughnessy'; he wanted to sound Jewish because he thought it would help him advance more rapidly in the world of the theatre; he assumed the name Levey when brought before the courts in Dublin for payment of a debt in order to avoid being charged.[15] But in Michael's affectionate memoir, The Chapel is on Fire, he reports the recent discovery that his great-grandfather, Richard Michael, was born

Levey, the son of a Dublin solicitor and that he changed his name to O'Shaughnessy and then back again to Levey. Michael himself was born in Wimbledon in 1927, the son of a civil servant, O.L.H. Levey, and an English mother.[16]

However distant these Irish connections were, Michael would have looked upon me, if not favourably then at least with interest, because I was Irish. But it was late 1973 when I was appointed to the gallery. British soldiers were being killed by the Provisional IRA on an almost daily basis in Northern Ireland and, in March that year, the notorious Price sisters (with accomplices) planted four car bombs in London, killing one person and injuring almost 300. It was the first Provisional IRA attack on mainland Britain and it was to herald an intense campaign of bombings, mainly in London, that would continue throughout the year and into the years that followed. Conservative Party Central Office, the Old Bailey, the Stock Exchange, Victoria Station, Kensington Police Station, the Household Cavalry, as well as several pubs, post offices and Tube stations were among the targets that first year.

An assistant keepership (there were then only three) at the National Gallery is the top job for any young art historian in Britain. Was 1973 the most propitious moment to hand such an opportunity, in the face of robust competition, to an Irishman? I would not have thought so. But it says something for the British that never, either at the time of my appointment or during my years in the gallery, did I ever encounter even a whiff of anti-Irish sentiment, in spite of the fact that the bombings and other atrocities continued; among them, the assassination of the British ambassador in Dublin in 1976 and, ultimately, the murder of Earl Mountbatten in August 1979.

Just as Brigid had (probably) persuaded Michael into being an atheist, a vegetarian and a socialist, she also persuaded him to be an 'Intellectual'. He certainly had the brains to be such, but he had other qualities – humour, graciousness, an ability to appreciate another's point of view – that are not generally the preserve of the intellectual. He once told me, apropos some friends of mine – a well-known academic couple who shared each other's art-history interests – that he did not really approve of 'these husband-and-wife teams'. But he himself was very much part of a husband-and-wife team, and it was Brigid's thinking which informed much of his personality and many of his actions, including the way he ran the National Gallery.

He had come to the gallery as an assistant keeper in 1951, having read English at Oxford following National Service, mainly in Egypt. Working his way up through the ranks – and writing several marvellous books and catalogues along the way – he was appointed director in 1973, leaving a vacancy at the bottom of the curatorial staff pile that was to be filled by me. His predecessor, Martin Davies, was a fine scholar who had worked all his life in the gallery but was an introspective and lacklustre director who, unlike Michael, shied away from publicity, either for himself or for the gallery. He did, however, once feature in the pages of the *Daily Mail*. Taking the Queen of Denmark (or was it Belgium?) around the gallery, he forgot to remove the carpet slippers he always wore at work and was photographed by the press padding along in them beside the queen: the *Mail* published the photograph together with a close-up of Martin's slippered feet.

Davies's quiet directorship, 1968–73, coincided with an altogether different directorship next door, in the National Portrait Gallery. There a flamboyant young Turk, Roy Strong, was by means of extrovert exhibitions – Cecil Beaton and the like – forcibly yanking a dull and fusty institution into the modern era and, in doing so, setting the pace for other museums to follow. When Michael Levey came in as director of the National Gallery, he took up the challenge but in his own measured – and scholarly – way, and through exhibitions, education programmes, publications and the like brought the gallery to the public's attention in a way that had not been done hitherto.

The hierarchy in the gallery in my time was Michael as director, Cecil Gould as keeper, Allan Braham[17] as deputy keeper and Alistair Smith,[18] Christopher Brown[19] and myself as assistant keepers. Some few years after I was appointed, two further assistant keepers joined the gallery, Michael Wilson and Dillian Gordon.[20] I remember them well but somehow they did not infiltrate my memory as much as the core group I joined as the junior in 1974.

Relatively speaking, the collection in the gallery, at little more than 2,000 pictures, is small, and furthermore it is, quite exceptionally for any museum, all on display. In addition it had, since the war, been fully catalogued in a series of scholarly catalogues initiated by Martin Davies and continued (among the staff during my time) by Michael, Cecil and Allan. Each curator had responsibility for a different 'school' – I had seventeenth- and eighteenth-century Italian and, later, British – and responsibility meant research, hanging, framing, decisions as to lending and cleaning, and anything else that might crop up. There were also different departments in the gallery: conservation, scientific, library and archive, framing, press, publications and, a recent one (established by Michael with Alistair Smith as its head), education. I think an Exhibitions Department emerged around this time too. But although all these departments had 'chiefs', the chiefs reported to us, the curators, and we were in overall charge. In time, I was in charge of 'framing', Allan Braham had 'library', and Christopher Brown 'press'.

There had, in decades past, been enormous public controversy over the cleaning (or, as some saw it, the over-cleaning) of gallery pictures, and as a result controls had been devised to, hopefully, prevent such controversies arising again. These controls gave enormous authority to the curators rather than the actual restorers and involved a particular ritual that was, in its way, quite terrifying. At least it was, initially at least, quite terrifying to me. It was also, in my view, quite demeaning to the restorers. For us curators, it meant addressing the full board of trustees and explaining to them the work that was proposed to be done – or else which had been done – on a particular painting and answering any questions that they might bring up. This took place in the conservation studio, when, with the exception of the chief restorer, the restorers – who actually did the restoration – would be shooed out to make way for the curators, and the board. If I (or Alistair or Christopher or Allan) thought a picture would benefit by being cleaned, we would discuss it with Michael Levey and see what he thought. Next, one of the restorers would be asked to look at the picture and give his views. (There were no women restorers in the gallery at this time.) Did it need to be relined? Might an x-ray or an infrared image provide any information? Would analysis of a paint sample by the Scientific Department tell anything? Should the obvious over-paints be removed?

A cleaning test would be made by removing one or two small squares of varnish and dirt to reveal what was underneath. The restorer would write a report. In addressing the board, having been fully briefed by the restorer, we the curators would explain what tests had been made, what work was intended, and the results that might be achieved by cleaning. The board would formally give their approval for things to proceed. When the cleaning had been completed, the painting was brought before the board again, when we reported on what had been achieved.

The trustees of the National Gallery are rather an august body. In my time they included the sculptor Henry Moore, the painters John Piper and Howard Hodgkin, Dame Veronica Wedgwood, Sir Isaiah Berlin, Lord Annan, Sir Eddie Playfair, Heather Brigstocke and Professor John Hale. These people were all immensely eminent in their respective fields; and as a general rule, they seemed to like very much their association with the gallery and were always very friendly. When I ran into Howard Hodgkin some twenty-five years after I left the gallery, he remembered me well; and not just that, he also remembered – oddly, and slightly to my embarrassment – that I had done a thesis on Irish sculpture. Had I been more clued-in at the time I was working in the gallery, I would have known to engage more with these enormously interesting figures and to have asked, for example, Veronica Wedgewood and Isaiah Berlin about their friendship with Elizabeth Bowen: there is a well-known photograph of them both dining with her in the discomfort of Bowen's Court sometime in the fifties.

It would have come as something of a shock to Michael to discover, within a fairly short time of my joining the gallery, that I was not remotely intellectual. Taking me out to lunch, where the rule was 'no talk of the gallery', he would open up several intelligent topics, only to draw from me an absolute blank. Literature?

'Mrs Bennett was a silly-billy,' I volunteered, 'but her heart was in the right place.'

'Isabel Archer was just a goose.'

Although he himself had published a book (with Brigid) on *Fifty Works of Literature We Could Do Without*, this was not the sort of 'lit crit' which he demanded.

'Have you read Disraeli's novel, *Coningsby*?' he might ask.

'Do you mean the prime minister?' I was able to reply. 'I didn't know he wrote novels.'

Philosophy?

'I went to the same school as George Berkeley,' I boasted, 'although he was a few years ahead of me.'

The joke fell flat, and flatter still when it became apparent that I knew nothing at all about Berkeley's thinking. Then he might try me on three of his hobby horses (all of whom he robustly identified with): Walter Pater (particularly Walter Pater), Ronald Firbank and Mozart. I knew that Pater and Firbank had both been 'lovers of boys' (but I had not read anything either had written, and nor could I when I later tried), and I knew something of Mozart's music, even if I was not all that clear as to how many 'high Cs' were expected of the Queen of the Night. And the production of *Don Giovanni* which I had seen the Dublin Grand Opera Society perform in the Gaiety Theatre did not at all compare to the version Michael had attended at the Salzburg Festival. Michael did not attempt these conversations in a spirit of condescension or intimidation: he was too kind for that. It was simply that he thought that that was the sort of conversation one should have over a civilised lunch. In a way, like many of his actions, it was a sort of performance for him rather than anything natural and, in addition, it served to conceal his gaucheness.

It may have crossed Michael's mind before too long that, not only was I not an intellectual, but – to his dismay – I might actually not be all that bright. It certainly crossed my mind, after several lunches with him over my first months, that that was indeed the case. But in selecting me from among the very many candidates who had applied for the assistant keepership, he had gone for me because I was 'unusual': I was Irish, I had not been to the Courtauld, my postgraduate thesis had been on a ridiculous subject of no relevance to the National Gallery and, on witnessing my relative timidity in the interview, he perhaps thought that I might be a 'still water which ran deep'. In my own defence, I might say that, on paper, I was very well qualified for the post. I had both undergraduate and postgraduate degrees in the history of art, and two years' experience in a major national gallery (of old masters), and I had already published more than many of my contemporaries. Michael's previous appointee to an assistant keepership, Christopher Brown, had by contrast a degree in modern history and a diploma in the history of art from Oxford and no museum experience; but his appointment fulfilled Michael's desire to pick out the unusual. In fact, Christopher was extremely intelligent, very open to learning, and frantically serious about his subject. And, on joining the gallery, he embarked without hesitation – and in terrific haste – along the road that would take him to being in time an internationally recognised scholar.

The National Gallery had in the past, as far as I know, rarely mounted temporary exhibitions: the permanent collection was exhibition enough. Michael changed all that. In 1974 – the year I joined the staff – was the hundred-and-fiftieth anniversary of the foundation of the gallery in 1824 and a big documentary exhibition was planned (and organised by Allan Braham) on the history of the institution. Michael felt it would be a good initiation for me to work with Allan on the project, and so it was. But very soon alarm bells sounded for me. The exhibition was to be designed by Christopher Dean, an architect resolutely of the modern movement who had done some work at the Tate, and it was to be slotted into the large gallery north of the Trafalgar Square vestibule. As Dean's designs materialised, I was shocked to find that his main aim was to disguise as much of the splendid (to me) Victorian architecture of the building as he could; Allan did not see anything wrong with this. This was all the more surprising as Allan – who was Courtauld-trained, and serious about his research – was primarily an architectural historian who had published books on the architect François Mansart, the architecture of the French Enlightenment, and the drawings of the Roman Baroque architect Carlo Fontana. But I thought it daft – and approaching vandalism – for an exhibition celebrating the National Gallery building as much as the collection to meddle with the architecture of the building it was celebrating. A huge, unwieldy block-like structure was installed incongruously to descend the main stairs leading up out of the vestibule. Michael referred to it jokingly as a lump of cheese – but he did not see anything wrong with it. This was an eye-opener to me but I kept mum. It did, however, express something of the thinking in the gallery – a disdain for all tradition – under Michael's directorship, and my sympathies always lay in a very different direction. After the exhibition, Christopher Dean moved on to redesign the early Italian galleries. The marble skirtings were removed or disguised, the ceilings lowered, and everything that smacked of 'decoration' hidden: the result was awful.

Alistair Smith was in a way the most 'offbeat' among us and had a genuine interest in contemporary art that was quite different, in my view, to being modern for the sake of being modern. He came up with novel ideas and Michael soon made him, quite rightly, 'head of exhibitions'. It was perhaps Alistair – or Michael and Alistair together – who came up with the idea for the small 'Painting in Focus' exhibitions that took place in the boardroom at this time; and it was certainly Alistair who inaugurated the series with an exhibition focusing on Holbein's *Ambassadors*. There followed Christopher Brown's focus on Van Dyck's *Abbé Scaglia Adoring the Virgin*, and I came next, with Caravaggio's *Supper at Emmaus*. Allan Braham chose *The Rokeby Venus* by Velázquez and, in order to prove (I think) that the positioning of Cupid in the painting was a physical impossibility, had a photograph taken of his four-year-old daughter in a similar pose. It was Alistair certainly who promoted the idea for the *Artist's Eye* exhibitions: a contemporary artist was invited to select some few works from the collection and show them in company with an example of their own work. The first artist so honoured was a very unlikely choice: the abstract sculptor Anthony Caro (1924–2013), whose work, consisting mainly of welded metal beams, definitely provoked some thought when exhibited in the company of Old Master paintings. It was Alistair too (I am almost sure) who later came up with the notion of an *artist in residence* programme whereby a contemporary artist was given studio space in the gallery and invited to show their own work: the first such artist was Maggie Hambling (b.1945).

When I came to the gallery, work was already well under way on a major extension to the building: opening to the rear, it was known as the Northern Extension. Designed by the Department of the Environment, it was hideously functional, with high and ill-proportioned galleries made even worse by sterile wall-coverings. It was opened by the Queen in June 1975 with a beautiful and original exhibition entitled *The Rival of Nature: Renaissance Painting in Its Context*. The building was, without a shadow of a doubt, the most inappropriate 'context' imaginable for Renaissance paintings, although it was certainly 'the Rival' of something: that something was, in my view, harmony. The Queen looked glum as she unveiled a plaque but then managed to smile at Allan Braham's tiny daughters when they gave her a posy. But she returned to being glum as she toured the exhibition with Michael and Alistair. Feeling no doubt that she ought to say something, she remarked on the very large scale of an altarpiece of the *Virgin*

Enthroned. (Alistair told me this afterwards.) Michael was nervous and was talking too much and the next thing Alistair heard him say to the Queen: 'The throne is quite enormous too. And perhaps, ma'am, not the sort of throne one would want to sit upon.'

The Northern Extension – it sounded like an addition to the Tube network, and was just as grim as the Northern Line is known to be – did allow scope for large loan-exhibitions. The first of these, *Art in Seventeenth-century Holland,* was organised by Christopher Brown, and set a high standard. Next (in 1977), Alistair brought in a rare exhibition, *Late Gothic Art from Cologne*, which uncovered – by means of illuminated manuscripts, sculpture, textiles, stained glass and paintings – a school of art that was largely unknown to British audiences. Then the finger pointed at me. Michael, leaving the choice of subject entirely up to myself, suggested that I plan, 'perhaps for the autumn of 1979', a large-scale loan exhibition. As I was in charge of the Italian seventeenth- and eighteenth-century school, it went without saying that my exhibition would be drawn from that area and – 'perhaps best, on account of economy' – that the loans would only come from British collections.

There had, over the decades, been several big exhibitions (and publications) in Italy and in London, which had served to revive an interest in Italian seventeenth-century painting, a period which had fallen very much out of favour in the early part of the twentieth century. The Bolognese painters – the Carracci and their followers – had been well covered by a succession of terrific exhibitions in Bologna; the Roman and Neapolitan artists had also been fairly thoroughly researched; light had been shone on the *Caravaggisti*, mainly through the publications of Benedict Nicolson and Christopher Wright. A young scholar, Charles McCorquodale,[21] was well advanced on his study of the Florentine *Seicento*; and Peter Cannon-Brookes[22] had imported from Milan an ambitious exhibition of Lombard Baroque paintings that was shown in Birmingham. The Lombard *seicento* painters produced pictures which, even by Baroque standards, are horrifically dark and gruesome, and it was rumoured that the Birmingham museum-going public was terrified that Milan would not take Peter's exhibition back again, and that Birmingham would be stuck with the pictures for evermore. If I wanted to select a school of painting that had not been covered (which I did), my choice was limited by these exhibitions. After deliberating between Genoa and Venice, I chose Venice.

The Venetian sixteenth century, with such stars as Titian, Veronese and Tintoretto, has always been very well known, and the eighteenth-century Venice painters, Canaletto, Tiepolo and Francesco Guardi among them, are also familiar: one of Michael Levey's first books, *Painting in Eighteenth-century Venice*, is a virtual love letter to them, it is so elegantly written. But the seventeenth century was largely a blank, and most art enthusiasts would be hard put to name even a single Venetian painter from that period. As I progressed with my researches I discovered (to my dismay) that this was for very good reason: the Venetian seventeenth-century painters were hardly worth knowing about. Their talent (with some exceptions) was, to say the least, indifferent. As I went about locating paintings in English country-house and museum collections, and as I did my research in the literature, it sometimes crossed my mind that this was 'Irish Church Monuments' all over again: I was – once more – toiling in a very infertile field.

I had some stars: Bernardo Strozzi, Domenico Fetti and Johann Liss, to name them. But, although the three of them worked in Venice at some stage, none of them was actually Venetian. Strozzi was Genoese, Fetti was a Roman who had worked in Mantua, and Liss was German. The other artists I gathered up included such 'household names' as Celesti, Pietro Liberi, Gian Antonio Fumiani and Alessandro Turchi but, by pushing my boundaries into the early-eighteenth century, I managed to include a painting each by the better-known G.A. Pellegrini and Sebastiano Ricci.

I did, however, have a very enjoyable time preparing the exhibition and writing the catalogue. The library in the National Gallery, which was more or less for the exclusive use of the staff, is superb and, in addition, there is a photographic library. It contains thousands of photographs of pictures in private and museum collections, as well as paintings that had passed through the salesroom or been held by dealers. It was relatively easy for me to make lists of the Venetian seventeenth-century paintings that were in British collections, and then it was a matter of going to see them. Very few art doors (museums, private collections, dealers) are closed to a curator from the National Gallery, and it is only a matter of proposing oneself to owners in order to be able to see whatever one wants. I went to Alnwick, to Burleigh, to Castle Howard, Kedleston, Corsham Court, Polesden Lacey, Weston Park and many more of the great houses of England, and was received in all of them with varying degrees of courtesy or suspicion. The suspicion derived, not on account of my Irish accent, but because of what I asked to see. A slightly eccentric Lord Methuen at Corsham Court was puzzled that I had no interest in his Van Dyck *Betrayal of Christ* but was instead fascinated by an odd picture of three women running furiously out of a building. This I knew to be by Sebastiano Mazzoni, but the correct subject matter – *Semiramus Queen of Babylon* – was only recognised when the picture went on show in the gallery. Lady Bradford had 'always hated' the Weston Park Zanchi of *Seneca and Nero* and was more than happy for us to borrow it: 'keep it if you like', she told me. George Howard at Castle Howard appreciated that his Fetti *Portrait of a Man* was superb, but questioned me as to how I could be so certain that it did not represent the composer Monteverdi (as traditionally believed); and he did give me lunch. At Burleigh, eventually among what seemed like thousands of pictures, I managed to locate the small Fetti *Labourers in the Vineyard* and, with further effort, recognise a Pietro della Vecchia. We asked to borrow the fabulous *Portrait of Vincenzo Avogadro* by Fetti from the Royal Collection. Oliver Millar, the surveyor of the Queen's Pictures – whom I did not know and had never met – did me the courtesy of ringing me up one day to say that, as the Queen was away, would I like to come and see the picture as it was hanging in the Palace. I said – and I can hardly believe my rudeness now – that I was very busy and did not have the time. Did I really refuse a personal invitation for a private visit to Buckingham Palace? I am afraid so.

I went to Venice a few times on research trips. On one of these, I ran into the art historian – with a special interest in the Venetian Renaissance – and Courtauld lecturer, Jennifer Fletcher, who was also there for research. I did not know her previously but we linked up in Venice and dined together several times. She was enormously good company and very amusing. Jennifer was 'a northern lass' and proud of it: she had retained something of her northern accent. She told me (along with much else) that when her colleague at the Courtauld, the novelist Anita Brookner, was in the process of introducing a northern character into a novel she was writing, it became apparent to Jennifer that Anita was using her as a basis for her 'research'. Finding Jennifer in her room, perhaps preparing a lecture on Crivelli, Anita would ask her something like 'What are you going to eat this evening?' Jennifer knew what Anita was up to and what she expected for an answer. So, although she might have planned a gourmet meal, she would – in order to oblige Anita – reply 'Tripe and onions with parched peas' or some such, and Anita would go away quite happy. In time, Jennifer reviewed my exhibition (very favourably`) with a three-page review in the *Burlington Magazine*.

The exhibition fell into place on schedule, the catalogue was compiled, an audio-visual progamme written and narrated by me was produced, and the pictures were hung (against dark green felt) in the Lower Floor Galleries, where the screens were reconfigured to install them. The conductor, Jane Glover, and the opera designer, Adam Pollock (whom I had once visited at his monastery at Battignano in Tuscany), had approached me during the run-up to the exhibition and had suggested putting on a semi-staged performance of Monteverdi's *Tancredi e Clorinda*: Monteverdi was, after all, Venice's best-known composer of the period. Michael was taken by the idea – there had not been music in the gallery for a very long time – and the opera took place in the pillared setting of the Dome, with the audience seated in the four galleries which opened off it, north, south, east and west.

The five of us – Cecil, Allan, Alistair, Christopher and myself – who worked under Michael were all completely different, both in character and background; and, when Michael Wilson and Dillian Gordon joined, they were both very different too. Cecil (who was in his late fifties) was old-style, part scholar, part connoisseur, and rather 'grand'; Allan was clever, knowledgeable, insightful, slightly nervy and attractively understated; Alistair – a Scot who did not seem like a Scot – was 'with it', outgoing, approachable and friendly; Christopher was very able, scholarly, and with an ambition that he never troubled to disguise. But in spite of our differences, or perhaps because of them, we all worked well together, although without any excessive camaraderie between us. As I remember it, there was little discord or unhappiness, and no one was not speaking to someone else. In the past, I think, Cecil and Martin Davies did not speak. We all got on with our own thing and respected each other's territory. This equilibrium, which was exceptional in the museum world, has to have owed much to the way Michael ran the Gallery (and managed the staff), and it was something which I often had cause to reflect upon when I was a director myself, and faced with some difficult colleagues.

Michael was adept at looking for, and finding, what roles suited each of us best, and, having identified that, he gave us our heads and encouraged us. During the planning of the hundred-and-fiftieth-anniversary exhibition, I asked him if he would like me to publish an article on a previous director, Sir Frederick Burton (who came from Corofin, County Clare), the centenary of whose directorship was in 1974. Michael was hesitant at first.

'Publish where?' he asked.

'I had thought of *Country Life*,' I said.

He tittered.

'But you would be in there with the *Notes on Ballet* and the photos of debutantes in twinsets and pearls,' he said.

He was not someone who would ever have looked at *Country Life* but, when he saw my face fall and when I said, 'Well, perhaps not', he recovered. I had only been in the gallery for a few months at this stage and had previously published several articles in *Country Life*.

'It would certainly bring the gallery to a different readership,' he said, 'although it's hardly the *Burlington*. But I like the idea and, as Burton was director at a propitious time, it could be very interesting. Do go ahead.'

I think it may have been this episode which put it into Michael's head that I liked writing and that I did not consider myself too grand to write for a general readership.

He himself had written several years previously a room-by-room guide to the gallery, which by this stage was out of date. To my delight, he asked me to write a new guide. There was also a Thames & Hudson, black-covered *World of Art* book on the gallery that had been written by Philip Hendy as long ago as 1958. Eva Neurath, the formidable managing owner of Thames & Hudson, approached Michael and asked him to write a new book; but Michael, in his great generosity, declined and proposed me instead. This was a very valuable introduction, and it led to Thames & Hudson publishing, in addition to the book by me on the National Gallery, the *Irish Art and Architecture* book which I had written (with Jeanne Sheehy and Peter Harbison) several years previously. The introduction to Thames & Hudson was valuable in other respects as well: the gallery book, which came out in 1977, remained in print until about 2005. My royalty statements show that it sold, in total, almost 150,000 copies earning me a total income of just over £50,000 which paid off my mortgage in London, and ultimately made it possible for me to retire at the age of forty-two.

Writing the guidebook simultaneously, I adopted a different tone for each. Michael's guide had been a continuous text, room by room, but in writing my version, I went for short notes on selected pictures and adopted what I hoped was a light tone. Michael liked this very much and encouraged me, although when Michael Wilson was revising the book years later (after I had left the gallery), he told me that my text was hopelessly politically incorrect. Perhaps it was. 'Claude's Hagar' I wrote – 'pregnant by Abraham – had fled in shame to the wilderness where she was visited by an angel who told her to return to work and stop being so silly'; Rembrandt's Saskia, 'although dressed as a shepherdess, had no intention of actually tending sheep'. The facetiousness extended to my introduction to the Dutch School. 'It does not do to think that the time-worn saddened people which Rembrandt painted may in fact have been very happy'; and in describing the Holland that one sees in Dutch pictures, I wrote: 'Although the sun rarely shone at any time of the year, it did sometimes set (Aelbert Cuyp); but days were short, so that light in any form remained something of a novelty.' When published, the guide attracted a lot of publicity, including a half-page interview with me in the *Guardian* and articles in the Irish papers by Maeve Binchy (in *The Irish Times*) and Mary Kenny (in the *Sunday Independent*). Maeve and Mary were introduced to me, over a very long lunch in El Vino on Fleet Street, by my friend Mary Geraldine O'Donnell. We had quite a riotous time, all four of us reminiscing about growing up in Ireland and all of us being terribly indiscreet. When the clock was already past four, Maeve and Mary suddenly came to their senses.

'Oh God!' they said. 'We're supposed to be doing an interview with you and we haven't taken a single note.'

I was rather glad they hadn't, as I had told several stories that I would not have wanted published. When Maeve's article was published, it was very gentle, and then I waited apprehensively for Mary's piece. (She still, at that time, had the reputation of being something of a tearaway.) But she was kind too, although she did wittily report my saying that, when one of my farming brothers visited my flat in Pimlico, he went out on my tiny balcony, only to exclaim: 'Is this all the land you've got?'

From what I have written, it should be obvious that, under Michael Levey's directorship, I thrived in the National Gallery and I adored every moment of working there. I learned a great deal, particularly about pictures. It was, after all, our job to look at pictures all day and every day: in the gallery, in the conservation studio, in the sales rooms and with dealers, and in museums and private collections across the world. The Gallery was a wonderful, happy, and inspiring place to work and I always had the feeling that I had arrived at the top of my career.

Endnotes

1. Born in 1918, Gould joined the National Gallery (after distinguished service as a pilot officer in RAF Intelligence during the war) in 1946 and rose to be keeper and deputy director. He retired in 1987. A specialist in Italian Renaissance painting, he wrote the catalogue of the sixteenth-century Italian paintings in the gallery. He referred to his popular *An Introduction to Italian Renaissance Painting* (1957) as 'the schoolboy's primer'. He died in 1994.
2. Distinguished historian of English painting and the Roman Baroque.
3. (1903–83). Appointed at the age of 30, he was the youngest-ever director of the National Gallery (1933–45). Writer on art, and later television personality.
4. Rudolf Wittkower (1901–71), one of the group of German art historians who fled Germany to Britain in the 1930s. Authority on Italian Renaissance and Baroque art.
5. Hendy (1900–80) was director of the National Gallery, 1946–67.
6. As a result of industrial action by coal miners, Edward Heath's government introduced a three-day working week in December 1973 in order to conserve coal stocks. The use of electricity was severely curtailed. As far as I recall we worked five days in the gallery, but in the gloom.
7. Obituary, *Daily Telegraph*, 29 December 2008.
8. Kate Levey: 'discoveringbrigidbrophy.com'.
9. As with his obituaries, the 'official' photo of Michael that is now most used (such as on the National Gallery website) shows him in a slightly more 'normal' suit.

10. For example an interview with Hunter Davies in the *Sunday Times Magazine*, 10 March 1974; and 'Brigid Brophy & Michael Levey: Why Wed at All?', *People*, 4 November 1974.
11. V.K. Janik, *Modern British Women Writers: An A–Z Guide* (2002).

12. Brigid Brophy obituary, the *Independent*, 8 August 1995; and *New York Times*, 9 August 1995.

13. As previous note.

14. *New Statesman*, 5 November 1965. Published in a volume of essays 'Don't Never Forget' (1966). Another article by her, relevant to the Troubles, 'A Solution for Ireland', was published in the *Spectator*, 5 June 1981.

15. R.T. Dudgeon, '*The Keyed Bugle*' (2004), p.13.

16. Michael's memoir of growing up as the only child of a devout Catholic father is *The Chapel is on Fire* (2000).

17. (1937–2011). A Courtauld graduate, he joined the gallery as an assistant keeper in 1962 and became keeper and deputy director in succession to Cecil Gould.

18. Born 1939. He read English at Aberdeen and then postgraduate art history at the Courtauld. Appointed an assistant keeper at the National Gallery in 1970 and later deputy keeper. Director of the Whitworth Art Gallery, Manchester, 1990–2005.

19. Born 1948. He read modern history at Oxford and then a diploma in the history of art (also from Oxford). Appointed as assistant keeper at the gallery in 1971, he rose to be chief curator (from 1989). Director of the Ashmolean Museum, Oxford, 1998–2014.

20. She remained in the gallery, as curator of early Italian paintings, until 2010 and compiled catalogues of the fourteenth- and fifteenth-century Italian paintings.

21. (1949–1996). A Courtauld graduate and freelance art historian and lecturer who published widely. His exhibition, *Painting in Florence, 1600–1700*, was shown at the Royal Academy in 1979.

22. (b.1938). Keeper of Art at the City Museum & Art Gallery, Birmingham, 1965–78, and keeper in the Department of Art, National Museum of Wales, 1978–86.

CHAPTER 11
THE TIME OF MY LIFE

The National Gallery, on account of the electricity restrictions of the three-day week, appeared to me on my first day there as a very gloomy place but, over the seven years I worked there, it proved to be far from gloomy in reality. Nor was my life outside of the Gallery in any way gloomy. I adored everything about living in London, the friends I made, being (relatively) well paid, travel and the cultural opportunities – theatre, music, exhibitions, the salesrooms – that London afforded. I bought a flat in Pimlico and walked to work every day across St James's Park. I had a lively time, and any responsibilities I had were only welcome ones. But, as I kept no diaries and saved very few letters, I have only memory, and a visitors' book, to remind me of those years. I did not observe the rule of having only those who stayed the night sign my visitors' book, and so I have names of the friends I made and entertained. I gave a party in May 1975 and invited from the art world Peter and Diana Scarisbrick, Christopher Monkhouse, Nicholas Thompson, Neil MacGregor, Jane Rick, John Martin Robinson, John Kenworthy-Browne, Gavin Stamp, John Redmill and several more. Other visitors at other times included Hugh Cobbe, Mary Geraldine O'Donnell, Adrian FitzGerald, Gordon Campbell-Gray, Colin McMordie, Tilman Mellinghoff, Denis and Della Howard, George Furlong, Penny Fairfax-Crone, Stephen Erskine Hill, Elizabeth Strong, Neil Burton, John Gilmartin, Speer Ogle, Colin Smythe, Derek Jennings, Jeanne Sheehy, David Marchese, Richard Wood, Jenny Phillips, Malcolm Rogers, Deirdre McKenna, Roy and Aisling Foster, Paul Spencer Longhurst, Angelina Morhange, Anthony Symondson, Ros Savile, Charles McCorquodale and Emily Lane. These are just names, but they were mainly people who were making their way in London, as I was, and many of them went on to higher things.

Of the friends I found, two of the closest also worked in museums: Hugh Cobbe in the British Museum and Malcolm Rogers in the National Portrait Gallery. I had not known Hugh at Trinity but, when I was preparing my William Kidwell thesis at Edinburgh, I had need to consult the eighteenth-century minute books of the London Painter-Stainers Company which were housed in the Manuscript Room at the British Museum and there, spotting me as a familiar face, Hugh introduced himself. It was the start of a lifelong friendship. Descended from the eighteenth-century archbishop of Dublin who had built Newbridge (Donabate), Hugh had been to school at St Columba's, was a Foundation Scholar in classics at Trinity and, later spent a year at Oxford studying Greek, and then to the British Museum, later the British Library, where, ultimately, he was Head of music manuscripts. Oddly, it was not Hugh's familiarity with Latin and Greek that gained him the library job in the first instance; instead, it was his knowledge of Irish. He had more than a *cúpla focal*, having (like Speer) been very well taught at St Columba's, and, as the library had no Irish specialist since the retirement of the distinguished Celtic scholar Robin Flower[1] several decades previously, Hugh fell into the job. But he soon escaped celticism and migrated to his real love which was music. He lived in Islington, entertained, had a wide circle of friends, was musical, and played the piano and organ. We had in common (and always laughed a lot about) Ireland and what it meant to have grown up there and, during my London years, we had many jolly times together. When, subsequently, he married Kate and had a family, I was made godfather to one of his daughters.

Malcolm Rogers, down from Oxford with a doctorate in English, joined the National Portrait Gallery as an assistant keeper in the same week that I came as an assistant keeper to the National Gallery, and we met soon thereafter. It became a friendship immediately. We had a similar outlook, shared many of the same interests, disapproved of the same things, were both getting to know the wider museum world in London, and were both interested in collecting; and yes, we were both ambitious. Malcolm was (and is) very clever, and had a very incisive wit that sometimes landed him in trouble, but more often was very amusing. Up at Oxford, he had met his friend Andrew, who worked in industry and had a cottage in the Cotswolds to which Malcolm went every weekend. Very soon I became a welcome and regular guest and, over the years, we had a great deal of hilarity. Twenty years later, Malcolm was overlooked when it came to appointing a director of the National Portrait Gallery and, taking his leave, went as director to the Museum of Fine Arts in Boston, where, over a period of twenty years, he was an outstanding success. He had the museum entirely renovated, built a new American wing, and raised well over $500 million in endowment funds.

I got to know John Kenworthy-Browne early on. We had a shared interest in British (and Irish) sculpture, as John was an acknowledged expert in the field (with a particular interest in the sculptor Joseph Nollekens) and had published very widely. About fifteen years older than me, he was sympathetic and gently entertaining, although with a tendency to denigrate himself that was quite unwarranted. A letter he wrote to me (dated 25 January 1980) when I was appointed director in Dublin was typical: 'It's a splendid appointment but sad because we lose you from London, and also 'cos now you are placed on a pedestal too high for me to reach.' But John, in his time, had reached up to many pedestals much higher than me. Educated at Ampleforth, Oxford and the Courtauld, he had been a regional representative for the National Trust and had set up and opened to the public the splendid Dyrham Park in Gloucestershire; he later worked for Christie's. He lived in a house on Hollywood Road in Fulham, where he entertained unaffectedly, mixing the young with the old, grandees with unknowns: at John's dinner table I met, among others, on various occasions John Pope-Hennessy, Anthony Blunt, the expatriate art historians (and experts on the neo-classical) Hugh Honour and John Fleming (they lived in Lucca), the American composer Aaron Copland as well as a younger generation that included Alistair Laing, Geoffrey Ashton and others. John had for many years enjoyed a special friendship with James (called Jim) Lees-Milne to whom he had been introduced by Harold Nicolson in 1958. The John and Lees-Milne friendship, 'largely-based on shared artistic interests, was essentially platonic in character and not sensual except incidentally'.[2] In spite of that when Lees-Milne's wife, Alvilde, who herself was the lover of Vita Sackville-West 'learned of her husband's feelings for John, she hit the roof but Lees-Milne made no secret of the fact that he was in love with John, an admission which led to terrible scenes'. There are many of John's letters to Lees-Milne, and photographs of John as a languid young man, among the Lees-Milne papers at Yale; and Lees-Milne's diaries contain several mentions of him, although (sadly) none of them very indiscreet.

> 7 January 1979. John K-B has presumably not returned from America yet: at least he has not telephoned. I have felt uneasy and unhappy. It is absurd that after twenty years and more I should mind as much as I do. I miss him when we are out of touch. Yet when I am with him I am frequently irritated. I just long for him to telephone and say he is glad to be back, and did not enjoy his visit much; and above all that John Pope-Hennessy was hell to him.

Aaron Copland and John had been friends since about 1958: Copland, John has written, 'was certainly affectionate towards me and always kind and generous, but the affection rather lessened before 1970'.[3] The two travelled together, to Paris and to Dublin, and met in London and New York. John introduced Copland to Harold Nicolson and on one occasion they called upon E.M. Forster in Cambridge. John never boasted about all these friendships; word of them just emerged over time. John could on occasion have a sniffy snobbery which I imagine his mentor, Lees-Milne (whom I never met), had in spades but, as I came to realise, John had a real gift for friendship; and because of all his associations, knowing him made one feel like the girl in the Edwardian music-hall song 'who had danced with a man, who had danced with a girl, who had danced with the Prince of Wales'.

I had, by accident rather than design, relatively few Irish friends in London. Jeanne Sheehy was now a lecturer in Oxford Polytechnic, and I would go up and stay with her and she would come to stay with me. The same with John Gilmartin, who was in the museum in Birmingham. Roy and Aisling Foster lived in a charming house in Bridstow Place, Notting Hill, and conversation around their dinner table was always guaranteed to be sparky; and the food was good too. Once, having dined with me in Pimlico, Roy kindly wrote (on 3 August

1976), 'I always feel we never see quite enough of each other (which I must cynically add, I think Proust says means that we're seeing each other just enough!)' But, if I had a few Irish pals, the dearth was more than compensated for by the existence of one particular Irish friend for whom the phrase 'larger than life' might have been specifically coined. Older than me by a few years, this was a woman stout in stature, singular in facial appearance, affectedly posh in her speech, unpredictable in her actions, outrageous in her conversation, ambitious in her social aspirations, uncertain in her education, and, above all, hugely resilient in the face of all adversity. She was passionately Catholic and a regular communicant at the Brompton Oratory, and, claiming somehow a connection with General Franco (whose photograph adorned her dressing table), she could sometimes – for effect – be frighteningly right wing. Contrary to what one might expect of such a person, her origins were far from obscure: she was the daughter of a bank manager in County Kerry and an *alumna* of the Sisters of Loreto. Her name was Mary Geraldine O'Donnell, known familiarly as Mary-G, and formally as 'The Princess of Donegal': it was by that spurious title that she was once announced into a Royal Academy reception. My friends were divided over my friendship with Mary-G. There were some who would only accept my invitations if I could guarantee that Mary-G would not be present, and there were others who would only come if she was to be included. I was amused by her because of the excess she brought to any occasion, the effect she could have on the unwary, and the general hilarity which, inevitably, trailed in her wake. She had a gift for finding interesting or notorious people, and was quick to establish friendships with them; but then, just when things were going really well, Mary-G would make some terrible *faux-pas* which would lead to a rift. As she was capable of laughing at herself, she would freely report such dramas with great laughter.

'Going back to Ireland once you have left,' she would say, 'can be tricky.'

'Tricky' was a word that she often used to describe the situations in which she found herself.

'The first time you go back you are made very welcome and have a fabulous time. The second visit is less enjoyable and you sense that there may be a problem. And the third time, you realise that YOU ARE the problem.'

This was rather the story of Mary-G's life. She lived, when I first got to know her, in a pillared drawing room (in reality just a bedsit) on Collingham Gardens, and there she would entertain: a cocktail party with a black butler, a swathe of newly acquired and unsuspecting guests, some few established friends, and generally a drama at the end of the evening. Mary-G sometimes managed to climb fairly high: when the Lucan nanny was murdered and Lady Lucan was left abandoned in her Belgravia home, her husband disappeared, Mary-G (who somehow knew her) moved in and almost became an unwitting Lady Lucan's spokesperson to the press. I once had Mary-G to lunch to meet my friend Derek Jennings: 'Dazzle', as he was called. Although Dazzle would have been appalled at the idea, I thought they had rather a lot in common, and so they did. At the lunch, they each dropped names in a spiralling crescendo, impressing each other by who they knew and where they had been until the moment – when I was about to serve the pudding – that it dawned on the two of them simultaneously that they were on the same game. Both of them had believed (as I had intended) that the other was a social ladder by which they might climb a step higher, and their mutual realisation that this was not the case rather caused their conversation to stall. Derek was at this time a civil servant in the Department of the Environment and worked under Dame Jennifer Jenkins (that name was produced fairly soon). But earlier in life, he had studied theology at university, became an ordinand in the Anglican Church (at the somewhat notorious St Stephen's House in Oxford). He later read history at York University, and was then received into the Catholic Church by Monsignor Alfred Gilbey. He lived (when I first knew him) in a fairly frugal flat in Dolphin Square. Adopted as a child, his parents were never much mentioned (one or other of them may have been American); and then he suddenly inherited a lot of money and was buying Turner watercolours at Agnew's. He was clever but complex – mixed up, I would say – and slightly ridiculous, but entertaining nonetheless. Ultimately, Derek was to climb much higher than Mary-G ever managed: her apotheosis was an invitation to an aristocratic wedding in Scotland where she became over-familiar with a royal duchess and was sent home, sozzled – thrown in among the detritus from the banquet – in the caterer's van; whereas Dazzle, in time, gave up the civil service, went to Rome to study for the priesthood at the English College, and was ordained by Cardinal Basil Hume. In the interim, he had somehow managed to dazzle Princess Margaret and had become one of her close friends. When he died prematurely (in 1995), Cardinal Hume was at his bedside.[4] Mary-G's demise was less illustrious. Diagnosed with Alzheimer's when she was only in her early fifties, she spent the last fourteen years of her life in a home in Sussex, her friends, and the high society which she had so avidly craved, strangers to her.[5] She was a generous, vulnerable, brave person with a sweet side that was often disguised under her outrageousness, and I came to be very fond of her.

The mention of Monsignor Gilbey reminds me. He may once have had ideas – very briefly, I would have to say – of converting me to Catholicism too. He was very adept at conversions and (as Catholic chaplain at Cambridge for more than thirty years) had performed a great number in his time. But, when confronted by me, he met with more resistance than he had bargained upon, and I soon saw him off. Retired, he lived in the Travellers' Club, where I was a member, and a truly delightful older man, Robin McDouall, was secretary. I had been introduced to Robin, and he organised my election to the club and befriended me. Gilbey cut quite a dash in his clerical garb of an earlier age: shovel hat (wide brim, shallow crown), breeches, double-waisted waistcoat, and frock coat. To me, he always looked as though he might have fallen from the stage of a Donizetti opera. When not in the Travellers', he was often to be seen (it seemed to me) attempting to hail a taxi from a bollard in the middle of Lower Regent Street. He was, it goes without saying, Tridentine Rite and anti-women in the Church, and he took his snobbery very seriously. Once, at lunch in Robin's flat, I was seated beside him. I thought it polite to pass him the salt.

'Dear me, no!' he sniffed. 'I wouldn't dream of salting Robin's cooking without having tasted it first.'

I was put in my place, as he no doubt thought, but my place – rather than his – was where I preferred to be, as I found him borderline sinister.

Sometime, not long after I had gone to the National Gallery, the collector and scholar Denis Mahon (1910–2011) made himself known to me. In his charming way, he flattered me by saying that he wanted to meet me, as I was now the assistant keeper in charge of Italian seventeenth-century pictures (his particular speciality). We also had in common that he was Irish: his mother – Lady Alice – was the daughter of the Marquis of Sligo, and his fortune derived from the family merchant bank, Guinness Mahon, which had been founded in Dublin in 1836. He lived in some splendour in the house where he was born, 33 Cadogan Square, sharing it with his mother until her death, aged ninety-three, in 1970. It was at Number 33 that his extensive collection of seventeenth-century paintings was hung. I did not see much of Denis initially, as he was very much *persona non grata* in Michael Levey's National Gallery. He had been a trustee (1957–64, and again 1966–73) and had made himself rather a nuisance: Denis specialised in making himself a nuisance. His worst transgression was to force the trustees to buy a *Salome with the Head of John the Baptist* attributed to Caravaggio, even though neither the director, Martin Davies, nor Michael Levey believed that the picture was by the artist. Michael was furious, and remained so. Mahon meddled with the government too: advocating the acceptance of works of art in lieu of estate duty, campaigning against museums being given powers of de-accessioning, and fighting entrance charges being introduced in museums. When it eventually came to making his final will (he died, aged 100, in 2011), he devised a complex arrangement (via the Art Fund) to ensure that, if any of the recipient museums ever de-accessioned or introduced entrance charges, his bequests would be forfeited.

As a contradiction, Denis in person was quite delightful: dapper, smiling and humorous, solicitous and kind, a bachelor – but a little boy really.

But, although he made a point of meeting me, he did not invite me to come and see his collection. In fairness, he invited very few people to Cadogan Square at this stage. 'All my pictures have been seen in exhibitions,' he would make as his excuse.

In the autumn of 1975, a major exhibition of the work of Federico Barocci (d.1612) took place in Bologna. Denis was very involved in its organisation, as he was in all the big seventeenth-century Italian exhibitions that took place in Bologna in these years. The National Gallery lent its *Holy Family* to the exhibition, and I was delegated to escort it there (on a freight 'plane). I remained in Bologna for almost a week and took part in all the celebrations – lunches and openings and receptions – which marked the inauguration of the exhibition. Denis, who spoke Italian in a very precise English way (very E.M. Forster, I thought), was at the centre of everything, and fêted wherever he went. He and I were billeted in the same hotel. But, although Denis was so sought after, he seemed to prefer his evenings to be more relaxed; and each evening, at about seven o'clock, the telephone would ring in my room and he would ask me if I would care to dine with him. (He loved his food.) His conversation over dinner – more of a monologue, really – was effusive and informative. He dwelled, of course, on all his battles, and how at different times he had insisted on this and only accepted that. It was he who, as long ago as 1957, had urged the trustees of the National Gallery to reach a compromise with Dublin over the Lane Pictures. 'There has to be an arrangement,' he insisted, 'you can't overturn someone's will, codicil or no codicil. The law is the law.' He told me about his (very public) row with Anthony Blunt at the time of the big Poussin exhibition which Blunt had organised for the Louvre in 1960: Mahon had demolished Blunt's connoisseurship in the pages of the *Burlington Magazine*. 'Anthony got the dating of the pictures all wrong,' he said, 'I simply had to correct him.' The topic, even still, fifteen years later, obsessed Denis, and I was made privy to it in full. He delighted in telling it: 'Anthony, of course, was always jealous of me because I could afford to collect and he couldn't. That was the rub.'

But, over the evenings of our companionship, he did not invite me to come and see his collection.

When I was planning my Venetian seventeenth-century exhibition, I saw that Denis had only one painting which was relevant and which we would want to borrow. This was his *Fall of Phaeton* by Johann Liss. The letter went out from Michael Levey requesting its loan, and Denis immediately assented. I had never seen the picture, and it would have been usual, in the circumstances, for an owner to invite me to do so. But Denis did not observe this convention.

Yet again, he did not invite me to come and see his collection.

Outside the world of work, I made other happy friendships and contacts during these London years, a number of which I still retain. Then one evening, during my last months there, I met someone who was different and with whom I sensed an immediate rapport: a rapport that has endured to this day – almost forty years. This was a young man nearly a decade younger than me: a product of the London School of Economics and a 'banker with brains' by profession. His name is Alex. Level-headed, intellectually curious and sensitive, he rarely takes the stage in this memoir but he is always in the wings. Today in retirement a magistrate in London, he is from a background that is a world away from my own; and it is that, I think, which has suited me just fine.

James White mentioned to me a few times that George Furlong, who had been director of the National Gallery of Ireland from 1935 to 1950, was still alive, and that I should look him up. He lived on Thurloe Street, near South Kensington tube station, and James gave me the address. I contacted George, and was invited round to meet him and his friend Rex Britcher. George, who was quite small, was in his late seventies by this time, but was still alert and active. Neat in his dress, with only a flowered tie as a hint that he was 'artistic', he had a high-pitched voice but otherwise was not unduly precious. Rex was more cumbersome (he was a vet by profession) but he was genial and friendly and, after decades of being together with George, it was obvious that he was still devoted to him.

They owned the entire house in Thurloe Street, and almost every room, from the ground floor up to the attic, was furnished as a reception room, with exquisite furniture, 'objets', furnishings, porcelain, pictures and sculptures. The dining room and kitchen were on the top floor. George, who came originally from Tipperary, was not from a wealthy background but, by the time I met him, it was obvious that he was very comfortably off indeed: he and Rex had owned a Rolls Royce and for years (with Rex at the wheel) they had every summer toured on the Continent in the Rolls, taking in Michelin restaurants, five-star hotels, music festivals, and 'the cure' at some German spa or other. George spoke French and German, as he had studied at the Sorbonne and in Munich and Vienna. When they went to the opera at Covent Garden, Rex always booked tickets in the second or third row, so that George could hear and see quite comfortably. They most liked to give small drinks parties at six o'clock, when chairs would be arranged in a circle around the ground-floor drawing room: 'there are chairs for everyone', George would command in his falsetto tones. Inevitably, their guests were from an older generation, but most had a connection to the worlds of music and art, and I was always happy to be invited.

George had hated his fifteen years (1935–50) as director of the National Gallery in Dublin, and he hated Ireland as a result. He was not bitter about it but he could become quite angry when describing some of his experiences. 'Can you imagine,' he would say, 'during the war, and the Minister for Education told me to remove the best pictures from the gallery in a way that no one would notice and store them in an old schoolhouse in County Mayo. I mean, how could you remove the best pictures so that no one would notice? The ignorance of it!' George would also complain that there had been 'no one in Ireland' that you could talk to. But Mrs Leask (who had known him) told me that there was no one in Ireland – 'except Lady Fingall' – that George *would* talk to. But, after his death, it was revealed that George must have been talking to someone, particularly during the war: he had been a 'whisperer'. 'Whisperers' were recruited by British Intelligence to disseminate, through deceptive 'careless talk', misinformation that was intended to reach German ears.[6] As it happened George would not have needed to whisper very loudly. His counterpart in the National Museum, an Austrian archaeologist, Adolf Marr, whom de Valera had appointed Director of the Museum in 1934 was *Gruppenleiter* (group leader) of the Dublin Branch of the Nazi party *Auslandsorganisation*. In time, Marr was arrested and accused of using his position as Director of the National Museum to plan Hitler's invasion of Ireland. The poet John Betjeman, who was press attaché at the British Embassy in Dublin, was in charge of the whispering campaign – with directions received from London – and George, from his desk in the director's office of the National Gallery – *my* office – ran the operation. As a State employee of a neutral county, this was surely a dangerous thing for George to engage in. I sometimes heard it said that George's sound financial situation stemmed from property dealings he made in London during the war, but now that I know of his deep involvement with British Intelligence I wonder if it was this connection which made it possible for him to retire from the gallery at the age of fifty-two and live very comfortably thereafter.

In 1977, the flamboyant director of the Metropolitan Museum in New York, Tom Hoving, conceived the idea of bringing a huge exhibition of early Irish artefacts (from the collections of the National Museum, Trinity and the Royal Irish Academy) to the Met and, thereafter, to tour America. Such an exhibition, which was to include exceptional treasures like two parts of the Book of Kells, the Tara Brooch, the Ardagh Chalice and St Patrick's Bell, had never been organised before, and it was only after a great deal of persuasion in many quarters that it happened at this time. It opened at the Met, to huge acclaim, in October 1977. I was still at the London National Gallery at the time but I was to be in New York, lecturing or on some other business, at the time, and as my kinsman, Ted Smyth, was a diplomat at the Irish Consulate, I asked him if he could somehow get me invited to the opening. Ted came up trumps and arranged for me to be invited, not just to the opening, but to the glamorous and exclusive dinner which was to take place beforehand. The dinner was held in the Carlyle Hotel, a few steps from the museum. The seating was at circular tables of ten, with the 'top table' in the middle. There was seated (among others) the Irish Minister for Education (the classicist John Wilson), Tom Hoving, the Director of the National Museum (Brendan Ó Riordáin), Professor Frank Mitchell from Trinity (who had written the catalogue) and, beside him, Jacqueline Kennedy. I was intrigued to observe this placement. Professor Mitchell, who had lectured me at Trinity when I was an undergraduate, was an exceptionally cultured and charming man, but he had a peculiar speech mannerism. He would say something, 'St Patrick's mission was mainly confined to the north of Ireland' and then, in exactly the same tone of voice, he would repeat himself verbatim as though he had never uttered the phrase in the first instance: 'St Patrick's mission was mainly confined to the north of Ireland.' I knew, as all the world did, that Jackie Kennedy only ever spoke in a sort of breathless baby-whisper, and so I was tickled at the thought of the conversation that would have been taking place between her and Frank Mitchell: she being confused by him repeating himself – 'Newgrange is about contemporary with the earliest Pharaohs', 'Newgrange is about contemporary with the earliest Pharaohs' – and her whispered responses being misheard – or not heard at all – by him.

In my memory, I see Jackie wearing green that evening but I have come across photographs of the event that show that she was actually in white, accented by a stole in blue. Her gown, shoulderless and full-length, the blue stole pinned at one shoulder and draped diagonally across the body, was Greek-inspired: she was, after all, a Greek widow by this stage. The ensemble derived its design from the antique Greek chiton, and I remember thinking it was not a success. Nor did I think that Jackie (whom I did not actually meet) was nearly as fabulous and glamorous in the flesh as she was in photographs. The googly eyes, the big mouth, and the permanent rigid smile that meant very little, but was so photogenic. Nor was I sure that it was quite the thing for a lady of her age to sit down to dinner with bare shoulders.

I was seated, understandably, on the very perimeter, and when I found my table, I saw that a most bizarre-looking old woman whom I did not know, and whose name on her place-card meant nothing to me, was already settled to my left.

'This is going to be a tough evening,' I thought when I spotted her.

The initial impression was that she had attempted – with some success – to make herself look Japanese: the look, perhaps, of the royal wife of a prominent Shogun in centuries past. But when I first caught sight of her, I could only think of Katisha in Gilbert and Sullivan's *Mikado*. I had seen the legendary Dublin contralto (and actress), Heather Hewson,[7] magnificently perform that role several times with the Rathmines & Rathgar Musical Society; and here I found myself – or so it seemed – sitting beside her in New York. It was the hair, glistening black as coal newly-hewed from the coal face, swept back from her forehead to the crown and curled back over her ears at the sides. It seemed to be waxed rather than lacquered but it was not a wig: of that I became certain. If her face had been lifted – and if it had not, she would have been unique among the American women in the room – it was not strikingly obvious: the nose was long and sheer, the mouth well shaped, the chin pointed. Her *maquillage* aimed at drama, with even her ears slightly rouged, her lips crimson, and her cheekbones 'raised' by the deft application of rose-coloured powder to the cheeks. Her ensemble – a high-collared tunic in a fabulous brocade of chrysanthemum flowers woven in gold thread – also took up the courtly Japanese or Chinese theme. It was worn with luxurious black trousers. Her jewellery was limited to chunky enamelled earrings and several finger-rings that were also huge.

'Who could she be?' I wondered. She could not be very important, or she would not have been placed, as it were, so far 'below the salt' at dinner. I also doubted that she was some Irish-American of note. Distantly connected to the Met – a minor donor, perhaps? Or someone's mother, possibly, wheeled in from the Bronx for the biggest night out of her life. I instantly appreciated that it was my duty to make her evening enjoyable, and that I should be attentive. She soon told me that when the Met 'events people' had telephoned her and asked her who she would like to sit beside, she had replied, 'Someone new, someone I've never met before'; and that was how she got me. I complimented her on her ensemble and remarked on the fabulous chrysanthemum brocade. She was easy and engaging to talk to, but revealed little about herself except that she seemed to have travelled quite a lot, was well read, knew very little about Ireland, and was quite fastidious about a number of things. I only recall some of our conversation. I said that I found Jackie to be much less glamorous in person than she was in her photographs, and I remarked that I did not think her dress that evening was all that stylish. She became quite angry at this.

'English women have no sense of how to dress at all,' she countered. 'They are so dowdy, they have no chic. Your Princess Margaret is the worst of all.'

Later, she asked me if I knew 'Cecil'.

'You would like Cecil very much,' she said, 'and he would, I'm sure, like you too.'

When I probed, I realised she was talking about Cecil Beaton.

'I know,' she said. 'I have something I want to send to Cecil and perhaps, if I gave it to you, you would take it to him in London? That way, you would meet him.'

I said that that would be nice but, by this stage, I had decided that she was given to fantasy, and I did not put much store by anything she said. Towards the end of dinner, she asked if I would accompany her to the exhibition opening. I vaguely agreed, but I knew that I would want to get out of that: I did not want to be encumbered with her for the entire evening. I felt I had already done my duty and I wanted to meet other, more interesting people. And so, I rather dumped her as soon as we got up from the table, and went on to the opening in other company.

I was staying with a friend in New York, Bob Nikirk, the librarian in the Grolier Club. I got home late and, in the morning, he woke me up, as he could not wait to hear my news.

'How did you get on at the big evening?' he said. 'Who was there? Who did you meet?'

'Jackie Kennedy was there, but I didn't meet her,' I said.

'Who were you sitting beside at the dinner?'

'Some old trout,' I replied. 'I haven't a clue who she was.'

'What was her name?'

I recalled the place-card.

'Diana somebody. Vreeman, or something.'

'NOT Diana Vreeland?' he exclaimed. 'You sat beside Diana Vreeland?'

'Who is she?' I asked.

'Do you mean to say you have never heard of Diana Vreeland? My God! She is the most powerful woman in Manhattan, in America. She has been telling American women what they must wear, and what they mustn't wear, for decades. First at *Harper's Bazaar* and then as editor of *Vogue*. She is now the bigwig at the Costume Institute of the Met. She did the fabulous Russian costume exhibit there last year. She is Jackie Kennedy's best friend: she tells Jackie what she should wear. Was she terrifying?'

'Not in the least,' I replied. 'She was rather nice. In fact, she asked me to accompany her to the opening, but I got out of that.'

He roared with laughter as he went off to get me a coffee.

'The only person in the world who has never heard of Diana Vreeland,' he shouted out, 'and he is staying in my apartment! I just have to call my buddies and tell them.'

How dumb had I been? I had sat beside a legend of the twentieth century and failed to recognise her. I had not accompanied her, as she had asked, to the exhibition, where I would certainly have been introduced by her to Jackie and, for that matter, to everyone else as well. I had brushed aside her suggestion that I take a package to Cecil Beaton in London in order that I might meet him. I had dismissed her in my mind as a dressed-up old thing on the biggest night out of her life; I had patronised her. I had done everything wrong that it was possible to do, and I had missed out on opportunities that had been put on a plate before me. The only conclusion I could come to was that I still had a lot to learn about the world. I thought of a well-known maxim and fashioned it to myself: 'You can take the boy out of County Meath, but you can't take County Meath out of the boy.'

The seventies in Britain is thought of as a dismal decade: 'The end of something – the tired, miserable hangover after the long party of the Swinging Sixties.' The lacklustre and stuffy Edward Heath, prime minister from 1970 to 1974, defeated in the end by the miners; Harold Wilson briefly returning between 1974 and 1976, to be succeeded by Jim Callaghan, in office from 1976 until the 'Winter of Discontent' in 1978–79. It was the decade when inflation reached almost 30 per cent and a bailout of £2.3 billion was required from the IMF. It was a decade of power cuts, an energy crisis, political impotence: the Labour government lost its majority in 1976 and was obliged to enter into an unsatisfactory pact with the Liberal Party and, to an extent, the Ulster Unionists. The IRA campaign of terror, both on the mainland and in Northern Ireland, continued unabated. The seventies was a decade of picket lines: above all, picket lines. Carmaker British Leyland was driven to bankruptcy (and subsequent nationalisation) by strikes in 1975; Ford motor workers also went on strike; then lorry drivers, followed by public-sector workers, the miners, waste collectors, railwaymen, even gravediggers. On 22 January 1979 there was the biggest strike in Britain since the General Strike of 1926. Britain was on its knees. It was no wonder that many people, as it were, 'took to the hills': emigrants outnumbered immigrants for the first time ever.

This was the decade when I lived in London and, although it seems ungracious of me to say so, I had – in spite of the surrounding malaise, by which I was only mildly inconvenienced – an absolutely fabulous time. And when the time came for me to leave, after only a brief six and a half years, it is fair to say that I was heartbroken, as I had had the time of my life.

Endnotes

1. (1881–1946). English-born Celticist and translator from Irish, poet and scholar. Deputy keeper of manuscripts at the British Museum from 1929 and compiler of the museum's catalogue of Irish manuscripts.
2. Michael Bloch, *James Lees-Milne: The Life* (2009).
3. H. Pollack, *Aaron Copland: The Life and Work of an Uncommon Man* (2000).
4. Obituary in *The Tablet*, 28 January 1995.
5. 'Mary Geraldine O'Donnell: Socialite who was always to be seen at the best parties', obituary, *The Times*, 21 April 2008.
6. Paul McMahon, *British Spies and Irish Rebels: British Intelligence and Ireland, 1916–1945*

(2008). Gerry Mullins, *Dublin Nazi No 1; the Life of Adolf Marr* (2007); Eunan O'Halpin, *Spying on Ireland: British Intelligence and Irish Neutrality during the second World War* (2008).

7. A stalwart of the R&R from 1954 until her death in 1995, she was the daughter of the Professor of Music in Trinity, George Hewson. Her mother, Mabel Home, was also a gifted singer.

CHAPTER 12

To the Land of Saints and Scholars

On my birthday (9 May) in 1978, James and Aggie White, who were in London on a visit, took me to lunch at the Bath Club in Brook Street. They did not know it was my birthday so that was not the reason for the lunch. No, it was something entirely different: almost as soon as we sat down, James came to the point. Would I apply for the directorship of the National Gallery of Ireland when it became available, as he wanted me to succeed him? I said I did not know, I would have to think; I dissembled by protesting that I knew that I was much too young to be considered.

But Aggie would have none of that nonsense.

'Colm Ó Briain was only 31 when he was appointed director of the Arts Council,' she said forcefully (Aggie always spoke forcefully), 'so your age has nothing to do with it.'

'What age are you?' James asked.

'I'm thirty-two today,' I said.

But James was not to be diverted by turning the lunch into a birthday celebration.

'That means that if I stay on until next year, when I will be sixty-five, you would be 33. That's not too young.'

Then he brightened up.

'Thirty-three,' he said, 'the same age as Jesus Christ!'

'And look what happened to Him!' I countered.

He chuckled, but Aggie, who was devout and did not care for blasphemy, only frowned.

As the discussion proceeded, I said that I was preparing a big exhibition of Venetian seventeenth-century painting which would open at the National Gallery in September of the following year and that I was, therefore, completely committed until that time.

'That's all right,' said James. 'I'll stay on till then.'

In October 1979, just after my exhibition opened, the advertisement for the Dublin directorship appeared. I was exhausted by the work involved in the final heave of getting the show up and running, and elated that what had been about three years' planning and preparation had come to fruition. Dublin and its directorship was about the last thing I wanted to be bothered with, and I set off for three weeks' holiday, staying with Speer and Henry in Rome. When I returned, James telephoned me to say that my application had not been received, and where was it? I put him off by saying that I would send it in later that week.

After a few weeks, James telephoned me to say that Bill Finlay[1] and Terence de Vere White (the chairman and vice-chairman of the board of governors and guardians) would like to come and see me in London, and an appointment was made for them to come to the gallery one afternoon. Unexpectedly on the day in question, the Minister for the Arts, Norman St John Stevas, asked to come and see my exhibition at the very hour that Bill and Terence were due. Michael Levey, doing what he knew to be correct, asked me – as curator of the exhibition – to accompany him in showing the Minister round, and I had no option but to have someone else greet Bill and Terence, explain to them what had arisen, and ask them to wait for me. This, I knew, seemed like gamesmanship on my part, and I felt very guilty and embarrassed. When I met up with them I brought them to my office and offered them tea. Bill – 'a dapper figure with wavy hair combed back, always attired in a well-cut suit and even a flower in his buttonhole'[2] – was not very forthcoming (caution, as I was to learn over the years to come, was his nature) and Terence, who had a shy side, also seemed uneasy. I kept a note of this encounter and I am horrified to read that

> I let it be known that I did not think it was any great honour to be sought after for Dublin and that I had a very good job and lots of prestige where I was. While this was sinking in, I added that I thought I would find life in Dublin personally intolerable.

Recovering from this, Bill asked me what I would like to do with the Dublin gallery. I said I would see it as an absolute priority to produce catalogues of the collection, and with that I handed him a copy of the Washington *Illustrated Summary Catalogue of Paintings*.

'First of all,' I said, 'a catalogue like that of the complete Dublin collection.'

He glanced at the catalogue, but no more than that, revealing thereby that he was unfamiliar with the responsibilities of a museum.

I did not record what else was discussed but it was a stilted and formal conversation and nothing even approaching a rapport, or warmth, was established. (There was very little rapport or warmth between Bill and Terence either, even though they had known each other all their lives.)

Sometime shortly after this meeting, I had another visitor from Dublin. One day, the porter rang through to my office to say that Mrs Hunt was in the waiting room and would like to see me. I had to think for a moment as to who 'Mrs Hunt' could be, and came to the conclusion that it must be Mrs John Hunt, and so it was. I did not know Putzel (or John, who was dead by this time) very well but, when I worked in Dublin in the early seventies, I had been invited to their home, *Drumleck* in Howth, several times to look at their wonderful medieval collections.[3] Putzel, who was German, was a small woman – and plump by the time I knew her – elderly, with a winning little-girl smile, and a little-girl manner to go with it. She spoke (the German accent still lingered) as though imparting a confidence, and it was said that if she came within the proximity of any medieval object – even an unseen stone in an open field – her body would react by vibrating violently, rather in the manner of a metal-detector. She was quite delightful and utterly sweet. But what you saw with Putzel was not necessarily always what you got.

I invited her to tea in the gallery restaurant, and it soon became apparent why she had called upon me.

'There's word in Dublin,' she said, 'that you are going for James White's job.'

I said nothing.

'You must do no such thing,' she said. 'It would destroy you.'

'Dear me!' I thought. 'This is rather alarming.'

'There will be lots of good candidates for that job,' I said. 'I would be considered much too young. Even if I did apply.'

'No, you wouldn't,' she said. 'But why would you want it when you have a marvellous position here in this gallery? Dublin would be far too small for you, after this.'

She continued in this vein until our tea was over, thanked me by saying how nice it had been to see me, and then made her way out into the November fog of Trafalgar Square.

'How kind and thoughtful of her,' I thought afterwards, and I said as much to a friend some time later.

'Don't be idiotic,' he said. 'Kind and thoughtful indeed! Couldn't you see what Putzel was up to?'

'Up to?' I asked.

'Yes. Putzel wants that job for her son, John, but he is too young at the moment and, if you get it, the post will be blocked for decades and John will be forever out of the picture.'

'Could anyone really be that devious?' I asked.

'Yes. Putzel could,' came the reply.

When I got around to examining the details of the Dublin director's post, I realised that it would be a drop in salary for me to take the job, and this fact, together with my other anxieties about leaving London, and a job I loved, gave me cause to ponder. As a result, I wrote to Terence de Vere White (on 24 October 1979) to ask his advice. I did not know Terence well at this stage, but I knew him a little and felt he would be a source of wise counsel, as indeed he was.

> 'I do think that if you had ambition to become a gallery director, Dublin, at your age, would be a good appointment even if you moved on later,' he replied (on 5 November 1979). 'However, I don't know what you ask of life and I agree that in Dublin you would be much sought after. The extent to which you would cultivate the public out of office hours would be up to you. In my view the gallery is ticking over well now but the next director will have more labour trouble than his predecessor. I think it would be wrong to apply and sit for interview if you didn't mean to accept.'

On receiving this, I wrote to James (12 November 1979) setting out my worries:

> The crux of the matter is that I am very happy in my present job, where I have lots of opportunity and, indeed, a future. To change to Dublin would mean a great deal more responsibility, a great deal more effort, and a certain loss of freedom. I finished the letter by asking him to withdraw my application. 'I expect you will be disappointed at my decision,' I added, 'particularly as I know that you did all in your power to get the salary raised.'

James was someone for whom the impossible was always possible, and that was one of the keys to his great success. Within days he telephoned me to say that the salary had been upgraded and that I now had no excuse. The interviews were on Thursday and Friday next, and he expected me to be there. I did as James told me and booked my flight to Dublin forthwith in order to attend the interview.

When the whole interview process was over, I wrote a note for myself about what had happened.

> I flew to Dublin from London on the Thursday morning for my first interview that afternoon. When I arrived, there was bright sunshine: this was 12 December. My sister-in-law, Hilda, met me and we had lunch in Davy Byrne's. I then went to the gallery and, from that moment, everything was farce. A subcommittee of three board members – Bill, Terence and the chairman of the Board of Works, John McCarthy – was conducting the preliminary interviews. There was no waiting room in the gallery, and the other candidates and myself were left to hang around the front lobby with our hands in our pockets in a state of extreme embarrassment at running into each other. I met Andrew O'Connor and Pat Murphy (of ROSC)[4] and simply did not know what to say. The staff of the gallery appeared at intervals to see the goings-on. It was all ludicrous.
>
> I was the last to be interviewed. All three interviewers were half-asleep and, not surprisingly, after a day of

131

interviewing in the stuffy boardroom, very tired. I did not record anything of what they asked me, and when I asked them what the purchase-grant was, they did not know. It was up to me to tell them. (I had looked it up.) I asked if they thought it was likely to be increased, and they said of course not, and that there would be no point in asking the government for an increase, as they had the Shaw Fund. They gave me a time when they would like to interview me again the next day.

It was during this preliminary interview that I realised that James White's long-hatched plans to have me as his successor were about to encounter a stumbling-block. On the boardroom table was a large coffee-table book on *Impressionism*. (None of my books was there, as far as I could see.) The author's name was unknown to me but I learned subsequently that he was from Philadelphia. I knew all the curators in the Philadelphia Museum of Art (I had been there and had lectured there on more than one occasion) but the Impressionist author was not anyone I had ever encountered, or even heard of. But somehow he had applied for the Dublin directorship and his candidature was being taken seriously, above all by Bill Finlay. So seriously, in fact, that (as I learned much later), James and Aggie White were delegated to take him out to dinner and ascertain if he would be socially acceptable in Dublin. In the restaurant he struggled, in the American way, with his cutlery (which he called flatware), folded his napkin neatly at the end of the meal, and did not drink wine – in fact he did not drink at all. His conversation was lucid although not very entertaining. He vouched that he had no Irish ancestry and expressed a preference for getting to bed early. In spite of all these shortcomings, he passed muster with the Whites. But, inevitably perhaps, he was to fall at the last hurdle: towards the end of the meal he mentioned – apropos of something or other – his 'first wife'. The words – 'first wife' – sounded an alarm for the Whites. The mildly favourable impression they had formed over dinner was shattered.

'Could this man be divorced?' they wondered.

Dublin was not ready for this. Aggie and James had been happily married for almost forty years: a divorcee in the gallery would be out of the question. The news was conveyed to Bill. But so determined was he – for reasons unfathomable – to have this unknown American as director, that he waived the objection aside and pressed ahead by inviting the candidate to a second interview.

The following morning the entire board interviewed the three shortlisted candidates: the American, Pat Murphy and myself. Sixteen of the seventeen board members were there, the missing member being the Lord O'Neill of the Maine (Terence O'Neill). Françoise Henry had travelled specially from her secluded retreat in France. Having retired from UCD in 1974, she was seventy-seven at this time and very infirm, an infirmity not helped by her huge size. It was recognised by the other board members that it had been an enormous effort for her to get to Dublin for the interviews – she was in a wheelchair – but she had told James White that she was determined to be there. She took her lunch in the boardroom rather than join the others in the restaurant. Seated in her wheelchair at the end of the table, she did not move much, and it seemed to me as though she was somehow propped up, and if she wasn't wearing an overcoat she looked as though she was. Even in such august company as Alfred Beit, Lord Moyne, Senator Ned McGuire, Terence de Vere White and Bill Finlay, her presence completely dominated the room. I recorded that she asked me which were my favourite pictures in the collection, but I didn't record what I replied. Ned McGuire asked me if I would see the social side of the gallery, such as concerts, as a good thing. 'Yes' was my answer to that. Lord Moyne was generous enough to remark that, although he had never seen me before, he had heard me, as he had sat through the audio-visual presentation in my London exhibition. If any of the others said anything, I did not keep a note of what they asked. The interview did not last long. Subsequently, I recorded for myself what happened next:

> When I emerged, James took me aside and asked me where I might be contacted later. When I said that I might be going to visit my mother, he became impatient.
>
> 'I mean where now?' he said. 'Where will you be this afternoon?'
>
> I said I would be lunching in the University Club with Michael Wynne.
>
> 'Fine', said James, 'I'll call you there about 2.'

After lunch, Michael and I went up to the ladies' drawing room in the club, and James called me to say I had got the job and that I was to come back to the gallery for the board to formally appoint me. I replied that I really could not accept just like that.

'I already have a job,' I said. 'I would have to tell Michael Levey that I would be resigning before I could accept another job'.

James became irate.

'Listen,' he said, 'the board brought you over here for an interview and, when you have an interview, the board expect that you want a job; and now the board have offered you a job, and they expect you to take it. Come into my office straightaway and speak to Michael Levey on the telephone.'

I was rather taken aback by this directive. I had discussed everything with Michael Levey before coming to Dublin. His advice had been that I could not possibly decide whether I wanted the Dublin directorship until I was actually offered it. It was then, and only then, that I could decide. I had actually asked Michael, What shall I do if they offer it to me over the table? They would never do that, was his response. Feeling wretched, I telephoned Michael from James's office. I told him what had happened and asked him what I should do.

'Am I just to end the agony and say yes?,' I said.

'That's probably the best thing,' he advised.

The board called me in again and Bill announced that they were pleased to offer me the directorship. Someone made a comment (which I did not record) and I countered with a quip (I didn't record that either) but Pat Scott the painter laughed. I did record that: I did not know him, but he was a human and sympathetic presence in the midst of the turmoil in which I found myself.

When I came out of the boardroom, James was with the gallery registrar, Miss Nellie McCarthy. He was composing a letter to the Minister for Education (John Wilson) seeking the Minister's approval for my appointment. Miss McCarthy was despatched to the Department in Marlborough Street with the letter. No word came back immediately, and no Nellie appeared either, in spite of several phone calls by James to the Department. He became angrier and angrier while I sat there. Eventually the Minister telephoned. 'Yes, yes,' I heard James say, 'of course he speaks Irish. He has his Leaving Cert.' Eventually, Nellie came back, breathless, with the Minister's letter of approval, and James sat down at his desk.

'Now, the press release,' he said, taking up his pen. 'What schools did you go to? Trim National School. We have to put that in, it appeals to "the people". Other schools? Good, that's finished.'

I suggested that it might be appropriate to say that I was an Assistant Keeper in the London National Gallery.

'Do you think so? Well, OK then.' He jotted it down. 'Now, have you a photograph of yourself?'

'Well, not about my person,' I said.

He picked up the 'phone. 'Is that the *Irish Times*? James White here. We've got a new director of the National Gallery. I'm bringing him down to be photographed.'

James bundled me into his car and dropped me at the *Irish Times* with the press release, and he drove off. I went in and was photographed. All day the sun had been shining but when I emerged, the heavens opened – an omen, I thought: so much rain that the furthest I could get was to the pub opposite. It was a Friday night and the pub was packed: cigarette smoke and the smell of beer filled the air. This is the real Ireland, I thought, dirty, drunken and wet. This is what I am coming back to. I ordered a drink. Then I came to. I went cold with shock and horror at the position in which I found myself. London was over for me, and I was back in Ireland, where I had started. I had one or two more drinks, as I could not move out of the pub on account of the rain. Eventually, I left, and managed to get as far as the more congenial surroundings of the Hibernian Hotel, from where I telephoned my mother with the news. I saw some friends there drinking champagne and, without them knowing my situation or my confessing to it, I joined them. I went back to Speer's flat in Fitzwilliam Street (he was in Rome), where I was staying, and later that night went out to dinner with my friends John Gilmartin and Jeremy Williams.

And that was my day, the day I was appointed director of Ireland's National Gallery.

James White had, of course, a keen understanding of human nature and, more to the point, he knew me well and also understood my character. Had I gone back to London and taken time to reflect, James knew that I might well have bolted and not taken up the job. The board's face-to-face appointment of me, the Minister's approval, the press release, the photograph in *The Irish Times*, all militated against that eventuality; James knew it, and planned it that way. He did not do so with any ill intentions. He himself loved the gallery, he had worked with me and knew me well, and – rightly or wrongly – he thought I would be a suitable director. Afterwards, he was thrilled that he had pushed my appointment through.

'It's as though his own son had been elected director,' several people reported to me.

However, it had been a close-run thing – as I was to learn many years later – and James had nearly lost.

Bill Finlay evidently persisted in his support for the American, and after the second interviews advocated his appointment. Bill was a skilled and adept chairman of a meeting (as I was to appreciate in years to come); with great courtesy and a gentle calm, he had the capacity to cut through any discussion and get to a decision, and the decision was almost always the one that he wanted. He was not a bully in meetings but he was very clever and had enormous dignity, and very few people ever had the courage to challenge him. And so, when he came down on the side of appointing an American director of the gallery, it seemed like a done thing. But on this occasion Bill had not counted on the colossus lodged in her wheelchair at the end of the table: Professor Henry. The protégé of her hated rival, Anne

Crookshank, I might have been, and her attempts, six years previously, to get to know me better may have fallen flat, but Françoise was prepared to rise above all of that. She bestirred herself – a Vesuvius – and stopped Bill Finlay in his tracks. To the astonishment of the other board members, she spoke up.

'You've GOT to appoint the Irish candidate who is properly qualified and trained,' she said.

The board wondered if she meant me or Pat Murphy.

'If you do not appoint Mr Potterton, serious questions could be asked afterwards. His only disadvantage is that he is very young.'

Bill, who did not care for the idea of 'serious questions being asked afterwards', capitulated, and I was appointed.

Françoise retreated after the meeting to her former stomping ground, the Department of Art History which she had established in UCD in 1965, and there she was joined by her erstwhile colleagues (one of whom, years later, was the source of my information).

'We've got Mr Potterton,' she said. And then she elaborated. 'I wasn't going to be dictated to by a banker' were her very words. Thereafter, she returned to France, never made it to another board meeting, and died two years later.

Reading the above account, much of it written at the time, thirty-five years ago, I think I sound like an arrogant little twerp: at least, I sound like that to me. The National Gallery of Ireland is a wonderful gallery with an extensive and extremely interesting collection. As a gallery, it is highly esteemed in the museum profession worldwide. To have been appointed its director was a tremendous honour, and an opportunity that many professionals, a great deal more distinguished than me, would grasp with enthusiasm. In the past some superbly gifted individuals have held the post and been satisfied with it. My dismay at being appointed stemmed not from any feeling that the gallery was inferior but rather on account of the fact that it was not the right time for me. I did not think I was too young but I was too engaged and satisfied with the job – and the life – that I had to want to move at that stage. Had the directorship become vacant ten years later, when I would have been in my early forties, I would probably have taken it on with enthusiasm, and been glad to move from London. But that was not how the dice had rolled.

I went back to London, and my lovely flat, on the Sunday, and in to work on the Monday. For some days, I did not feel like sharing my news with any of my colleagues, and Michael Levey did not tell them either. There was a letter from him on my desk.

> It is a great pleasure to welcome you back, with many congratulations, as a Director, and of a major National Gallery. Not since Kenneth Clark probably has anyone so young achieved such a post . . . think of that.[5] Our loss is undoubtedly Dublin's gain. I am sure yours will be a prosperous and impressive reign – and I hope too it will be a happy one for you. We're proud that it should be our colleague who has been chosen.

Other letters came, a great many of them, in the following weeks. From Maurice Craig, 'I heard with unfeigned joy of your appointment'; from Professor Frank Mitchell; from the painter Howard Hodgkin, 'I wanted to talk to you and congratulate you.' From Rosalie Mander of the National Trust, Nancy Balfour of the National Art Collections Fund, Richard Ormond in the National Portrait Gallery, the chairman of the National Gallery, Professor John Hale, and from Terence Hodgkinson and Neil MacGregor in the *Burlington Magazine*. Madge Ashton, the widow of a V&A director, also wrote, and Jennifer Montague from the Warburg Institute, and Tim Clifford from Manchester. '*Un petit mot seulement pour vous féliciter très chaleureusement de votre nomination à la tête du musée de Dublin*' came from Pierre Rosenberg in the Louvre; *i miei rallegramenti più vivi per la sua designazione a Direttore della National Gallery of Ireland*' from Professor Rodolfo Palluchini in Venice. And then from a Dublin wit and friend, John McBratney: 'I sense with the appointment of Charlie Haughey as Taoiseach and you as Director of the National Gallery within a week of one another that once more our little island home will be called by the other nations of the world the Land of Saints and Scholars.'

Press reports of my appointment struck a positive note: 'a local boy who has made very good, very fast' wrote Victoria Glendinning in an article headed 'The Homan Factor' in the *Times Literary Supplement* (8 February 1980); and there were more in similar vein.

I had stated in Dublin that I would not be available to take up office until six months later; this was agreed, and so I embarked upon the last months of my London life. The time went all too quickly. Michael Levey gave me a pep talk before my departure.

'You must decide, above all, to enjoy it,' he said. 'Remember to bear that in mind.'

With that thought in my head, I set out – indifferent scholar though I was – for the Land of Saints which, for much of my time there, was the Ireland of Mr Haughey.

Endnotes

1. William D. Finlay (1921–2010). A barrister, later dean of the Law Faculty in UCD, and subsequently governor of the Bank of Ireland. He had only just been appointed to the board of the gallery at this time and need not necessarily have known what was required of a director. His interests were shooting, fishing, wildlife and music rather than art.
2. Obituary by Charles Lysaght, *Irish Independent*, 17 October 2010.
3. Now in the Hunt Museum, Limerick.
4. Patrick J. Murphy, passionate art collector, later Chairman of the Irish Arts Council and the Irish Contemporary Art Society and, from 1980, Chairman of ROSC, Advisor to the State Art Collection and Member of the International Council of the Museum of Modern Art New York. His early career was in business working with the Guinness Group in Ghana, Malaysia and London. He has published a monograph on the artist Patrick Tuohy and also a Memoir, *A Passion for Collecting* (2002).
5. In fact, Roy Strong was appointed director of the National Portrait Gallery in 1967 at the age of 32, but Michael would not have considered the NPG 'a major national gallery'. Kenneth Clark was 30 when he was appointed director of the National Gallery in 1933.

CHAPTER 13
OFFICIAL AND OTHER SECRETS

There is a general view that the decade of the 1980s in Ireland was, economically speaking, the most dismal decade in the history of the State. Statistics can lie but the fact that the national debt, which was an impressive IR£7bn in 1980, rose to IR£23bn by 1986 says something; and the something it says is that the country was in a parlous condition at the time, and living well beyond its means, on borrowed money. Unemployment was over 13 per cent. The Irish pound, only introduced after the break with sterling in 1979, was devalued in 1986. Income-tax rates were staggeringly high. I see from a payslip of 1985 that my gross monthly salary was IR£1,855, but total deductions for tax and other contributions amounted to a punishing IR£1,003. It was not a very nice time to be in Ireland and, as a State employee attempting to run a State-funded institution, I was in the thick of it. Metaphorically speaking, I was as a potato in this Irish stew. And it was not very long before I was mush.

But this is not a 'misery memoir', and the above is merely a background sketch. Unfortunately, much of the foreground is not a great deal better. Nevertheless, if there are dark bits on this canvas, there are bright bits too. And as a restorer approaches the cleaning of a picture, I will concentrate on the dark parts first and then move on to the lighter areas: those which depict the aspects of being director of Ireland's National Gallery that I most enjoyed.[1]

When Terence de Vere White warned me in his letter that 'the next director will have more labour trouble than his predecessor', he knew what he was talking about. Staff unrest (among both the professional and the warder staff) had surfaced in the last years of James White's tenure, and the need to address it had reached the board. James's reaction was to be offended by this, and the board sought to sweep it under the carpet. James had always loved working in the gallery, and he thought that everyone else should feel the same way, irrespective of their conditions. It was he who had recruited most of the staff (and had some of them trained), and he took it personally that they would (as he saw it) turn on him in this way. Although still his ebullient self, he was, underneath, disappointed in his last years. But the problems were nothing to do with his administration: they stemmed from the structure of the gallery.

The gallery, and the powers of the board, were established by an Act of Parliament in 1854. Based on that, the staff were the employees of the board, but an anomaly arose in that they were paid by the government. They were not civil servants but were employed 'under the State'. Staff numbers in the gallery were tiny, and what had happened over the years was that many of the modern conditions of employment (including salaries) adopted by the general civil service had not filtered down to the gallery staff and, realising this, they were at this time seeking to remedy the situation. As they were not civil servants, they could not be represented by any civil service union, and consequently had joined other unions: the ITGWU (Irish Transport and General Workers' Union) in the case of the warder staff and the Federated Workers Union for the professional staff. The unions then had to find someone to negotiate with – they could not negotiate directly with the civil service as represented by the Department of Education – and as the director is the servant of the board, it was, in the absence of there being such a thing as a Personnel Officer in the Gallery, to the Director that the unions turned. But the director, no more than the board, did not have the capacity to grant any concessions without first of all obtaining sanction from the Departments of Education, Public Service and Finance and the delays (and obstructions) involved in those negotiations led to frustration on the part of the staff. There was frustration on the part of this director too, as dealing with the various Departments – so many of them, but particularly Education – was not something which anyone would wish on their worst enemy. There were individual grievances too. My successor in the post of temporary cataloguer, John Hutchinson, had now been temporary for seven years and, understandably, wanted to be made permanent. I agreed with him wholeheartedly, but when I told him what my brother Elliott had once told me – that the postman at Rathcormick had been temporary for thirty-five years – he was not reassured.

Was all of this complicated? I quote from a letter received from, jointly, the Departments of the Public Service and Education:

> Following a letter from the Minister of Public Services, requesting that the two Departments should consult on the question of the letter from the Federated Workers Union, it is recommended that the Board of Governors and Guardians might meet Representatives of the Union and the State. The hands of the Board of Governors and Guardians are completely tied by an Agreement made in 1960 between the Board of Governors and Guardians and the Ministers for Finance and for Education whereby basic conditions of service so far as they relate to salary or retiring age, pension rights, annual leave, working hours, general conduct and similar matters require the approval of the Minister for Finance (now the Minister for the Public Service). If the Federated Workers Union wish to obtain negotiating rights in the Civil Service which would normally cover the professional people in the Gallery, they (the Union) would have to discuss this with the Department of the Public Service. If, following these discussions, it was decided that the professional people in the Gallery were outside the Civil Service Conciliation Scheme, then the only recourse would be the Labour Court. The Agreement is a confidential document between the Board and the Ministers and, whilst the Union might be told about it, they should not be given a copy of it.

This was all gobbledegook as far as I was concerned, and I had very little patience with it. But the reality was that, as Director, I had to have patience with it.

When I took up office, it did not take me long to assess the situation. I could see that all the staff were completely justified in their unrest, and I was totally on their side. At meetings with the union representatives, and the unlucky member of staff who had been chosen as shop steward, there was very little discussion, as I was in agreement with everything they had to complain about. The difficulty arose when I tried to seek remedies from the various Departments, as these were never easily obtained. In order to help steer myself through the maze, I sought advice, initially from Charles McCarthy, the professor of industrial relations in Trinity and, subsequently, from the Federated Union of Employers, but the advice I received did not lead to my being able to avoid frequent confrontations in the Labour Court, where I found myself alone and faced with my colleagues, who were backed up by the professional services of a union official. Outside the arena of the court, I was generally able to have friendly relations with the union representatives, but there was one exception: the ITGWU man was one Eamon Gilmore,[2] whose stern dislike of me (and, more particularly, of what – personally – I represented) was palpable. In a later incarnation, he was invited by the Queen of England to dine at Windsor Castle but, for my part, I would not want to invite him, even for a cup of tea.

All of this union negotiation, and the days I spent in the Labour Court, was, for me, a very far cry from writing a guidebook to the London National Gallery or researching the Venetian 'seicento', and I cannot say that I enjoyed any of it in any way. The Labour Court was just that: a court. And, for the most part, I found my experiences there both harrowing and very disturbing.

Other staff difficulties arose from a public-service embargo on recruitment at this time. Three staff, over all grades, had to leave (through natural wastage) before one new person might be recruited. This diminished the warder staff particularly, leading to many of the rooms in the gallery being almost permanently closed.

On my list of miseries, the Office of Public Works (OPW) would rank very high. The chairman of the OPW is 'ex officio' a member of the board of governors and guardians of the National Gallery on account of the fact that the building is vested in the Office of Public Works. The OPW is, therefore, by that means made aware at first hand of any difficulties or requirements pertaining to the building, as any such problems are brought to the attention of the governors and guardians. On taking up office, it did not take me long to see that the gallery building – both the public rooms and behind the scenes – was in a shocking condition. There was much that was actually dangerous. Some of the electric wiring in the older parts dated from before the war. The air-conditioning in the newest wing was so unreliable that it ran the risk of causing more damage than it prevented. Security provisions were scant. All of this I soon brought to the attention of the gallery board, and set about convincing the OPW to institute a programme of repairs. Some gestures were made by them from time to time, but nothing substantial was ever put in hand. I tried to cultivate the chairman of the OPW and convince him of the gallery's needs, but the first chairman I so cultivated retired after two years, his successor died not long after taking up office, and there then came in a third chairman, Pascal Scanlan, with whom I started over again. He eventually appointed a young architect from the office to draw up plans for a major scheme, but putting this scheme into effect was postponed from one year to the next. Eventually, I came to regard it as nothing more than a pipe dream, and my hopes of ever getting anything done evaporated. It was this experience over the eight years of my directorship that frustrated me most, and in the end contributed more than anything to my decision to resign.

In my early years, frustrated by a lack of action, and embarrassed and ashamed of the dilapidated state of the public galleries, I thought of raising funds through sponsorship in order to have the rooms at least redecorated. I had, without much difficulty, obtained sponsorship for gallery publications, exhibitions and bursaries to fund work-experience in the gallery for young graduates. I had not needed the permission of the board to do this: I only required them to open bank accounts in the name of the board to receive the monies I raised. But to take over what was the responsibility of the Board of Works and proceed independently with our own funds was a different matter, and for this I felt I needed to be directed by the board. I sensed that Bill Finlay, as chairman, would want to consider very carefully before embarking on this go-it-alone route, and for that reason I had to come up with a plan as to how I might persuade the board to instruct me.

Terence O'Neill (the Lord O'Neill of the Maine), a former prime minister of Northern Ireland, was an immensely eminent figure who had been a governor and guardian of the gallery since 1972. Living in England, he did not come to every board meeting, but he was always very friendly towards me, persistently inviting me to look him up in London and lunch with him in the House of Lords, followed by an insider's tour of the Houses of Parliament. For long, I did not take up his flattering invitation but, after about two years in office, I did so; and I did so with more in my mind than an inspection of the House of Lords. Lord O'Neill was a charming and very approachable wise man, and it was easy for me, over lunch, to bring up my shame at the gallery's appearance and lead him to suggest my raising funds privately to have the galleries redecorated. We agreed that he should write me a letter for circulation to the board in which he would propose such an approach. This he did. Dated 29 January 1983, he wrote:

> Dear Homan, While visiting the Gallery recently, I could not help noticing how shabby the wall coverings have become. Could something be done about this? I realise of course that money is not plentiful at the present time, but I would have thought that with the same enterprise as you have shown over publications, redecoration could be undertaken room by room. What I have in mind is that prominent Irish companies could be asked to contribute a sum of money sufficient to cover the cost of redecorating one room each. A suitable plaque could then be displayed in each room to let the public know of the generosity of that particular company. I would be grateful if this suggestion could be considered at our next meeting, as otherwise the Board of Works may take years to come to grips with the problem and many of us may not be here to see the redecoration. Yours, Terence.

The procedure for board meetings was that I drafted the agenda, discussed it with Bill Finlay, and sent it out to board members some ten days in advance of a meeting. Only very rarely did Bill make any amendments. But on this occasion things went very badly wrong. I wrote to Lord O'Neill (on 19 April 1983):

> I thought I should write to let you know how matters went over your letter although you will of course receive the

Minutes. Basically everything was very unsatisfactory. Bill
Finlay's attitude to the whole question was both contorted
and negative. In the first instance he asked for the matter
to be put on the Agenda as 'Deterioration in the condition
of the rooms'. I was abroad when the Agenda was sent out,
but it would have been my intention to circulate copies of
your letter to the Board; this, however, was not done. Bill
then asked that I should not refer to your letter at all, but
that I should say at the meeting that 'some Board members'
had raised the matter with me. I made it clear to Bill that
what I wanted out of the discussion was the suggestion that
we should raise funds for the redecoration – but Bill
deliberately sidestepped this one. The net result was that
the Chairman of the Board of Works was left to report back
at a later meeting as to what, or when, the Board of Works
would do something. I am trying to see when I would be
in London mid-week to take up your invitation to see the
Dilettante Society portraits,[3] and then we could also talk
about other things.

I was furious that my plan had backfired so completely. I was familiar
with the words 'the chairman of the Board of Works would report back',
as I had heard them many times before and I did not welcome hearing
them again; and I felt frustrated by Bill's reluctance to let me go ahead.
Afterwards, I said to him that, in my view, when a board member asked
for a letter to be circulated, it should be circulated. It was the only
occasion during my directorship when I confronted him directly. 'Let
me turn it over in my mind,' he said.

He may have done so but it was noticeable that our relationship,
which had always been good – but somewhat distant – developed into
something more friendly, even affectionate, thereafter.

Almost five years later, in October 1987, when still nothing at all had
been done about renovation or redecoration, the billionaire
philanthropist Dr Tony Ryan,[4] who had recently been appointed to the
board, raised the possibility at a board meeting of fund-raising by the
Gallery for a renovation scheme which the Gallery itself would
undertake. His question came out of the blue but it was immediately

clear to me what he meant: he personally would fund a refurbishment. How did the board react? The minutes record that Dr Ryan's 'point was noted for consideration'.

Reading through all the above, it is obvious that, in dealing with the civil service – be it the Departments of Education, Finance, Public Service, the Taoiseach or the Board of Works – I had many shortcomings, and the same applied to my dealings with politicians. The fault lay with me: I was not up to this aspect of the job. I lacked the required tact and patience and, added to that, were other factors that contributed to my failure. I see from my diary that a Minister Boland – Minister for what, I cannot recall – was once persuaded by his civil servants to call me in and threaten me with the *Official Secrets Act* because I had criticised his Department publicly. In the view – I am convinced – of civil servants, I was just young, and I was back from England with big 'English' ideas. My religion (yes, my religion, make no mistake about that) did not help, and the fact that I came from a 'Big Farm' background in County Meath only compounded my difficulties as, in Ireland, owning any land is often perceived (because of history) as a stain on one's character. I rapidly established a popular public profile, and that did not go down well either. I freely admit to an occasional (unintentional) stand-offish manner; condescension (again unintentional) is not unknown to me. I can have a sharp tongue, and tact is something I only have in limited supply.

What chance had I? None.

But if I experienced such difficulties in dealing with officialdom, I had no such problems with the governors and guardians. From the very start, guided by Bill Finlay, they were unanimously and unequivocally supportive, and agreeable to everything I asked. Bill understood perfectly the role of a chairman, and he appreciated that the chief executive (me, in the case of the gallery) must be the one to direct and manage the running of the organisation. There were times – like when I would wish, fruitlessly, that he would go and bang on the Minister's door – when his strict observance of this protocol led to my frustration, but the benefits were considerable, and contributed greatly to any success I might have had. The board never turned down a picture I proposed for purchase, they never instructed or required me to do something which I myself had not asked for, they allowed me tremendous freedom, and they never censured me. They allowed me to bid for pictures at auction, and not just in Dublin but also in London and New York. I see from Peter Somerville Large's history of the gallery that I was allowed to spend up to £250,000 on a picture without their approval. (I had forgotten about that.) They agreed to a moratorium on temporary exhibitions for a period of two years after I took up office. They agreed to my closing the long-established restaurant and replacing it with a more contemporary one. They agreed to charging admission for temporary exhibitions, and, by setting up an Exhibition Fund, agreed to keep the monies so raised (rather than hand them back to government, as was required). They then agreed to the practicality of having a gallery vehicle for transporting pictures, and paid for it, on my suggestion, out of the fund. They agreed to my charging guests for their drinks at gallery openings. They allowed me a three-month sabbatical so that I could complete my Dutch catalogue. I could go on. And then, when I made my most fantastical proposition of all, one that required a tremendous leap of imagination on their part, as well as a supreme confidence in me, they agreed. I proposed that they purchase with Shaw Funds a house and garden adjoining the gallery, Number 90, Merrion Square. The house was to be sold by tender – a potentially complicated process – and I was delegated to deal with all that that required. When our bid of IR£80,000 was successful and the sale went through, I had *carte blanche* to oversee and plan its restoration, with Austin Dunphy as architect.

It was peculiar, really, that Bill and the board should have had such confidence in me when the civil service and the politicians had none at all.

Having listed my miseries above, and got them out of the way, it is time for the Mrs Lincoln question.

After her husband, Abraham, was assassinated at the theatre, she is said to have been asked, 'Apart from that, Mrs Lincoln, how did you enjoy the play?'

And so, aside from my woes, how did I enjoy being director of the National Gallery of Ireland? Unlike Mrs Lincoln, I can reply, unreservedly, 'I enjoyed it hugely, thank you.'

Things got off to a start with rather a bang. It was June 1980 when I took up office. James White asked me to come to the gallery on the Friday, his last day, before I started on the Monday. He had been on to

The Irish Times (again) and had a photographer on hand, who took photographs of me and him together. James was wreathed in smiles and, remembering that Michael Levey had told me to enjoy the directorship, I tried to smile too.

The big art event in Dublin that summer was Rosc, an exhibition of international contemporary art, which took place every four years. Somehow, by this time, it had spawned other ancillary exhibitions, one of which, *Chinese Paintings from the Sackler Collection* was to be shown in the National Gallery. I failed to see the relevance of this, either to the gallery or to the appreciation of contemporary art, but it had all been arranged, and who was I to object? The main aim, as I quickly realised, was to get an American colossus of art philanthropy, Arthur Sackler,[5] to Ireland, and live the dream that he was going to shower us with benefactions. Michael Scott the architect, and the genius behind Rosc (and many other art projects), was probably responsible for the Sackler presence – the man, his pretty young wife and the exhibition – in Dublin: the episode very much smacked of the optimism for which Michael was notorious. Festivities were planned: a dinner at the American Embassy, another in the Burlington Hotel, the exhibition opening in the gallery; and, to fill a gap in the schedule, I was asked to host the Sacklers for Saturday lunch in the National Gallery.

This proved to be a disaster. The gallery restaurant at that time catered almost exclusively for politicians from the Dáil and civil servants from Government Buildings, whose preference was for a lunch of meat and two veg, Mondays to Fridays. On Saturdays and Sundays, when bona fide Gallery visitors might have wanted something to eat, the restaurant hardly functioned at all. But I did not know this. I invited some other guests to meet the Sacklers but we all sat there at the inelegant wooden tables and waited. Eventually a waitress appeared but everything on the menu was 'off'.

'Ah no! Not on Saturdays,' was her persistent refrain.

I squirmed with embarrassment but, underneath, I was livid.

If this lunch did not finish off any hopes that I might have had that Dr Sackler would be the saving of the National Gallery, the exhibition opening certainly did. It too was a disaster.

Liz Shannon, the wife of the American ambassador, described the event in her diary.[6]

We all trooped down to the National Gallery for the Opening. The place was mobbed. Bill (the Ambassador) had prepared a very nice speech, welcoming the Sacklers to Ireland, describing the aims of Rosc and officially opening the exhibit. Unfortunately the microphone in the Gallery did not work so no one could hear his speech. Brian Lenihan, the Foreign Minister, was going to introduce Bill, but decided at the last moment that it would be better for Michael Scott to do it but then Michael could not remember Bill's surname; but since the microphone wasn't working anyway, scarcely anyone heard.

Mrs Shannon does not record where the new director was in all of this: had I fled the fiasco?

The next event was the dinner at the American Ambassador's Residence, in which I was included. I was exactly one month into the job and it was the first time in my life that I had been invited to an embassy. The Shannons were a stylish couple, young(ish), educated, Democrats (Jimmy Carter was president at this time), and they entertained with a clever combination of formality and informality. They liked people to be entertaining. Instead of sitting at either end of their long table, they sat opposite each other in the middle, and it was clear that they saw themselves as a double-act. I remember some of the guest list from that evening: Tim O'Driscoll from Bord Failte, Michael Scott (of course), possibly John Meagher the architect, the attractive Mary Scott (Michael's erstwhile daughter-in-law) and a very recent recruit to this coterie, Dr Tony Ryan. Tony was, in Michael Scott's eyes I'm sure, a 'sub' on the team: if Dr Sackler did not play ball, Tony would take his place on the field. And, as it happened, that is what transpired. Tony and his company GPA subsequently became the sponsor of Rosc and, after that, much else in the Irish art world as well. In time, he was perhaps the most generous art patron that Ireland had ever known. But that night he was very much a novice. Sitting opposite me and beside Mary Scott, he said very little and I think that, as for me, an embassy dinner may have been a new experience for him. I noticed from across the table that he had the 'bedroom eyes' which women find devastating.

Liz Shannon clinked a crystal glass as soon as dinner was over.

Silence descended, and the ambassador rose and made a speech. He gestured round the table, introducing the guests one by one, and saying nice things about all of us. Someone replied. Then Liz clinked again and called upon Michael Scott to speak. Michael rose to his feet.

'You've all been listening to me for decades,' he said. 'I've been making speeches all my life. There's not a thing I could say that you haven't heard before.'

Everyone laughed.

'But there's someone else here tonight,' he continued, 'and none of us have ever heard him speak at all. And it's time we did.'

Everyone looked at each other.

'Yes,' said Michael, 'we would like to hear from the new director of our National Gallery, so Homan Potterton, the floor is yours.'

It was very unexpected, very unexpected indeed, but somehow I managed to get to my feet and make an impromptu speech of sorts, possibly on the theme of being thrown in at the deep end.

The dinner in the Burlington Hotel, also in Dr Sackler's honour, was on the Sunday night. Further excruciation, but of an entirely different nature, awaited me there. The guests, about eighteen of us, were all drawn from the world of contemporary Irish art: the movers and shakers, as it were, who were behind Rosc (and much else besides). Again speeches loomed. After several people had spoken, Anne Crookshank (who had written the catalogue for the first-ever Rosc exhibition) got to her feet. She was always a tremendously amusing speaker, her piercingly exaggerated voice rising in decibels and interspersed by peals of her own laughter: she was also, always, totally unpredictable in what she might say. That night was no exception. The other speakers had all spoken about art, about exhibitions, about the need for a museum of modern art in Dublin (eyes turned towards Dr Sackler at that), and about the effect that the Rosc exhibitions had had on Ireland's young artists. But Anne had another theme.

'We are so pleased to welcome you to Ireland, Dr Sackler,' she trilled, 'so pleased indeed. You see we are such a very small band of enthusiasts here, who are passionate about bringing art, and particularly contemporary art, to the people, and tonight we welcome you to our [pause] bosoms.'

Vibrating vigorously, she led the laughter.

'And nearly all of us enthusiasts are in this room,' she continued. 'You are meeting the crème de la crème.'

More laughter.

'And do you know what it is about us, Dr Sackler?'

The distinguished guest gave no indication that he had a clue what she was talking about.

'The thing about us – and I'll go around the table one by one – is that we are nearly all . . . [long pause] . . . Protestants.'

She then proceeded to point out Gordon Lambert, Pat Scott, Cecil King the painter, Deborah Brown the sculptor, Robin Walker and finally – with the words 'our latest recruit' – me. I was mortified.

Everyone, of course, knew that I was Protestant but it was not an aspect of my make-up that I necessarily wanted to trumpet abroad: I had more sense than that. And now Anne had, as it were, blown my cover.

Following these Rosc celebrations, I was reminded of Terence de Vere White's words to me: 'I agree that in Dublin you would be much sought after.' Is this what he meant? Was it all to be like this? Then I realised that, in spite of the embarrassments, I was rather enjoying myself.

Apart from the microphone – and the restaurant – there were many other things in the gallery that did not work the way I would have liked. Simple things, like the telephone, for example. True, we had telephones, but we did not have our own switchboard. Instead we were linked to the switchboard of the Department of Finance. In order to make a telephone call, one picked up the receiver and waited. And waited. Eventually the operator in Finance would say in a sulky voice, 'Yes?' You told her the number you required and she dialled it for you. If anyone called the gallery, they also came through Finance. 'Rialtas' was how the operators answered the phone (it means 'government'). Most people calling the gallery were confused by this but Speer Ogle loved it. As he had once worked in the Arts Council (An Chomhairle Ealaíon), he knew about this sort of thing, and pronounced his Irish in a very exaggerated way. (He had been to St Columba's.) On one occasion, when at the Council, he telephoned his friend David Hendricks and was answered by David's assistant, Diane Tomlinson.

'Who's calling?' she asked.

Disguising his voice, Speer said exaggeratedly, 'An Chomhairle Ealaíon' (pronounced 'on-hoar-la-ay-lea-on'). Diane went through to David.

'There's someone on the phone, I can't quite catch the name, but it sounds very much like a whore from Lyon.'

Whenever Speer called me and the operator in Finance answered 'Rialtas', he would ask her what she said. She might repeat 'Rialtas' once, or perhaps twice, but would then become embarrassed. 'Who do you want to speak to?' she would repeat. 'I want to speak to you,' Speer would say, 'and for you to tell me what this word means.'

It was the little oddities like the phones – and a plague of feral cats in the basement stores – which made my first two years rather a roller-coaster. The gallery was permitted, under a 1967 Act of the Dáil, to lend pictures to government offices, as well as to Irish embassies abroad, on a long-term basis. I discovered that a total of 589 pictures were out on this basis; over the years, some of them had been mislaid and others damaged. I set about retrieving them but I was met, in many cases, by an extreme reluctance. Evening receptions for delegates attending international conferences in Ireland (that had nothing to do with art) were frequently held in the gallery, and many proved to be very rowdy affairs: I eventually persuaded the board to put a stop to them. I had the security adviser to the National Museums in the UK, Nipper Read – the man who had caught the Kray twins – come and do a report on security in the gallery. I announced that I wanted to establish 'Friends of the Gallery' but so many people wrote in wanting to be my friend that (without saying so) I put the plan on the long finger. I got the attendants to shed their dull navy blue uniforms and dressed them instead in Irish green blazers: I wanted them to have scarlet waistcoats with brass buttons as well, but that was a step too far.

In the same period, I was able to put in place some people that I could work with. Raymond Keaveney was my choice (although appointed by the board) for the vacant post of assistant director, and no one could have been better; I swapped an unsatisfactory registrar for a topper; sent a secretary packing; and found in England a recent Edinburgh graduate, Adrian Le Harivel, who proved to be a dynamo in assessing and recording the entire collection while compiling the three volumes of *Illustrated Summary Catalogues* that I was determined to push through. I raised sponsorship and used some of the funds to offer bursaries to young graduates for a six-month employment in the gallery.

Some terrific young people came through the gallery in this way, and I loved working with them. One, Barbara Dawson,[7] came to me at the end of her six months and told me that she was leaving, as her mother had told her that she was wasting her time and that there was no future in gallery work. I told her that my mother had said exactly the same to me not all that long ago.

'And look where I am now,' I added.

As I liked her, I found some further funds and asked her to stay on.

The secretaries in the gallery – two of them, one of whom was my secretary – were, by tradition, novices seconded to the gallery from the Department of Education. When I took up office, one of them, Rita Frawley, had been in the gallery for a number of years. She was excellent but she soon returned to the Department, and promotion. Without reference to me, her replacement turned up. This girl could type (slowly) but as far as other secretarial duties were concerned, such as dealing with telephone callers and keeping my diary, she was completely at sea. I was sure she had a promising career in the Department of Education but it soon became clear that she did not have a promising career with me. I saw no reason why we should accept these girls and I put it to the Department that the gallery should be allowed to recruit its own secretarial staff. The response, as usual, was: 'I don't know that we could allow that, but we'll see.' Nothing happened and after a while I took matters into my own hands and, one Friday afternoon, told the two girls in question that they were no longer required in the gallery and that they should report to the Department on Monday morning.

I had someone in mind as my own secretary. This was a girl (actually a little older than me) who had trained as a personal secretary in the head office of the Bank of Ireland and then, as an older student, had gone into Trinity and taken an honours degree in French and art history. She was called Honor Quinlan and she came to work for me. I did not have to teach her anything about what I required but she found that she had to teach me quite a lot about what a secretary expected of a chief executive – and, to my great advantage, she did. I liked her very much and we had a perfect accord. She kept my appointments diary scrupulously, marshalled my contact with the staff, received visitors, arranged my travel and, privy to my private life, was always discreet. She dressed well and was always, in her words, 'perfectly groomed'. But it was in the realm of the telephone that Honor came into her own. She did not easily allow people to actually speak to me, nor did she permit me to make my own phone calls. She would make them for me, get whoever it was on the line, and then put me through. She observed a strict protocol on this but the protocol ran into difficulties when she had occasion to get me Bill Finlay on the phone, as she frequently had to do. Bill was the governor of the Bank of Ireland and his secretary was, therefore, a former colleague of Honor: she too was trained in telephone protocol. As far as I could fathom, although I never quite got to the bottom of it, if Honor telephoned for me to speak to Bill, it was Bill's secretary who should put Bill on the line first and then Honor would put me on. But Bill's secretary did not see it like that and she would try to insist that Honor put me on the line first. Between the two of them, it was a miracle that Bill and I ever managed to speak on the telephone at all.

In the matter of my appointments diary, Honor was also assiduous. If someone had an appointment with me, the hour was to be strictly observed. On one occasion, the official from the Department of Education due to meet me at noon rang at 11.30 to say that 'there would hardly be time now as he needed at least an hour and a half with me and perhaps he might come in the afternoon'. Honor would have none of this.

'No, Mr Heneghan. The director never sees anyone for more than half an hour, so you will have plenty of time. Come at noon as arranged.'

He came.

When I met someone one night at dinner, it came up in conversation that I would like to play bridge, and this lady said she would arrange a four and invite me. She subsequently rang the gallery with the invitation and got Honor.

'Bridge, Mrs Fuller? Did you say bridge? The director doesn't play bridge.'

'But I met him and he told me he did.'

'He has never been invited for bridge before. Are you sure?'

'Perhaps I got it wrong but no, come to think of it, he definitely said he would like to play.'

'I'll see if I can put it to him and ring you back. Your name again was ...?'

It sounds like Honor was a dragon but she was not a dragon to me. On the contrary, with her well-judged efficiency, she smoothed my life considerably. She resigned after about four years and was succeeded by another Trinity art history graduate, Janet Drew, whom I also liked very much. Young, stylish and personable, she projected an image of the Gallery that was exactly as I wanted. She proved to be efficient, and I soon taught her all that Honor had taught me.

The office of registrar is provided for in the Act of Parliament that established the gallery. It was the registrar who traditionally handled the gallery's finances, records, management of the attendants, and general day-to-day administration. An early registrar was a Mr Killingly, who was dismissed in 1872 for 'great negligence and irregularity in the discharge of his official duties'. A subsequent registrar was Walter Strickland, the author of the *Dictionary of Irish Artists*, and he was succeeded by the poet James Stephens, who had no qualifications for the post other than his literary eminence. Another writer, Brinsley McNamara, came after him. But from about the 1960s, the Department of Education exerted a stronger hold, and the registrar became an official seconded from the Department. Nellie McCarthy – she who had extracted the letter from the Minister securing my appointment – retired after years in the post as I came in, and the Department put in place a successor, who proved to be unsatisfactory. As a replacement, I insisted on interviewing some few possible recruits to be provided from the Department, and I selected another McCarthy, this time a Mary. She was, as it transpired, a wonderful choice. The finances side was child's play to her and her straightforward manner – she came from Kerry – appealed to both the warders and the professional staff. She did not put up with any nonsense but was very fair and approachable, and cheerful to work with, and she cut through red tape as though it did not exist. She was to become enormously helpful to me in my dealings with the various Departments and I became very fond of her. Attractive and young, she had been unlucky in love but had taken it on the chin.

Once when a post of typist-secretary became available, we advertised; Mary later came to me to say that she did not know how she was going to select the five or six candidates for interview as there had been hundreds of applications.

'Give them up to me here,' I said, 'and I'll go through them.'

Half an hour later I went down to her office.

'There,' I said, 'we will interview those six.'

'How on earth did you sort them so quickly?' she said, her face beaming in admiration.

There was a knock on my door some ten minutes later. Mary came in.

'I know what you are up to,' she said with a grin, 'and I am not going to let you get away with it.'

Of the candidates I had chosen, four had been to Rathdown the other two were from Alexandra College (both Protestant schools).

'All right then,' I said, 'add in a couple from the Holy Child Convent, Killiney.'

Mary went away satisfied.

Of the (many) arenas where I might have been more politically tactful in seeking to ingratiate myself with government, one was exhibition openings. Ministers, particularly those whose Departments had any connection with the Gallery, expected to be asked to perform such openings but I did not see the need to invite them to do so at all. They had no interest in the gallery as far as I could ascertain, apart from lunching in the restaurant, and only wanted a platform to display themselves to their own advantage and, hopefully, get their photographs in the newspapers. Apart from that, their speeches – written by their civil servants – were invariably excruciatingly tedious and, by my reckoning, very few of the people invited to gallery openings had any interest in anything any Minister had to say. Furthermore, they were always late in arriving. And so, with one or two exceptions, I ignored them. Gemma Hussey, then Minister for Education, I invited to open the Walter Osborne Exhibition, but she was someone who was interested and informed about art and could be relied upon to make a good speech (but she did arrive late). Otherwise, I invited Seamus Heaney to open the James Arthur O'Connor Exhibition, Lord Killanin (the distinguished president of the International Olympic Committee) to open something else, and my kinswoman, Thekla Beere (the retired first woman Secretary of a Government Department –Transport and Power), to speak at another event. Some openings were muted six o'clock affairs but for the big exhibitions I arranged something much grander. I made them black-tie, set 9.00 p.m. as the hour, had a piper in the forecourt, the gallery façade illuminated, and a red carpet in the lobby. There Bill Finlay and I would receive the 300–400 guests who had been invited. It was all a bit ridiculous (particularly as I then made guests pay for their drinks) but it was fun and slightly glamorous, and people liked it: invitations were very much sought after. Following one of these events, Professor James Meenan,[8] the President of the RDS and a Gallery Board member, wrote to me (12 May 1985):

> Annette and I were delighted to be asked the other night. There are two pleasures about such invitations – one, to be there: the second, to be reminded that something in the country is still being well and imaginatively run.

For one such occasion – I can't remember the exhibition – I invited President Hillery to perform the opening. This time I decided to go further over the top and have trumpeters in the minstrels' gallery at the end of the great room upstairs. They would announce with a fanfare the arrival of the president. But my plans for the night did not go smoothly.

Exceptionally, because it bordered on the absurd, I made a note of what took place.

> I was telephoned by the Department of the Taoiseach some days beforehand.
>
> 'You've got the President coming to open an exhibition?' said the caller.
>
> 'Yes,' I replied cautiously.
>
> 'He should have been asked to do that through this office.'
>
> 'But he has accepted and he's coming,' I said.
>
> 'Yes. But that should have been arranged through the Taoiseach's Office.'
>
> 'No,' I said, 'the protocol is for the invitation to go directly to the President's Office at the Áras, and it is then up to that office to seek the approval of the Taoiseach's Office.' I hadn't a clue whether this was the case or not but I sounded (I hope) quite confident on the matter.

The official rang off but on the day of the opening, I had another call.

'What are the arrangements for the President's visit to the gallery this evening?'

'Well, guests are invited for 9.00 p.m. and President and Mrs Hillery have been asked to arrive at 9.30 p.m. They will be received at the entrance by the chairman and myself and escorted upstairs to the reception. On his arrival there, he will be announced by a trumpet fanfare, followed by the national anthem. He will then move to the dais, make a speech declaring the exhibition open, and then, with Mrs Hillery, be escorted round the exhibition by the chairman and myself and introduced to guests as appropriate. He will then leave'.

The official it seemed was noting all this down and that was the end of the conversation. He called back half an hour later.

'You can't have a trumpet fanfare', he said.

Intrigued, 'I asked why.

'No, It has to be the Presidential Salute.'

'Exactly', I said. 'I know all about that. And, as the trumpeters are the army trumpeters, they will be very familiar with the Presidential Salute and also the arrangement of the national anthem that should be played in the presence of the President. There is a variant, you know.' That was the end of the matter and, apart from Mrs Hillery complaining to me that the walk up the back way (in order for them to first appear at the top of the stairs) was very long, the evening went off splendidly.

It was this sort of behaviour on my part that did not stand me in good stead at all. I knew that. But I also knew what I wanted for the gallery – be it a fanfare or something more lasting – and I did not care to be obstructed. I was impatient and, more to the point, I was confident that I knew what I was doing.

In the early years, my principal contact in the Department of Education, with whom I conducted most negotiations, was a Mr

Heneghan: Paddy Heneghan, to be precise. His brother was the head of the College of Music, which was a recommendation as far as I was concerned. Paddy was a brick wall to start with but gradually – very gradually – he started to crumble and I came to appreciate that he was actually a very nice man. It took him somewhat longer to discover the same about me. But, having spent decades in the Department of Education, he had become conditioned by the culture, a culture in which nothing was possible if 'the rules' did not provide for it, and in which every answer had to be 'no'. We had lots of meetings about staffing but I don't think anything ever came of any of them.

One day Mr Heneghan (as I always called him) told me that he was going to Rome the following week.

'On holiday?' I asked.

'For the canonisation,' he replied. 'The wife and I are going with a group from the diocese.'

(I think it must have been the canonisation of Maximilien Kolbe in 1982.)

'That will be very interesting,' I said, 'and is it all arranged by the diocese, your seats and everything?'

'Oh, we won't have seats, nothing like that, we will be among the crowds in St Peter's Square.'

'I might be able to help you,' I said.

Paddy looked puzzled.

'Our hotel is already all booked with the group,' he said.

'But I could possibly get you seats for the ceremony,' I said.

Had I stated that I might be able to get him an audience with the Virgin Mary, he could not have looked more doubting.

'Give me the name of your hotel and I'll see what I can do,' I said.

He scuttled from my office as soon after that as he could.

I rang Speer, who at this stage was working for the Vatican: he was reading the news on Vatican Radio.

'Are you in a position to get tickets for the canonisation on Sunday?' I asked.

I explained the circumstances to him. He was as piqued as I was by the thought that two Protestants like him and me could arrange tickets for a canonisation for a Catholic couple like Paddy Heneghan and his wife. It seemed preposterous.

'I'll do what I can,' said Speer, 'and leave the tickets, if I get them, into his hotel.'

Speer got two seats in the very best position, on top of the colonnade overlooking the steps of the Basilica, with an unobstructed view of the altar which had been set up for Pope John Paul to perform the ceremony. Paddy and 'the wife' were within a few feet of the Pope.

When he came home, he brought me a bottle of whiskey.

'Oh!' I said, to confuse him further, 'I'd rather you had brought me a bottle of holy water.'

To my disappointment, however, my Roman intervention brought me no miracles nor did it even noticeably improve my standing in the longer term with Paddy or the Department of Education and I continued to soldier on.

Endnotes

1. In an interview with Vera Ryan, published in 2006, I have described some of my experiences as director. Vera Ryan, *Movers and Shapers: Irish Visual Art, 1940–2006.*
2. (b.1955). Elected to the Dáil in 1989, leader of the Labour Party, 2007–14, Tánaiste and Minister for Foreign Affairs, 2011–14.
3. These exquisite eighteenth-century British portraits hang in the clubhouse of Brooks's, and I lunched there with Lord O'Neill on 24 November 1983 in order to view them.
4. (1936–2007). A self-made billionaire, founder in 1975 of the aircraft leasing company Guinness Peat Aviation and, in 1985, co-founder of Ryanair. Ryan was a prolific and munificent donor, particularly to the arts. He thought nothing of funding a marine-science research institute at Galway University (in 1992) and paid for a splendid building to house it: to pay for the renovation of the National Gallery would have been a project dear to his heart, I feel sure.
5. (1913–87). He endowed museum galleries at the Metropolitan Museum, Princeton, Harvard, the Smithsonian and the London Royal Academy.
6. Elizabeth Shannon, *Up in the Park: The Diary of the Wife of the American Ambassador to Ireland, 1977–81* (1983), p.278
7. Director of Dublin City Gallery The Hugh Lane, since 1991.
8. Professor of Political Economy in UCD from 1961 (d.1987).

CHAPTER 14
In Demand

Outside of the gallery, my appointments diaries record that I kept up a pace, which rather astonishes me in reconstructing it now. Michael Levey in London did not do this. He lunched lavishly with someone every day but at six o'clock he went home to Brigid and their basement flat on the Old Brompton Road. He did not accept invitations: any invitations. Even the Queen knew not to invite him to so much as a garden party at Buckingham Palace, as he would not go. According to newspaper profiles, he and Brigid, and Brigid's girlfriend, the poet Maureen Duffy, watched *Match of the Day* on television together and wrote books in the evenings.

Social life in Dublin, as I soon found out, was a great deal more demanding than that. I deemed (rightly or wrongly) that the success of the gallery depended very much on my being known to the public and getting around, so I went (almost) everywhere and to (almost) everything to which I was asked. James White had done that, and it had stood him in very good stead. I thought I should follow his example.

I lectured to the Medical Missionaries of Mary in Drogheda, spoke to the Irish Country Women's Association in An Grianán, addressed the Tullamore Chamber of Commerce, the Lady Graduates of Trinity College, and the Rotary Club of Fingal (where I nabbed a new gallery sponsor). Abroad, I lectured in the museums in Charlotte (North Carolina), Philadelphia, the Kimbell in Fort Worth, the Morgan Library and the Getty. I proposed the toast of the arts at an Ulster Arts Club dinner in the Agricultural Hall, Belfast: 'a dreadful drunken evening where I was heckled vigorously', I recorded in my diary. I had 'forty American blue-rinse to tea in my office' and, on the invitation of Henry

Mount Charles, went to a David Bowie concert at Slane Castle. I went to the North Galway (or was it the Galway Blazers?) Hunt Ball and, although I did not know her, somehow stayed the night (hair-raisingly) at Bermingham with Lady Molly Cusack Smith: 'Somerville & Ross she might well be, but I do not like her,' I wrote. 'And she is an atrocious snob.' I dined as the guest of Tony O'Reilly at Castlemartin: 'Lots of Americans. We did not sit down till ten, and then dancing till 4. I did not enjoy myself but Tony is a very genial and welcoming host.'

I sat on the board of the Royal Hospital, Kilmainham (newly restored), it was some sort of arts venue then, before it became the Irish Museum of Modern Art (IMMA), I was also on the boards of the National Self-Portrait Collection in Limerick and the Castletown Foundation and sat on some Department of Foreign Affairs committee which made me Ireland's representative at meetings in Paris. I cannot fully recall what this was all about (was it UNESCO or Council of Europe?) but it was to do with arranging international art exhibitions. At one meeting I was asked if I could arrange for some museum or other to borrow the Book of Kells: I gave a very definite 'no'. This committee also brought me to Tokyo to celebrate the opening of a big exhibition of paintings in a department store. I came home the recipient of gifts of pearl cufflinks a camera, and a small wooden casket on which my name had been burned in Japanese lettering. Another committee of which I was a member selected the designs for Irish postage stamps. As accounting officer for the gallery's government funding, I attended the Public Accounts Committee annually. I opened Kilkenny Arts Week, judged the Taylor Art Prize in the RDS – and the Texaco Art Competition – and selected a sculptor to make a bust of the composer John Field for the National Concert Hall. I delivered the Hermione Lectures in Alexandra College and presented the prizes at Sandford Park School. Marian Finucane, Pat Kenny, Mike Murphy and others interviewed me on the radio. I was made an honorary member of the Royal Hibernian Academy and sat for my portrait to the president, Carey Clarke. I had for long admired Carey Clarke's work at the annual exhibitions of the RHA and thought him a very fine portraitist. On meeting him one day, I said as much to him and he replied 'why don't I paint you?'. I was not averse to the idea so, without offering him a commission, I agreed to sit. His method was to do several charcoal sketches of a subject from the life to get the character and likeness and then use photographs for reference when it came to painting the background. Sketches and photographs were all taken in my office over a few sessions and the oil portrait was completed (without my knowing it) with Carey's meticulous and painstaking care. I was no longer living in Ireland when it was exhibited at the RHA[1] but a friend wrote to tell me that as I looked so very stern in the picture, it must have been painted on a day when I had had a very difficult meeting in the Department of Education.

My daily routine was sometimes interrupted to show visiting dignitaries – generally sent by the Department of Foreign Affairs – around the gallery. A Saudi prince (or perhaps a cousin of the Emir of Qatar) came in a flowing white robe with red-chequered ghutrah on his head: idiotically (and quite inexplicably) I stopped before the Mantegna and explained the subject matter. Judith, a Jewess, has decapitated the Assyrian Holofernes.

'Yet another example of Jewish aggression,' my guest laughed.

He had probably been educated at Harvard.

And then the invitations: hundreds of them. I have kept some, all annotated in pencil by Honor: 'accept' on some, 'regret – previous engagement' on many more. I was bidden to dinner at every foreign embassy in Dublin, from the Chinese, the Indians, the Russians and the Turks to the British, the French and the Germans. Some were more enjoyable than others. 'Dinner, informal' at the Spanish Embassy and the comment in my diary 'They have met all the wrong people.' I was invited by the President and Mrs Hillery to a (rare and almost-private) dinner at the Áras when Mrs H (who was a very gracious hostess) complained to me that the house was not really geared for entertaining. I expressed surprise at this.

'No,' she said, 'there are, for example, no dishes for avocados.'

State dinners for visiting heads of state at the Castle, were splendid, although I was passed over when Ronald Reagan came, and had to make do on different occasions with the presidents of Israel and, later, India. I watched the jumping at the Horse Show from the box of the president (of the RDS); I dined as guest of the Benchers of the King's Inns and lunched on the invitation of the army chief-of-staff at McKee Barracks. I was a regular at Maureen Cairnduff's 'First Fridays' on

Waterloo Road. Mrs Frank Duff invited me to 'Dinner & Dancing to Miss Bay Jellett & her Orchestra' at Brooklawn, Alfred Cochane to 'Lunch on the Lawn' at Corke Lodge, and Mrs Donald Weir to 'Dinner & Disco. Dress Romantic'. Mrs Patrick Duggan, Mrs Michael Maughan, Mrs Timothy Counihan, Mrs William P. Fay, Melanie Stewart, the Countess of Mount Charles, Mrs William Hederman, Mrs Brian J. O'Connor, Lady Davis-Goff, Lady Killanin, Mrs Kenneth Rohan, Mrs John Mahon, Mrs John Reihill, Mrs Peter Delamer, Mrs William O'Reilly, the Principessa di San Martino Biondi-Morra and many more were all 'At Home' to me on one occasion or another. These invitations were almost pre-war in their archaic formality (and this was the 1980s), but the hospitality was lavish, with butlers (generally the same butlers, but different houses) circulating with laden silver trays.

I was bidden for weekends in the country. To Glin, where the heating in the bedrooms was supplied by small electric fan heaters. This, the Knight of Glin explained, was because American paying guests could not bear the noise they made and, as a result, would turn them off. The saving on electricity bills was considerable. He teased me when I asked if I might see his dairy herd by telling me that he thought that 'that would be too near the bone'. It did not seem too near the bone to me: I was proud of the fact that I was a farmer's son and I could certainly tell the difference between an Ayrshire and a Friesian. I knew precisely where to find the udder on a cow and when it came to attaching a milking machine to the teat, I was fully adept: while still a schoolboy, I had spent a summer milking my brother Edward's herd. I resisted the temptation to tease Desmond in return by letting him know that the Pottertons had many more acres in County Meath than he had in County Limerick, and better land too; but we were never posh.

I was also invited my first summers to weekends at Glenveagh as the guest of the Philadelphia millionaire Henry McIlhenny. This was a signal honour, as most of Henry's guests – and there was always a minimum of ten or twelve – were imported from America and around the world: very few Irish, and very selective ones at that, were invited. But I had been recommended to him by a Donegal neighbour, my friend Peter Braddell, whom Henry drew on as a source for some younger – and congenial – blood. It was all quite magnificent. All tartan, and loads of loud floral chintzes on the chairs (which I thought perfectly hideous) and spectacular Landseer oils (now in the Philadelphia Museum) on the walls. A formal tea at a round table with tea served from a samovar and, at lunch and dinner, a different dinner service (all exquisite) for every meal. The outdoor pool, which was built into the black lake, was always heated, steaming away twenty-four hours a day. In general the Donegal rain pelted down, making visits to the beautiful gardens something of an ordeal. A large sweep of lawn, hidden away so that one came upon it, was enclosed by trees and surrounded by exquisite plantings. No matter what the weather, it always seemed sultry in that area – it was a microclimate – and many of the shrubs that thrived there had been imported by Henry from different parts of the globe.

Henry had a Donegal man, Patrick Gallagher – who first came to work for him at Glenveagh when he was sixteen – as butler. He served him for more than thirty years, in Philadelphia and around the world, and Henry never travelled without him. Patrick's sister, Nellie, was for many years cook at Glenveagh. Through the Gallagher connection, local boys and girls were recruited as serving staff at Glenveagh: they were dressed up in country peasant costumes that Henry had invented to suit, as he thought, the Donegal setting. They sometimes danced and sang after dinner to entertain the guests. It was all quite fabulous. Henry had a dry wit and was very amusing and he liked his guests to be amusing too. I once asked him if he had been in the war.

'Oh yes!' he drawled. 'I was at all the very best engagements in the Pacific.'

Needless to say, James Lees-Milne had once been to Glenveagh, and probably more than once. He wrote,

> Glenveagh is a miniature Ludwig of Bavaria castle, but oh! so tame if you compare it with Neuschwanstein. It is 1870 or 1880 and there are not enough towers and battlements. The outside is parsimonious. The inside has been made very attractive by Henry McIlhenny, and is filled with Landseers. He has eight gardeners, eight indoor servants, twenty thousand acres and twenty-eight miles of fencing to maintain. He is a friendly, absurd, cosmopolitan Society American millionaire queen. But shrewd, philanthropical, and a genuine connoisseur of the arts, with good taste.[2]

I never told Henry (because I did not know at the time) that I had a family connection with Glenveagh. My maternal grandfather, Spencer Tong, had – as a young man – worked there as a sort of steward in the 1890s. The castle had been built between 1870 and 1873 by Captain John George Adair, an American millionaire of Irish descent, who had assembled (by fair means and foul) an estate of over 40,000 acres of Donegal mountains, forests and lakes. The identity of the castle's architect is uncertain but it may have been an amateur (a cousin of Captain Adair), John Townsend Trench (1834–1909). Captain Adair died in 1885 but his wife, Cornelia (née Wadsworth), lived on until 1921. In a letter on 'Glenveagh Castle, Letterkenny' writing paper (dated 20 April 1896), my grandfather wrote to his sister:

> At present I am very busy opening sewage drains all round the Castle and it is no easy job through the solid rock in places, and they are six feet deep. You would think it was some big railway job to see the gang of men. I have 14 working now. I expect I will have a very busy summer, what between road making, turf cutting, and I have to get a lot of timber cut, also have to see after the making of a laundry house in a cottage two and half miles away and to fit another cottage up for a family and have to see after the work in the Castle. In all conscience I am badly paid, the man before me had £150 a year for doing far less and a horse to ride, etc but I am not complaining. Mrs Adair is a very sharp lady and I would not like to be the one to vex her. If she were here constantly, there is no power on earth would hold me in it. However, I will stick it out for this year. Mr Browne got me the use of the dining-room if I wish and to keep this as my bedroom.

On one of my visits to Glenveagh, after Henry had already decided to part with the castle (he sold it to the Irish State), I asked him if, when he was leaving Ireland, he would give two busts by the eighteenth-century Irish sculptor Van Nost to the National Gallery.

'Sure,' he said, 'but I'll leave them to the gallery in my will. Is there anything else you would like?'

I pointed to a little painting of *Lovers in a Landscape* by the Irish artist Thomas Bridgford that was hanging in his bedroom.

'That,' I said, 'we have nothing by the artist in the collection.'

'I love it too,' he said, 'and it has always been in my bedroom, but your gallery would be a good place for it eventually.'

He was as good as his word, and when he died suddenly a few years later (in 1986), the busts and the painting came to the gallery. I also stayed with Henry in Philadelphia at his magnificent house on Rittenhouse Square. Chock-a-block with exquisite furniture and masterpieces by, among others, Renoir, Pissarro, Degas, Cézanne, van Gogh, Seurat, Toulouse-Lautrec, Vuillard, Matisse and Rouault, it was a huge and unique privilege to be able to wander those rooms and enjoy such incredible treasures. Of course, I wished I could ask him, as I had done for the Bridgford and the Van Nost busts, for some of those pictures for the National Gallery, but I knew that all were destined for the Philadelphia Museum, to which Henry was devoted and of which he was the long-time chairman.

Weekends as guests of the Baron Brian de Breffny and his Finnish wife, Ulli – a wealthy Bahamian widow – at Castletown Cox in County Tipperary were also very luxurious and splendid, although they paled into insignificance by comparison with Glenveagh: everywhere paled into insignificance by comparison with Glenveagh. The de Breffnys had restored the house, decorated it with taste, furnished it attractively, and made it very pleasant indeed. Bathrooms were in plentiful supply, the heating worked, beds were comfortable, cut flowers arranged by Ulli scented every room, the company was interesting, and Brian and Ulli were solicitous, generous and thoughtful hosts. The food was fair but the Indian servants, whom Brian had years previously brought from India (his first wife was Indian), were unpredictable and occasionally – at least so it seemed to me – sinister and menacing. The major-domo would follow everyone around, in the expectation, it seemed, that every guest was a potential thief.

There might be about ten house guests, among them very often the elderly novelist Molly Keane, an adorable bird-like naughty little person. I had first met Molly at the launch of her novel *Good Behaviour* that took place in the National Gallery in 1981 when she signed my copy for me. As everyone knows, she had had an earlier successful career as a novelist and playwright writing under the pseudonym, M.J. Farrell, but her last novel from that time had been published as long ago as 1952. She was 76 when *Good Behaviour* came out and the press pounced on this as well as the fact that she had been almost silent for thirty years. Molly was given to telling how, as a young writer, she was obliged to write secretly (almost 'under the blankets') as her parents would not have approved and she only wrote to supplement her dress allowance. Nor did her parents read her books. After I got to know her slightly through meeting her at the de Breffnys, I said to her on one occasion that I sympathised with her having had to write in secret as my parents, like hers, put little store by books either. This produced an instant reaction and the public persona was momentarily dropped. 'But my mother was a well-known published poet,' she said with great indignation, 'she was a regular contributor to *Blackwood's Magazine* and there were lots of books in our home.' Her mother was indeed a poet, writing under the name Moira O'Neill, and her *Songs of the Glens of Antrim* (1900) was very well-known.

Brian liked his guests to be correct. A lady who, for effect, asked me at breakfast (within Brian's hearing) if I had managed to find her earring in my bed was never invited again. But, as a rule, we all behaved, although, when left to ourselves in the library, we might titter together at photographs of Brian's 'family' in silver frames on the mantel-shelf. We all knew that he was not the Baron de Breffny at all. (It was a title that Brian claimed descended through O'Rorke ancestors – which he did not have – from the Princes of Breffny.) But some of us knew that he was actually Brian Leese, from a modest background in Isleworth, Middlesex. At one stage, Brian announced that he was going to Russia to do family research. (He was a genealogist.) This caused some comment.

'What?' said a Dublin wit, 'to prove once and for all that he is Anastasia?'

But we, as guests, did not mind in the least about Brian's foibles. We were there to have fun, and Castletown Cox with Ulli and Brian was a lovely place to be.

Staying with the painter Derek Hill at his home, Churchill, in Donegal was for me, on the few times I went there, a muted affair, and a far cry from the exotic house parties that Derek had hosted in his heyday. There would be no other guests, dinner would be simple (his famous cook, Gracie, was old by this time), and Derek would go to bed early.

I liked Derek – he was very likeable, and as he knew and had known absolutely everyone, he was fascinating to talk to. Of course, he was very 'grand' but he genuinely enjoyed meeting and getting to know all sorts of people, and he could be very kind. Initially, I got to know him as he would call on me in the gallery to bombard me with his long-running and frustrated plans to donate his house and collection to the State. He foolishly imagined that I might have some sway with the civil service but, needless to say, I had none. When the deed was eventually done, Derek asked me to perform in 1983 the opening of the Glebe Gallery (in the stables), which formally marked the handover of Churchill to the State. He had discovered that the house, a former rectory, had once been lived in by a Reverend Homan, whom he was convinced had to be one of my ancestors – he probably was – but I am sure it was because I was director of the Gallery (rather than being Homan) that he asked me to officiate at the ceremony.

However, in its very early stages, my friendship with Derek had suffered a severe setback.

At one stage in the early 1980s, Anne Crookshank, to everyone's shock, was diagnosed and hospitalised with cancer. But Anne was not going to go down lightly.

'I'm the one person cancer is not going to beat,' she announced to the Adelaide Hospital doctors and nurses (and to everyone else), and nor did it beat her.

When she was back in harness, Roger Stalley, Marcella Senior (who had a responsibility for the college pictures), Mary Boydell and I conceived a plan to raise subscriptions and have Anne's portrait painted for Trinity. On the suggestion of Anne herself, I think, we decided to commission the portrait from Derek. Derek was delighted and set to work on his next stay in Donegal, painting Anne at her home in Ramelton. When the portrait was delivered, we were shocked. This was an Anne that few had ever seen. She was seated relaxedly in a high-backed chair with some pretty china in the background. Her hands (badly painted) crossed, her gaze directed downwards (Anne never looked downwards), and a gentle smile on her handsome face. Where was the redoubtable figure who stalked Trinity leaving everyone in her wake in awe? Not on this canvas, by any manner of means.

Roger, Marcella, Mary and I conferred and, as Derek in his letter to me accepting the commission had (unwisely) written 'and of course I never insist on a sale if my portrait does not find favour', we decided to turn down the picture. Roger, Mary and Marcella looked at me, and on the spurious premise that, as it was me who had been the contact with Derek, it was me who should write and tell him of its rejection. This was not a task I relished. Derek had a furious temper, he was extremely sensitive to any hint that he was being ignored (or rejected), and he was capable of pursuing revenge.

I don't recall how he replied to me but he certainly identified me personally as the villain of the piece, and he pursued retribution in a manner that only he could have devised. He persuaded a 'Mrs J.M. Clarke of Maidstone' to buy Anne's portrait – Anne had never heard of Mrs Clarke, and nor had I – and, in turn, offer it as a gift to the National Gallery. It was his way of testing me, to see if I would have the audacity to turn down the picture a second time. But, of course, I had no desire whatsoever to do so. It was a charming picture, it looked like Anne (albeit an unfamiliar Anne) and as it was my view that, as a distinguished scholar of Irish art, she was well worthy of a place in Ireland's National Portrait Collection, I recommended its acceptance to the board. Furthermore, there were now two portraits – we had subsequently commissioned a portrait from the noted English artist Lawrence Gowing – for the price of one, and both in public collections. We allocated the balance of the subscriptions after the portrait had been paid for to the History of Art Department in Trinity to establish a student prize in Anne's name

I visited Derek on one occasion only in his house (and studio), Sundial House on Holly Hill in Hampstead, and sometimes he shared more intimate conversation with me than I feel he would have done with everyone. When he met Alex, he was charmed by his looks and asked me if he could paint him; but, foolishly – and to my lasting regret – I did not take up the offer. At the opening of a Mildred Anne Butler exhibition in the Bank of Ireland, Derek introduced Alex to (of all people) the fabulously glamorous Contessa Marina Cicogna of Venice. There is an extraordinary surviving photo (taken by Derek) of the

Contessa and Alex smiling into each other's eyes, deep in conversation. The photograph, in a way, sums up Derek: he adored grandees but he also always looked for something in unknowns.

Of all the enjoyable times I had, one particular social occasion stood out and, because I was so impressed by what I witnessed, I wrote (exceptionally) a *compte rendu* of it afterwards. This was a dinner, as the guest of Sidney and Nesbit Waddington (Mr and Mrs Waddington), at Beaulieu, County Louth. Nesbit had been manager of the Aga Khan's stud farms in Ireland and was himself a noted horseman.

> 27 July 1982: Dinner at Beaulieu, one of the most beautiful houses in Ireland, and rare. Red brick and render, late seventeenth century. Perfect, although the house is now a bit shabby. No sons have been born here for a few generations and it has descended in the female line: Nesbit & Sidney have no son either. They are old but dignified and, although they are probably much richer than most of the Anglo-Irish gentry, it is still all a bit sad. A sunny evening, so the drive from Dublin is pleasant. I arrive on the dot of eight: no cars outside, I ring the bell and there is not a sound. I ring again and again. Soon another car arrives and my anxiety that I have come on the wrong night is assuaged. All the passengers are in black tie: I had not looked at the invitation carefully and am in a suit. Nesbit comes out and is charming, silver-haired and handsome. They have a house-guest in whose honour the dinner is being given: Lady Delamere from Kenya. Supremely elegant, tall, and very beautiful. But later in the evening I notice that she is probably somewhat older than she looks. Mrs W carves the turkey herself and the maid wears a printed cotton frock, no apron and certainly no cap either. Service is awkward. It seems like a big night for them whereas in the past they must have entertained frequently and very splendidly.

Indeed they had, The Waddingtons' daughter, Gabriel, was a debutante in the last season (1958) that debutantes were 'presented' at Court. So was Fiona MacCarthy who has described going to stay at Beaulieu for Gabriel's dance together with a number of other debs.[3]

> The house was run quite formally, more grandly than in many English houses I had stayed in: a maid had been instructed to unpack for us and laid out our clothes for the dances. At the same time there was an underlying sense of strain, as if the household were stretched to its limits by the influx of twenty or so self-centred and boisterous young people. The ball was held in the two-storey hall ... architecturally splendid, carved, moulded and adorned with coats of arms, the spoils of war and sporting trophies which included the huge horns of an ancient Irish elk. Like all Anglo-Irish parties this one had a tribal vigour. The portraits of the ancestors looked down as if admiring its abandon. It ended with us going out to paddle in the river at 5.30 in the morning.

My evening at Beaulieu (one of several) was altogether less vigorous I am glad to say. I continued my account:

> All the paintings need attention. There is a room full of Jack Yeats, whom I don't care for all that much, but seeing so many together, I think again.
>
> Lady Delamere is wearing diamond and sapphire drop earrings: the sapphires are the largest I have ever seen, even in a museum. She also has huge diamond rings, and four long ropes of boulder-size pearls. She is quite spectacular – and not at all what County Louth can be used to – but the fabulous *bijouterie* looks perfectly natural on her. Eight to dinner and I am seated beside her. She is superbly gracious and very easy to talk to but a life in Kenya has had its inevitable effect. I ask about Kenya, is it difficult for whites there now, etc?
>
> 'No, Kenya is perfect. There is no political trouble and the blacks are charming. True, it was wiser for me to sell some of my land and now, of course, I only have a small

farm of 40,000 acres, but the climate is wonderful. And I have a cottage by the sea that I can fly down to every weekend.'

'And what about Jomo Kenyatta and the Mau Mau?' I ventured.

'Oh, that's all in the past. Kenyatta was a marvellous man, he was our friend. He often stayed with us.'

The sapphires blazed, the pearls wobbled on her lovely chest, the diamonds winked and blinked, she held herself very erect.

'You see, the difference between Kenya and the rest of the African states,' she continued, 'is that the white settlers in Kenya – and it is, I know, snobby of me to say so – but the white settlers were all gents in the first place. So now the life there is peaceful and perfect.'

But I wondered if Kenya was really as peaceful and perfect as she said.

I had a vague recollection of reading somewhere about Kenya's decadent 'Happy Valley set' in the 1930s and '40s but I did not dare ask Lady Delamere if she had known any of them.

Four days later, and lunch at the Canadian Embassy in Killiney. A young(ish) bachelor, Alan Sullivan, is the ambassador: outgoing and fun-loving, he has made a lot of friends in Ireland. The house is Victorian classical grandeur with huge gardens and a magnificent view down to the sea. Although the week has been sunny, this was a bank holiday so, inevitably, the weather had turned nasty. Drinks in the garden before lunch a bit chilly: some Americans from the American Embassy and some Dutch from the Netherlands Embassy and two missing guests. I ask Alan who is expected. Eileen Mount Charles and her house guest, he says. Lady Delamere, it appears, has by now moved her bivouac from Beaulieu to Eileen's home in Kilmessan. They are very late in arriving and time ticks on. Alan becomes concerned. 'Oh dear, I wonder where the girls are?' he says. Lady Mount Charles and Lady Delamere are both very glamorous women but 'girls' is not a description of them that would immediately spring to my mind. More Bloody Marys are brought out, and more, but still no sign of 'the girls'. Half an hour later, Eileen bounces through the French window: she is wearing tailored culottes and looks terrific. 'Very Happy Valley,' I thought. She is followed by an ashen-faced Lady Delamere. The sapphires are smaller today, the diamonds slightly fewer, and only some of the pearls are worn as a choker. She is introduced.

'I've had a quite appalling morning,' she says. 'Eileen's maid came in at crack of dawn with a very muddled message.'

Gripped by her words, and fascinated by her appearance, we all waited to hear what the message had been.

'There has been a coup in Kenya,' she said.[4]

Some few years later, I was travelling to New York and at Heathrow picked up a book to read on the plane. It was *White Mischief* by James Fox, 'the brilliant best-selling reconstruction of a murder that scandalised Africa'. Before reading very far, I came across the name Delamere: the 3rd Lord Delamere, who had gone to Kenya in 1901 and by 1906 was farming 160,000 acres there. And then I came to the mention of Diana Caldwell – later in life (according to the index) 'Delves-Broughton, Colvile, and Delamere'. It took me a while to work out that this was the Lady Delamere that I had met, and that it was she who had been the cause of (and also a suspect in) 'the murder that scandalised Africa'. She had been at the very centre of the Happy Valley set and, among them, very much 'happier' than most. She had gone to Kenya in 1940 with her second husband, Jock Delves-Broughton (he was 56, she thirty years younger), and had immediately embarked on a very public love affair with the Earl of Erroll, who was murdered a few weeks later. Delves-Broughton was tried and acquitted of the murder.[5] He committed suicide shortly thereafter. Diana then married one of the largest landowners in Kenya, Gilbert Colvile, and, after twelve years of marriage inherited his huge fortune and then married the 4th Lord

Delamere, and inherited 'his' huge fortune too. Pearls, for one reason or another, featured prominently in the Delves-Broughton murder trial, just as they had featured prominently in the memorable encounter which I had with the quite incredible Diana Delamere.

And did I, as Director of the National Gallery, meet any less-exotic people? Aware of the possible hazards, I was cautious at the outset in the friends I made. Against my natural instincts, I took to being discrete in my conversation. And I knew that, on no account, must I ever, ever 'frighten the horses'. Having assailed the fortress that was Honor, Ann Fuller became the focus of my bridge playing and, with Desiree Short and Brian Coyle, we formed a regular four. Through the same friendships, I took to the stage – although I could not act – in drawing-room theatricals: *The Importance of Being Earnest* (I played both butlers, Lane and Merriman) and *An Ideal Husband* (the more taxing role of Sir Robert Chiltern). Although these were essentially private performances directed by Ann Fuller in a private house (Ferndene, the Cruess Callaghan home in Blackrock), the press became interested. 'It was in the role of Merriman that Mr Potterton excelled,' wrote Ruth Buchanan in *The Sunday Tribune*. 'The opening night audience included the British Ambassador, Sir Alan Goodison, his wife Rosemary, and the wife of the Argentinian Ambassador, Senora Del Campo.' She did not mention that the Argentine Ambassador, knowing that his British counterpart was attending, could not be there as diplomatic relations between Britain and Argentina had been severed at the time on account of the Falkland's War.

Ann Reihill was appointed to the board of the gallery by the Fine Gael government, and she and I soon became good friends: she was a sympathetic ear when I needed to air confidential gallery worries and always a source of wise counsel. With her husband John, she entertained sumptuously at their home, Deepwell, in Blackrock. Through Desirée, I met two young men – her upstairs lodgers, Brian Walsh and David Murray – who became valued younger friends. I spent happy weekends with Jeremy Williams and his amusing mother at her delightful home in County Kilkenny and I had Sunday suppers *en famille* in the elegant setting of 32 Lower Baggot Street with John Gilmartin and his parents. I got to know Jeffery and Tessa Lefroy and went to Carriglas. My neighbour, occupying a single room in the house where I lived on

Merrion Square, was Humphrey Langan, a congenial elderly bachelor in reduced circumstances who shared many of my interests and was a fount of saucy gossip of Dublin in the past. Alistair Rowan (my former tutor at Edinburgh, then in UCD) and Ann-Martha invited me; and Rosemarie and Sean Mulcahy were other friends from the past with whom I was close. Gordon Lambert, to whom I had originally been introduced by Speer years previously, was also a friend. And gradually there were many more.

But, in order to maintain the whirl – and to escape from it – it was necessary for me to have some 'down time', and for that I went to London every second or third weekend. There, in order to sustain a friendship, all talk of Dublin and its National Gallery was strictly embargoed: and that, in large part, was the saving of me.

As to how I was perceived in Dublin by the general public, the often-acerbic critic of the *Irish Times*, Brian Fallon was as good a judge as any. 'He gave Dublin all he had,' he wrote of me in a half-page *Assessment* (29 November 1986).

> Rather slight and pale, with something slightly boyish in his manner and looks ... most people find him approachable though not bonhomous, with an easy but cool civility which keeps them at a certain distance. Though in demand on Dublin's cocktail circuit, he is not in essence a socialite and outside his work has a reputation for being a rather private man. He is a Director of the modern age – highly skilled and specialised with a strong academic grounding ... but ... regarded as very hard-headed and a man who plays his own hand shrewdly. He is, too, much respected by his staff.'

Tom Ryan the artist perceived a different persona and lampooned me as somewhat precious in a cartoon that showed me dining with the more outré members of the RHA.

Aside from all my frivolity and giddiness, I did also actually do some work in the gallery; in fact, quite a lot of work. My main priority was catalogues of the permanent collection: I was determined to push these through. They were, I thought, essential to the ordering of a museum collection yet many, if not most, museums and galleries never get round to publishing them at all: the task is said to be too enormous and the curators have not enough time, is the general excuse. Yet, in order to have any public-access programmes, such as education and exhibitions, it is vital to know in some depth what is in a permanent collection. A complete catalogue of all the oil paintings – more than 2,000 of them – with basic information and thumbnail illustrations of everything was my first project: an out-of-date computerised checklist (compiled by Michael Wynne ten years previously) was all that Dublin had, and the catalogue before that, which was selective, dated from 1932. *The Illustrated Summary Catalogue of Paintings*, largely the result of a young Adrian Le Harivel's huge energy (but aided by several low-paid graduates), was published eighteen months after I took up office. To mark the occasion, 300 'rarely seen pictures' were taken out of store and shown in an exhibition titled *The Best of the Cellar*: Garret FitzGerald, Taoiseach at the time, came and opened it. The catalogue required a vast number of paintings to be photographed that had never been photographed before; many had to be surface-cleaned by Andrew O'Connor and Sergio Benedetti in the gallery's conservation studio, and all had to be examined. It was, in retrospect, rather a breathtaking project to have been completed in a year. I persuaded Allied Irish Bank to sponsor the publication (they paid the entire production costs), and the catalogue was published by Gill & Macmillan. In time, two similar catalogues, of the watercolours and drawings, and the prints and sculpture, appeared, so that, by the time I retired, the entire collection had been published – for the very first time since the opening of the gallery in 1864.

Parallel to this project were fully detailed, in-depth catalogues of the oil paintings, school by school. My expertise was seventeenth- and eighteenth-century Italian paintings but Michael Wynne had researched that part of the Dublin collection for many years and it was appropriate that he would be delegated to compile that catalogue, which he did. I took on the Dutch paintings of the same period, in which I had no expertise whatsoever – and which I did not even specially like. Rembrandt is by no means my favourite painter: too much mucky brown paint in many of them, clumsy wads of flesh, and eyes welling up with tears that many people find 'moving'. But aside from him, and one or two other painters, Dutch pictures are relatively easy to catalogue as they are (unlike Italian seventeenth-century paintings) generally signed. The two-hundred-or-so-strong Dublin collection, consisting of many *petits maîtres*, is a fine collection, and I found out quite a lot about them (mainly in respect of their provenances). Most had been purchased at Christie's in London by Henry Doyle who was Director from 1869–92. All of the Christie's catalogues, annotated with the names of purchasers, are in the library of the London National Gallery and, allowed as a privilege to work there, I went through the catalogues and identified Doyle's purchases, gleaning much further information about the paintings in the process. I had sessions in the library of the Dutch Art History Bureau in The Hague. This was the type of gallery work I most enjoyed, as it was what I had been educated and trained to do, but, as the director, I had to grab what time I could to complete it. The catalogue, when it was published in 1986, passed muster with scholar reviewers.

Rembrandt attributions are a minefield and, almost as a pattern, they can vary from one generation of art historians to another. For example, the lovely *Lady with a Glove* in Dublin (who looks as though she has a cold) was known as a Rembrandt from at least 1826 and, when it was sold in 1880, it created a sensation by fetching the highest price ever paid for a Dutch picture: thereafter, it was known and celebrated as *The Demidoff Rembrandt*. The painting was subsequently owned by Hugh Lane and exhibited by him in London in 1913: it was then that the attribution to Rembrandt was first challenged. Rembrandt scholars of the day weighed in: Dr Wilhelm Bode said it was definitely by the master, and Cornelis Hofstede de Groot (the great scholar of Dutch painting at the time) agreed with him; but another great scholar, Abraham Bredius, said it was not (but by Rembrandt's pupil Ferdinand Bol). Since that time, there has always been a question mark about it. I think it is a very fine painting and I catalogued it as 'Studio of Rembrandt, meaning that it was painted in his studio . . . if not actually by the master himself'.

In the case of the *Head of an Old Man*, I agreed with a recent suggestion by the reputable Horst Gerson that it is a fake and I pointed out that (consistent with a fake) it is painted on two pieces of seventeenth-century oak stuck together, although the wood of the two panels is not from the same tree. The painting had been accepted as a Rembrandt by all the early-twentieth-century scholars. Foolishly, perhaps, I did not have the picture (which I greatly dislike) cleaned: an earlier x-ray reveals nothing. It has since been cleaned but its status as a 'Rembrandt' has not been confirmed or further rejected.

The exquisite small *Interior with Figures* was purchased in 1896 as by Willem de Poorter but catalogued by my predecessor, the distinguished Walter Armstrong, as a Rembrandt in 1914. Some scholars agreed with him but others waved different attributions – such as Gerard Dou and Jan Lievens – at it. I had the picture x-rayed, and what was discovered underneath – a portrait similar to Rembrandt's early self-portraits – led me to catalogue it as 'painted by an artist very closely associated with the master in the years 1628–30'. I am sure that, in time, it will be accepted as a genuine Rembrandt.

Such are the vagaries of art-historical scholarship. I did not mind in the least if I was to be proved wrong in any of these assessments: the important thing was to get the catalogue out and, thereby, facilitate discussion.

I commissioned catalogues of the other schools. Rosemarie Mulcahy in Dublin was a world-acknowledged expert (above all in Spain) on Spanish art, and she knew the Spanish pictures in the gallery very well. She was also very efficient in her scholarship and could be relied upon to 'produce' – which she did. Her catalogue came out in 1988. No one in Dublin had any expertise in the Northern schools of painting, and so I looked for scholars outside of Ireland, and young scholars at that. Older established experts are always too much occupied for the slog of compiling catalogues (and are too eminent to be bullied into action). I found David Oldfield, a graduate of McGill with a doctorate in art history from the University of East Anglia, to do the German (and subsequently the Flemish) paintings, and a Dutch graduate of Leiden University working in the Rijksmuseum, Amsterdam, Christiaan Vogelaar, to write the Early Netherlandish catalogue. In all, six of these catalogues were published: there were to be another three (Early Italian, French and British); and one of the very few regrets I had about leaving the gallery was that I had not had the series completed.

Very thorough catalogues were also published for temporary exhibitions: among them occasional recent acquisitions, *Walter*

Osborne, James Arthur O'Connor and the *Irish Impressionists*. The latter, by Julian Campbell, derived from his doctoral thesis on Irish painters in Brittany in the late-nineteenth and early-twentieth centuries; but, to Julian's horror, I dreamed up the title in order to make the exhibition more marketable. There was no such thing as 'Irish Impressionism', and very few of the painters in the exhibition painted in a style that was truly Impressionist. But the exhibition drew enormous crowds. The painter Tom Ryan who, as President of the Royal Hibernian Academy, was on the board of the gallery, brought to the board's attention, in a jocular way, the nonsense of the term. He also drew a very funny cartoon for me of visitors to an exhibition lying on the floor to view paintings that are attached to the ceiling. I am pointing to the ceiling and saying, '... and after our Irish Impressionists, we are showing the Irish Sistine Painters.' In an effort to promote the gallery (and Ireland), exhibitions from the permanent collection were sent abroad. 'Masterpieces' to the National Gallery, London, and 'Master European Drawings' (with a catalogue by Raymond Keaveney) and 'Dutch Paintings' to tour museums in America.

The public liked the exhibitions of the gallery's acquisitions, and the catalogues that accompanied them, all the more so as we published the prices that had been paid. I also very much liked making acquisitions. The procedure followed (at least in my time) was that the director finds appropriate acquisitions and, in presenting them to the board, makes the argument for their purchase, or (in the case of gifts and bequests) acceptance or rejection. Many things were offered to the gallery by dealers or private individuals but, if they didn't get past the director, they were not considered by the board. I also actively sought out suitable acquisitions in the sale-rooms and elsewhere: on one occasion I picked up for £40 in Portobello Market an eighteenth-century print of the gallery's wonderful painting by Castiglione. At the other end of the scale, £356,000 was paid at auction in London for an oil by the German painter Emil Nolde. Some purchases required more energy on my part. My diary records that, on 13 May 1983,

> I flew to New York via London. Leave Dublin 4.30, arrive New York time 9.30. Saturday 14th May: View sales at Sotheby's and Christie's. V. good Impressionist & Post-Impressionist paintings. Flight back to London 7.30 pm.

> Monday 16th May: 9.30 am flight to Dublin. Prepare
> papers to bid for Pissarro Flowerpiece. Tuesday 17th May:
> Round-up Board to get authorisation for bid of quarter of
> a million on Pissarro. Phone the bid to New York.
> Wednesday 18th May: We bought the Pissarro for
> £218,000. Very pleased.

In one unusual instance, I failed in my pursuit of an acquisition. George Furlong once told me that at some stage during the War, the Italian government or some major Italian museum requested the loan of a painting from the National Gallery of Ireland for a temporary exhibition in Italy. George was very friendly with the Italian Ambassador of the day, Vincenzo Berardis (Ambassador in Ireland from 1938–44). Due to this friendship, George supported the granting of the loan (most other countries refused on account of the then regime in Italy). In gratitude for George's support, Ambassador Berardis offered George an Italian Government decoration; but this George refused. 'I wasn't going to accept a decoration from Mussolini,' he told me. As a result of his refusal, the Italian Government subsequently presented a painting by the contemporary Italian painter Giorgio de' Chirico to the National Gallery. The picture was despatched through diplomatic channels and when it arrived at Iveagh House in Dublin (the headquarters of the Irish Foreign Service) that is where it remained in spite of George's persistent requests to have it forwarded to the National Gallery to which it rightfully belonged. The painting (one of a series by the artist of horses and classical ruins on a seashore) was no longer in Iveagh House when I became Director of the Gallery so I mentioned it to Noel De Chenu, the Principal Architect of the OPW, and asked him where it was. I told him George's story and pointed out that as the painting properly belonged to the National Gallery, I would like to have it back. Some time later, Noel told me that he had located the painting. 'That's great,' I said, 'When and where can I collect it?' But Noel was too pleased to have discovered such an important picture for the State Art Collection that he had no intention of giving it up and I, for my part, decided against taking up yet another challenge to officialdom; and so George's De' Chirico never reached its rightful home.

Homan at a reception in the National Gallery hosted by Arts Minister Ted Nealon, February 1984. L to R: Victor Griffin (Dean of St Patrick's); Brendan O'Riordain (Director of the National Museum); Garret FitzGerald (Taoiseach); Bill Finlay; Homan Potterton; Minister Nealon and (partly concealed) Wilfred Lockwood (Director of the Chester Beatty Library). (Photo © *The Irish Times*.)

Thomas Ryan, PRHA (b. 1929), cartoon: *The Irish Sistine Painters*, 1984. Inscribed by the artist: 'And after our Irish Impressionists we are showing the Irish Sistine Painters. For Homan Potterton Dec 1984'. (Author's Collection.)

Garret FitzGerald (Taoiseach) with Homan Potterton at the opening of the exhibition, *Le Classicism Français*, in the National Gallery of Ireland, 29 April 1985. (Photo: Matt Kavanagh, © *The Irish Times*.)

Thomas Ryan, PRHA (b. 1929), cartoon: *The Director of the National Gallery dines with the RHA*, 1983. Inscribed by the artist with the title and 'For Homan Potterton'. Signed and dated 'T Ryan 6.12.'83'. (Author's Collection.)

The fume Potterton

HOMAN POTTERTON, wit, raconteur and aesthete par excellence provided entertaining company for luncheon at "Les Freres Jacques,"

A lunch date with Terry Keane. Cartoon by Jim Cogan, *Sunday Independent*, May 1988. As usual, Terry is stirring things up.

Thomas Ryan, PRHA (b. 1929), cartoon: *A visitor to the National Gallery of Ireland*, 1988. Inscribed by the artist: 'The Chairman of the Board of Governors and Guardians introducing an Important Military Visitor to the Director of the National Gallery of Ireland, circa 1988'. (Author's Collection.) The cartoon depicts Dublin's most notorious criminal, Martin Cahill, familiarly known as 'The General', who had been interviewed on television wearing an outsize green anorak.

Thomas Ryan, PRHA (b. 1929), Sir Alfred Beit, drawn from the life by Tom Ryan, PRHA, at a board meeting of the National Gallery of Ireland, April 1986. Pencil and watercolour on paper. Inscribed by the artist: 'All is lost! Sir Alfred Beit. Homan! for your collection. Thomas Ryan'. (Author's Collection.)

Following the board meeting at which the Beit Collection was presented to the National Gallery, December 1987. L to R: Bill Finlay (chairman), Lady Beit, Sir Alfred and Homan Potterton. (Photo: Michael Olohan.)

'Farewell, or The 'going of Homan', a Tragedy

Thomas Ryan, PRHA (b. 1929), cartoon: *Farewell, or The Going of Homan: a Tragedy*. Signed and dated: 'Thomas Ryan 9 June 1988'. The Governors and Guardians of the National Gallery lament the departure of their Director. The one female member of the Board is Ann Reihill. (Author's Collection.)

Seán O'Criadáin, whom I had known well years previously (as my Diary above records) was still in Dublin at the time when I was Director and he was still dealing in art, albeit in a smaller way. One day he got in touch with me to tell me he had something that he thought might be of interest to the Gallery. I went along to the lovely flat he shared with Peter Lamb on Pembroke Road to see (I can't remember what). The place was stuffed with interesting things and, while I had no interest in what he was offering, a small conversation-piece by Harry Robertson Craig hanging in a dark corner caught my eye. This was a portrait of Guillamore O'Grady (dating from 1951) at home in a lovely cluttered room hung floor-to ceiling with pictures. I knew of Craig because it was he who had painted Speer's portrait and Speer had known him well and often told me about him but I had never heard of Guillamore O'Grady. He turned out to be an interesting figure who had from 1908 to 1943 been Dublin Herald in the Office of Arms, Dublin Castle. The room in which Craig had painted him was his home at 9 Marine Terrace, Dun Laoghaire. In the painting he is being served tea by a young manservant. The picture greatly appealed to me and I asked Sean if he would offer it to the Gallery which he agreed to do at IR£3,500. The Board agreed to purchase it at that price and I was delighted. Its acquisition, however, set my brain to work and I came up with the idea that I would like to have myself painted in a similar charming way. The problem was I did not have a home in Dublin that was as gracious as O'Grady's and, nor, for that matter, did I have a manservant. I did, however, have the Director's Office in the Gallery, a room I had made very much my own by having it painted a dark green, the same green that I had years previously used for my rooms at 169 Rathgar Road. I had hung the office floor-to-ceiling with paintings from the cellar and furnished it with some of the Milltown furniture. It was, at the time, the nearest I came to having a room of my own in Dublin and I decided that that was where I wanted to be pictured. But who to paint me? Craig was only recently deceased at this time (1986–7) so I was too late for him. I did, however know an English artist who painted a lot of portraits in Ireland at this time and whose work I found appealing. This was Andrew Festing (b. 1941). Andrew became a portrait painter by a circuitous route that included Sandhurst, followed by a few years in the army. He then joined Sotheby's where he was Head of the British

Pictures Department. But he had always painted and in 1981, retired from Sotheby's and took up portrait painting full time, becoming a member and later President, of the Royal Society of Portrait Painters. I asked Andrew if he would like to paint me and he was encouraged when I said I did not want typical 'boardroom portrait' but a conversation piece. I showed him my office and said it was the setting I wanted. 'Are these all your favourite pictures?' he asked. 'Not at all,' I replied, 'they are just what I found in the cellar to fit the hang. I would like you to show the room as it is hung but in your painting could you insert into the frames as they exist representations of pictures that mean something to me?' He was immediately gripped by this novel idea and very soon his easel was installed in my office. The desk at which I am seated was not the desk I used (although James White did use it). I had a large table in front of the chimneypiece. The kneehole desk once belonged to the little-known Irish miniature painter, Charles Robertson (1760–1821) and was used by him as a worktable. Its design is based on that of a traditional architect's table and Robertson is shown seated at it in a miniature in the Gallery by Henry Kirchoffer (d. 1775). Desk and miniature were presented to the Gallery in 1901 by Robertson's grandson so it is an historic Gallery artefact and because of that I wanted it included. I was always tempted to think that it might have been the desk that Hugh Lane used when he was Director and that it was perhaps in one of its drawers that the notorious unwitnessed codicil to Lane's will was found after his death. But that was just speculation.

The fun of the portrait is in the transposed sizes of the paintings as depicted. The 'little' painting above the door is in reality an enormous canvas by Hugh Douglas Hamilton of the Earl Bishop of Derry, which I looked upon as one of my most important Irish acquisitions.[6] Carelessly, obscured (it seems) by the easel on the left was my first major purchase, Wheatley's *Portrait of the Marquis and Marchioness of Antrim*. Nonchalantly thrown on the floor is one of the most-expensive pictures I bought, Nolde's splendid *Women in a Garden*. The bronze horse on the right is Queen Victoria (a sensitive purchase: 'royalty') on a horse by the Irish sculptor John Henry Foley, and above her Walter Osborne's portrait of my most-admired previous Director, Walter Armstrong. The Steen above it was used by me on the cover of my Dutch catalogue; the Barry self-portrait had been the cover on one edition of my *Irish Art and Architecture* book; and the Strozzi, a much larger picture than Andrew shows, was on the cover of my Venetian Seventeenth-Century Painting Catalogue. With the exception of the antique bust on the floor in the foreground, everything else in the picture, including the books, meant something to me and Andrew showed all exactly as I wanted. The bust is there because he wanted a brighter 'mass' in that area to balance the composition. Andrew recalls many of the pictures being painted from postcards[7] but in some cases, I did arrange for the originals to be brought to the office for him so that he might work 'from the life' as it were. His method of work and the progress of the composition, I recorded in simple snaps.

The picture was exhibited in London at the Royal Society of Portrait Painters in 1987 (Cat. no.76)

Exhibitions and publications generally required some form of sponsorship, and I would pursue whatever (and whomever) I could in the hope of attracting funds. The idea of sponsorship was relatively new in Ireland at that time and certainly (as far as I recall) the sums I managed to raise were quite modest by comparison with what sponsorship means today. The gallery bookshop (in which I took much interest) was successful and, by increasing the range of prints and cards (on which the profit is very substantial), it became a source of funds for related activities. But the shop space was primitive: its improvement depended on the Office of Public Works, and that meant it was never improved, and so it struggled on.

And so did I.

And now, I have a hazy recollection, and the story I am about to tell is very much against myself, an admission of failure on my part; and not a failure in matters of administration – which might be excused – but a failure as an art historian and, worse still, within my own area of expertise: Italian paintings of the seventeenth and eighteenth centuries and, specifically, the work of Caravaggio. I had mounted a 'Painting in Focus' exhibition at the London National Gallery, which centred on the Gallery's Caravaggio, *The Supper at Emmaus*. As part of my research, I had seen and studied – in the museums and churches of Italy and elsewhere – most of the painter's works. I had read much of the extensive literature on the artist and I was very familiar with his technique, his life, and his chronology. Yet when, some years later, I was shown a Caravaggio – one that had been painted one year after *The Supper at Emmaus*, and for the same patron – that was hanging in a house no more than a few hundred metres from the National Gallery of Ireland, I failed to recognise it: a failure that could be seen as tantamount to a dereliction of duty on my part. It was inexcusable.

The Dublin Caravaggio, *The Taking of Christ*, was presented to the Dublin Jesuits in the 1930s by a Dr Marie Lea Wilson and hung in the Jesuit house on Leeson Street, where it was labelled 'Van Honthorst', a Dutch follower of Caravaggio. It has not been discovered where Dr Wilson acquired the painting but, as she was devout, she almost certainly bought it because of its religious subject matter rather than its artistic merit. It had been sold at auction in Edinburgh in April 1921 and had come from a historic Scottish collection, Hamilton Nisbet of Biel House. It was known from the Italian archives that Caravaggio had painted a picture of *The Taking of Christ* for his Roman patron Ciriaco Mattei, and that he had been paid for it on 2 January 1603; and it was known that William Hamilton Nisbet had purchased *An Imprisonment of Christ*– listed as by Honthorst – from the Mattei family in 1802.

The first Caravaggio scholar, Roberto Longhi, had speculated in print that, as both the Mattei Caravaggio and the Honthorst had the same subject matter, they may have been one and the same picture, and that it could have been the Mattei Caravaggio that Hamilton Nisbet had actually bought, rather than a Honthorst. But Longhi believed that the painting was lost. It was a young Italian scholar, Francesca Cappelletti, working twenty years later, who found the record of the painting in the Mattei archives and it was she who traced the picture's journey from Italy to the auction in Edinburgh in 1921. But there she drew a blank: the name of the purchaser was not recorded in the copy of the sale catalogue that she had found.

It took a restorer in the National Gallery of Ireland, Sergio Benedetti[8] – who knew about Italian seventeenth-century painting – to recognise that the painting in the Jesuit house in Leeson Street, rather than being by Honthorst, was possibly by Caravaggio, and to follow up by linking it to the history of the lost Mattei Caravaggio as pieced together by Cappelletti.[9] It was an astute deduction.

When the painting's discovery was announced – to international acclaim – in 1992 (four years after I left the gallery), it rang no bells with me. It was only a few years later, when someone reminded me, that I could vaguely recall that the picture had once been shown to me.

How could I have missed it?

It is not enough to say that my mind must have been addled with gallery administrative matters on the day I saw it and that as a result, I did not bother to go to the gallery library and do some preliminary research. Had I done so, I would have seen photographs of an identical picture in Odessa that was said to be a copy of a lost Caravaggio and I might have jumped to some conclusions and followed up (as Sergio commendably was to do) with further research.

I did not do that, and I have no excuse.[10]

Endnotes

1. See B. Arnold, 'A Master Craftsman: Carey Clarke, PRHA', *Irish Arts Review*, vol. 12 (1996), Fig. 15.
2. James Lees-Milne, *A Mingled Measure: Diaries 1953–72* (1994).
3. Fiona MacCarthy, *Last Curtsey: The End of the Debutantes* (2006).
4. The *coup d'état*, on Sunday 1 August 1982, was a failed attempt to overthrow the government of Daniel Arap Moi.
5. It is now believed that he was actually the murderer.
6. I write 'I' throughout in respect of purchases but of course it is the board, rather than the Director, who buys on the Director's recommendation.
7. Jenny Pery, *Andrew Festing: Face Value* (2015), p. 78.
8. Sergio Benedetti, 'Caravaggio's Taking of Christ: A Masterpiece Rediscovered', *Burlington Magazine*, vol. 135 (November 1993).
9. Francesca Cappelletti, 'I quadri di Caravaggio nella collezione Mattei', *Storia dell'Arte* (May–August 1990).
10. The story of the painting's history and discovery has been very well told in '*The Lost Painting: The Quest for a Caravaggio Masterpiece*' by Jonathan Harr (2005). As to any 'excuse' on my part, the fact that hordes of international experts failed to recognise a Fragonard at the Mentmore Sale (see pages 212–13) goes some way to explaining how I could have 'missed' a Caravaggio.

CHAPTER 15
Two Bequests

I did not have much contact with Denis Mahon after I moved to the Gallery in Dublin, and I do not recall him visiting me there. He knew the collection very well – it was after all, between Britain and Ireland, the best museum collection of Italian seventeenth-century pictures; and Mahon, I think, was very involved when Italian restorers came to the gallery in the late sixties and cleaned these paintings. I had been in Dublin for about five years when Denis did get in touch with me, inviting me to lunch with him in London and suggesting meeting at a hotel in Knightsbridge. It was no secret that he intended to bequeath some pictures to Dublin, and, over lunch, he talked about that. I knew from our times together in Bologna several years previously that he loved talking about his will. He also wanted to satisfy himself that my views on de-accessioning and museum charges coincided with his. They did, unequivocally. Towards the end of the lunch, he surprised me.

'Well now,' he said, beaming, 'I suppose, as you will one day be custodian of some of my paintings, it is only right and proper that you should see them. Have you time to come with me and we can look at them together?'

Had I heard correctly? Had he really invited me, after all this time, to come and see his collection?

We went to Cadogan Square, and he brought me into the enormous house and we made a tour. I remember (I hope correctly) a lofty staircase-hall lined with paintings, and then more of the same in the other rooms. I recognised some of the paintings, as they had been in many publications and exhibitions. But I do not remember much about the house. He chatted on about which pictures would go to which museums, and pointed out the five that were destined for Dublin. They were by no means the cream of the collection, but they were examples by the major artists – Guido Reni, Domenichino, Guercino and Annibale Carracci, with a French seventeenth-century painting (by Sebastien Bourdon) thrown in.

'We could have fared better,' was my private reaction, but I was not there to make a case.

Almost without thinking, I said to him: 'Have you decided what will become of your library?'

The question, as far as I was concerned, came completely out of the blue. I had never given it any thought beforehand.

'Well, the National Gallery is my main beneficiary, and I suppose it will go there,' he replied.

'But they will already have most of the titles,' I said. 'Their library, as you know, is very comprehensive. What will they do with the duplicates?'

He smiled his delightful smile and shuffled on his feet.

'I have been trying to build up the library in Dublin by buying historic texts,' I said. 'Would you think of us for at least some of your books? It would make us a study centre for the Italian *seicento*, which makes sense when we have the collection. And your own papers and notes on pictures have to be very important.'

'That's a wonderful idea,' he said. 'You are right. London doesn't need the books. I'll leave them to Dublin.'

In arranging to entertain me and show me his pictures and particularly those destined for Dublin, Denis had, as was his wont, some crafty ruse that he wished to discuss and negotiate. In order to facilitate the complicated provisions he had devised for his will, he wanted me to get my board's agreement to pay the National Art Collections Fund in Britain, the sum of $150,000 (yes, dollars) within one year of probate being granted on his estate. Because the Dublin gallery did not have charitable status in Britain there would be a tax liability on Denis's bequest and this sum was to provide for that. In seeking the Board's agreement to this at their meeting in October 1985, I reported details of the proposed gift of paintings as well as 'Mr Mahon's intention to bequeath his library to the gallery'.

I reported back to Denis the board's agreement and gratitude and then heard nothing more; but he obviously remained enthused by the library idea as in 2010, a year before his death, his books and archive were packed up in almost 1,000 boxes and despatched to Dublin. Known today as the Denis Mahon Library and Archive there is a special Denis Mahon Reading Room housed in No 90 Merrion Square. Coincidentally, this is the house purchased at my instigation by the board with Shaw Funds in April 1986.

My most vivid memory of the visit to Cadogan Square – and the one that has always stuck in my mind when thinking of Denis – is of a small domestic detail. The dining room, like all the rooms, was large: the polished table could accommodate twelve, perhaps even twenty, diners. But it was set for one, to dine alone, at one end: a formal place-setting, napkin, glasses, a silver cruet, a wine coaster were all in place. The chair was a carver, to match the set that was ranged around the table, at empty places, and awaiting guests who would never be invited and never arrive. Underneath the table, at the spot where the feet of the solitary diner were given to resting, the Turkey rug was bare: worn through to the webbing, over decades, by Denis's agitated little feet, as he planned further public battles and campaigns and devised ever more complicated stratagems for dealing with his own affairs.

It was here that Denis dined on his own, day after day, night after night, for all his life (although accompanied by Lady Alice until he was sixty).

The hole in the carpet was an image redolent of complete loneliness. It explained much about him: his obsessiveness, his intense activity, his machinations. He loved his pictures; he dined alone with them; they were his only intimate company. It was piercingly poignant.

When George Furlong died (in 1987), *The Daily Telegraph* asked me to write his obituary which I did. When it was published, George's partner Rex wrote (on 15 May 1987) to thank me:

> it was the kindest thing you could have done . . . George thought so much of you. There had been a burial at Tenterden in Kent, he told me, where there are two plots side by side. For some years George has made plans for this moment always with me in mind. All is left to me with instructions for disposal at my demise (which cannot be

far away). It is most important that when you are next in London that I see you, as I have now to remake my will to carry out his wishes and urgently need your advice. As you can imagine, I am devastated and alone after forty-five years.

When I had time to digest this letter, it certainly set my nerve-ends jangling. Protestants love wills, and the more complicated and devious the will, the more we love it. And then the words, 'George thought so much of you.' Had George, out of his affection for me, bequeathed some enormous sum to the gallery or was I, personally, to be the recipient of a thoughtful bequest?

In due course I called on Rex. George wanted a bust by Henry Moore to go to the Dublin Municipal Gallery: that, I advised, would not present any difficulty. More complicated was his wish to endow for the Friends of the National Collections of Ireland an annual lecture. The endowment amount which George had envisaged was, in my view, much too modest, but Rex was adamant that that was all there was. As it transpired (after Rex's death), the monies came to the Friends but either the word 'annual' was omitted in the correspondence, or else it was ignored by the committee; nor was there any mention of George. It was the Rex Britcher Bequest, and as such (from what I heard) a single lecture took place with a splendid party afterwards, and all the money was gone.[1] No one, understandably, had a clue who Rex Britcher was, and it was left to John Gilmartin (who had also known George) to get to his feet and tell the audience that Rex was merely a conduit and that the bequest, in reality, stemmed from George Furlong, who had been a distinguished director of the National Gallery.

As I was leaving the lovely house on Thurloe Street the day I called on Rex, he said to me, 'George left instructions that I was to give you something by which you would remember him.' I was slightly embarrassed, and hurried on towards the hall door.

'George was specific,' continued Rex. 'You are to have a jewel. I've not had time to deal with all his affairs just yet, but when you come and see me again.'

This was certainly something to ponder upon. A jewel? For a man? What sort of jewel? A ring for my finger, a pin for my tie, or links for my cuffs: what had George in mind? I had once read that Hugh Lane collected precious jewels, which he would place in an *epergne* on his dining table; and his guests were encouraged to fondle them after dinner as they circulated the port. Is that what George had in mind for me to do with his jewel?

Among George's closest friends was a couple, Denis and Della Howard, who lived nearby in an elegant house on Egerton Terrace. Della was Irish, and she and Denis entertained very graciously and very generously. I had come to know them very well during my London years. I saw less of them, understandably, after I went to Dublin, but some months after my calling on Rex, Della got in touch with me and asked if I would please come to drinks the next time I was in London, as 'dear Rex' would love to see me. At Della's party, Rex sidled up to me and, taking something out of his jacket, discreetly pushed it into my pocket.

'That's from George,' he whispered.

My heart raced. 'It's the jewel,' I thought, and I quickly finished my drink and said my goodbyes to Denis and Della.

I scampered round the corner from Egerton Terrace and made my way towards Knightsbridge. I stopped in a quiet spot and took out the little box which Rex had put in my pocket. I opened it. Inside was a pair of cufflinks of the type – with a swivelling spring mechanism – popular in the fifties and sixties. They were metal, coloured gold, and each featured a vulgar large yellow stone. They were by no means the sort of 'jewel' that my guests – or anyone else's guests – would want to fondle over the port. It was still quite early as I walked along Knightsbridge; I came upon a jeweller's shop that was open, and went in. Apologetically, I showed the links to the jeweller and asked him what the stone was.

'It's called tiger's eye,' he said. 'South African. It's sold there mainly as a souvenir.'

And then, having detected my Irish accent, he volunteered more.

'Rather like your Connemara marble in Ireland.'

I was disgusted, not because they were valueless, but because I had liked George and admired what he had achieved at the National Gallery of Ireland. I did not want to remember him as 'tiger's eye' (or Connemara marble). I went into Hyde Park and walked over to the Serpentine. It was a fine evening and a number of couples were boating, athletic business types were jogging, black-veiled Middle Eastern ladies were sauntering along on the arms of their fat husbands. Taking the cufflinks from the box, I looked at them and then threw them into the lake. The box, I put in a litter bin. I never regretted my action and today, whenever I walk by the Serpentine, I look at the tranquil waters and take in the beauty of the setting; and I think fondly of George.

Some few years later, I ran into someone I had known during my London years and whom I used to meet at George's little parties. This was Victoria Press, a wealthy American, a decorator, who lived in a splendid five-storey Queen Anne house on Cheyne Walk. She had superb taste and her house was sumptuous, with wonderful furniture, 'objets' and beautiful furnishings. Period rugs, velvets, silks and brocades cascaded through her every room. As I told her about the cufflinks – down to their final splash in the Serpentine – she listened intently. Then she smiled.

'The same happened to me,' she said, 'except it was silk.' I was intrigued.

> Rex said to me, in a heavy whisper, that George had wanted me to have some silk. Naturally I was fascinated, as George had known that I collected antique fabrics, and I could not help wondering if the silk was going to be a bolt of something eighteenth-century and wonderful that he might have picked up in Venice or Paris.
>
> She laughed. 'And . . . ?' I said. Rex rang up one day and asked if he might come round, and he did. But nothing was said about the silk and then, on leaving, he handed me a small package. When he had gone, I opened it and found a silk headscarf. The label, I think, said it came from Harrods or some such.
>
> 'How could he have been so mean?' I said. 'It wasn't necessarily meanness,' she said. 'Rex was just like that. It was merely a complete lack of judgement.'

Apart from the cufflinks, I remember Rex as a very welcoming and attentive host at George's little parties and his complete devotion to George was always touching.

Endnotes

1. This may be incorrect and somehow the lecture has been revived annually.

CHAPTER 16
OUR LEADER

When Jack Lynch resigned as Taoiseach in December 1979, Mr Haughey was elected leader of Fianna Fáil, and became Taoiseach. Feeling confident in his popularity, and with the hope of gaining a greater majority, he called a general election eighteen months later – and lost. Garret FitzGerald and Fine Gael took the helm. That was June 1981. The country was in crisis and as a means of solving it, FitzGerald proposed – among other measures – a tax on children's shoes. This was an emotive issue in a country where barefoot children walking to school was still a memory and, nine months after taking office, FitzGerald's government fell. That was March 1982. By putting together deals with independent TDs, Mr Haughey scraped back into office but, when the deals collapsed nine months later, Mr Haughey was out again. December 1982, and Garret FitzGerald is back. This time he managed to stay the course for almost five years but, like a spectre, Mr Haughey reappeared as Taoiseach in March 1987 and remained so until February 1992.

Throughout most of this period, I had remained in office as director of the National Gallery.

Early on, I had met Tony Cronin,[1] who was 'cultural and artistic advisor' to Mr Haughey (but was retained in the same capacity by Garret FitzGerald during the 1981–82 interregnum). Initially, I was not all that impressed by Tony. With his dishevelled appearance and cloth cap, he looked too much like an Irish '*littérateur*' for me, but when I learned more – he was a distinguished poet who had a lot of very innovative and original ideas about the promotion of the arts – I came to admire him. It helped that he showed very clearly that he approved of me and saw that I only wanted what was best for the gallery. In 1980 or 1981, I asked Tony if he thought that Mr Haughey would like to come and have lunch with me in the gallery, and this was arranged. It was my first time meeting him.

He is small and very wary, I noted, the suit expensive and, like the hair, well-cut. I talked of general things: it was not part of my plan to ask at this stage for concessions for the gallery.

He asked me where I came from. Even at this stage of my being acquainted with him, I knew that this was preposterous: the notion that he would agree to have lunch with anyone without first of all being fully briefed on exactly who they were and where they came from (and what use they might be to him) was laughable. In spite of Tony helping the conversation along, no rapport or warmth was established between Mr Haughey and me: but then, I did not believe he would allow such familiarity on meeting anyone for the first time. The lunch, if rather dull, went off without mishap: and that in itself, as far as I was concerned, was something.

In March 1982, the morning after Mr Haughey was voted into office, my telephone rang at 10 am. The Taoiseach wanted to see me immediately. I sensed what this was all about: he wanted to borrow pictures for his office. This was normal: the gallery lent pictures to most Ministers, as well as to other government offices. I went up to Government Buildings and was shown into his office. (I kept notes on all of this.)

It was a horrid little internal room, long and narrow, with a single window that looked out into a courtyard, the desk pushed up to one end; but none of this was Mr Haughey's choice. Mr Haughey was there; his desk was empty save for a large silver tray and an enormous silver coffee-pot. He did stand up when I came in. He pointed to the pictures on the walls and said that he would like them changed. There were also four outsize ugly plaster medallions of patriots embedded into the walls, and he said that he would like those changed too. I agreed with him on that but pointed out that that was the responsibility of the Board of Works. I went back to the gallery intent on replacing the pictures. But I did stop to think: this man has just been elected Taoiseach and, instead of doing what a normal prime minister, in any country, would do on his first morning in office – which must surely be to appoint a Cabinet – he is only concerned with having a silver coffee-pot and pictures that he likes on his walls. Was this real, or what?

Next day, and before I had time to send up replacement pictures for his office, there came a further phone call: this time, even more urgent.

The paintings which had always been in the Council Room had been changed, the official said.

(I had replaced them at the request of the FitzGerald-appointed Minister for Education the previous year.)

The Taoiseach wants them returned, immediately.

This was a group of landscapes by the early-twentieth-century Irish landscape painter Nathaniel Hone, which had been in the Council Room (where the Cabinet meets) since the time of my predecessor, Thomas McGreevy (who had retired in 1963). When they had come back to the gallery (at the request of Fine Gael), I had had them cleaned and had hung them with some prominence in the Irish galleries, where they might be enjoyed by the wider public for the first time in more than twenty years. I explained this to the officer who had called me, and pointed out that, if the pictures now disappeared again from the public rooms, it might occasion public disquiet and lead to adverse comment in the press. I was still told to put them back; and put them back – or some of them – I did.

The matter did not end there. The Taoiseach wanted to see me again. I went up to Government Buildings and was kept waiting for an hour and three quarters, and then ushered down to the Council Room, where the Cabinet had been meeting. They were all there, gathering up their papers: their leader was standing at the far end of the table. There was no apology for keeping me so long, and no gesture towards politeness.

'Potterton,' he said, 'I have asked for the pictures to be returned to this room and you have not returned them.'

I attempted to explain that they were hanging in the gallery but he interrupted me.

'I don't think you realise the dignity of the government's Council Room,' he said.

He strode over to a charming small Hone, waved his hand at it and said, 'Look at that, it's a disgrace. And that too,' he said, waving at another.

Noel De Chenu[2] the principal architect of the Office of Public Works, was also in attendance. A very cultivated and honourable man, he was an ally of mine, and always friendly towards me. He interrupted.

'Taoiseach, if I may,' he had the temerity to say, 'that is one of the pictures which has always been here.'

'It's not,' said the Taoiseach.

'It is,' said Noel.

'Well, even if it is, I don't like it.'

Mr Haughey turned his back on me, waved his hand in the air and, on leaving the room, said, 'Change them.'

I was boiling as I returned to the gallery and remained so. Nevertheless, I arranged to change the pictures in the Council Room.

In the meantime, the paintings that I had hung in the Taoiseach's office were taken down so that the room could be redecorated: Noel had been given orders similar to mine. He spoke to me and I said that the Taoiseach could have whatever paintings he liked if I could have peace. He told me, in confidence, that Mr Haughey could not say bad enough about me, but that he had been misinformed about what I had done: I had, according to Noel, an enemy in the Department, and he told me who this was. It was someone whom I had hardly encountered but who was known to be ambitious, both as a civil servant and, encouraged by his wife, socially as well. Subsequently, in talking to Mr Haughey, Noel told him (correctly) that I had said that he could come to the gallery and select whatever pictures he liked. At this, Mr Haughey exploded.

'What? Go near that little brat?' he said, to which Noel generously replied: 'Taoiseach, I know you don't want explanations, but Potterton is doing a very good job at the National Gallery.'

'F**k his National Gallery,' was Mr Haughey's response, 'it is not Irish anyhow. And nor is he.'

There one had it, from the horse's mouth as it were, the attitude towards the gallery in some official quarters, and towards me personally as well.

A day or so later, Noel rang to say that Mr Haughey would come to the gallery the following morning to select paintings. When Noel told someone in the Taoiseach's Department about the proposed visit, the official said, 'Christ, don't let him near Potterton or he will lynch him.' Fortunately I did not know about this exchange until later but nonetheless I was extremely worried about the impending visit as I was not sure if he was rude to me again but that I would be rude in return and resign on the spot to his face. To protect me, as much from myself as from Mr Haughey, I thought of the idea of asking Bill Finlay to come to gallery and greet the Taoiseach with me. I rang Bill and, without telling him any of the background (that would have been a mistake), I said that Mr Haughey was coming to the gallery the following morning, probably to select pictures for his office. As this would be his first visit to the gallery as Taoiseach, it might be appropriate for Bill to greet him. Bill was immediately taken by such an observance of correct form and courtesy, and agreed to come. As we waited together in the portico, the clock ticked past the appointed hour, Bill became agitated.

'Does his protocol person know that I will be greeting him?' he asked.

Ten minutes late, the Taoiseach and his entourage –

including Noel De Chenu – walked through the gates, and Bill and I went out to the forecourt to greet him. On seeing Bill, Mr Haughey's expression immediately changed. This was to be a different encounter from what he had planned: smiles and civility were called for, and that is what we got. On going into the gallery and towards the Irish rooms, I placed myself in the position – both by my demeanour and, walking several steps behind, with my presence – of attendance on Bill as chairman. I was, legally speaking, his servant, and not the servant of the Taoiseach – that, I made clear. Bill immediately grasped what I was doing and, addressing me as director, asked for my approval of anything the Taoiseach asked for or said. I addressed him as chairman in return. Only at the end of the visit did Mr Haughey and I speak to each other directly; by this point, he seemed to be in good humour. I had not thrown in the towel and resigned on the spot, and he left the gallery satisfied.

Some few days later, I was bidden to dinner by my friends Maureen and Ian Cairnduff and found myself seated beside Mr Haughey's *maîtresse-en-titre*, Terry Keane, whom I knew. To my surprise, she was fully informed as to what had taken place between me and her paramour. I found this astonishing: that I was sufficiently significant for the Taoiseach (who was, after all, governing the country) to relate our encounter to his mistress. At the same time, I was tickled by the notion that I had been the subject of pillow-talk between them. In reporting the visit to the gallery, Mr Haughey had told Terry that I had trailed round after him and Bill Finlay like a mouse (which was true). She then moved on to talking about him in more general terms, as she was given to do. Mentioning that he was manifestly such a bully in his public life, I asked her if he was perchance – as is often the case – a lamb in the bedroom. I knew that she liked this line of carefree conversation.

'Indeed not,' she replied, 'far from it.'

She then told me that she had deliberately irritated him

by telling him that I was perhaps every bit as smart as he was, as otherwise I would not be director of the National Gallery at the age of thirty-three. I was not at all sure that I took this exactly as a compliment but I fell in with her by asking her if she thought that I might also be as devious. On a subsequent occasion, she told me that when she had reported what I had said to Mr Haughey, he became livid and burst out: 'How could a little County Meath brat say he was as devious as me?'

This all took place following Mr Haughey becoming Taoiseach for a second time in March 1982.

In the summer of that year, a series of extraordinary incidents took place in Ireland that called for the Taoiseach to make public comment: a suspected double-murderer was apprehended by the Gardaí in the home of the attorney general. Attempting to distance himself from events, and from his attorney general, Mr Haughey described what had taken place as 'a bizarre happening, an unprecedented situation, a grotesque situation, an almost unbelievable mischance'. Pouncing on this statement – itself bizarre – the intellectual politician and commentator Conor Cruise O'Brien coined the acronym 'GUBU'. This term has found a permanent place in the language – in Ireland at least – to describe any political scandal to which a whiff of notoriety is attached.

The murders, of a nurse quietly sunbathing near the American Ambassador's Residence in the Phoenix Park and, three days later, of a farmer near Edenderry, were both violent and apparently without motive, but the Gardaí soon issued a description of the murderer. Some weeks elapsed, during which the public remained enthralled.

By this time it was August and, on holiday in England, I was spending a weekend with my friends, Andrew and Malcolm, at their cottage in the picturesque Cotswolds village of Uffington. On the Sunday morning they burst into my bedroom with a cup of tea and a copy of the *Sunday Times*.

'Homan,' they said, 'do you know about these murders in Ireland? The murder suspect has been found in the house of the attorney general. You always boast that you know everyone in Ireland, so tell us all about the attorney general.'

They were disappointed when I said I could not recall who the attorney general was.

'There have been so many changes of government,' I made as my excuse. 'What's his name?'

'Patrick Connolly,' they read out from the paper, and then they read on: 'Police in the Irish Republic have arrested a murder suspect, Malcolm MacArthur, in the home of the country's attorney general . . .' 'My God!' I said. 'I don't know the attorney general, but I do know the murderer.'

This indeed was GUBU. Now it was my turn to join with Mr Haughey and say 'grotesque, unbelievable, bizarre, unprecedented'. I had, in my time, known one or two criminals but this was the first occasion – as far as I knew – that I had known a murderer.

In addition to being a farmer and auctioneer, my father acted as a sort of land-agent for many people, advising them on the management of their farms, setting their lands, stocking their farms by buying their cattle and arranging for them to be sold, engaging labourers and dealing with contractors. One of his clients – who like many others became a friend of my father – lived outside Trim on a farm of several hundred acres with an attractive Georgian farmhouse called Breemount. This was Daniel MacArthur, a gentleman. On some occasions in the school holidays, my father would take my brother Alan and me with him as he visited clients and we would wait in the car, or get up to some mischief, while father discussed business. At Breemount, it was different, as there was a small boy of our own age there – Mr MacArthur's son – with whom we could play about the farmyard. He was called Malcolm and was an only child: he was also a lonely one. His parents' marriage was not a happy one – in fact it was a disaster – and his mother, Irene, was rarely at Breemount. Malcolm was very much neglected. This was sometimes discussed by my mother and father within the family's hearing and, as small children do, I took it in. I never knew Malcolm as an adult but I have happy memories of playing with him as a child in the sunny farmyard at Breemount. In light of what happened later, it is obvious that demons lurked there, but happily their focus was Malcolm rather than me.

In the autumn of 1984 a conference took place in the National Gallery, *Art and the Human Environment: Dublin – A Case Study*. This

201

had nothing to do with me or the Gallery: we merely lent the lecture theatre. It was organised by the Edinburgh arts entrepreneur and guru, Ricky Demarco, and brought to Dublin through the enthusiasm of contemporary arts enthusiasts in Ireland like Dorothy Walker[3] and Rosemarie and Sean Mulcahy[4] who had somehow fallen under the spell of Demarco at the Edinburgh Festival and had been taken up by him. It was one of those ridiculous 'big-thinking' events which somehow manage to get pulled-off in Ireland from time to time but generally with little or no permanent effect. On this occasion, Demarco managed to persuade a plethora of luminaries from the international contemporary arts world to come to Dublin. They included the British Minister for the Arts, Lord Gowrie; the charismatic French culture minister, Jack Lang; Anthony Burgess the writer; the Dutch hot-shot curator, Rudi Fuchs; Dominique De Menil, American art collector and philanthropist; and, a surprising invitee, the sacked Labour Prime Minister of Australia, Gough Whitlam. Some, or all, of these spoke at the Conference but, as I do not have a copy of the programme, I have no record of what they spoke about or indeed if many of them had ever been to Dublin before. As a sop to me, I suppose, I was asked to speak on the Sunday afternoon and, as the focus of the Conference was so vague and abstract, it seemed to me that I could speak about whatever I liked; and, as I most liked speaking publicly in those days about the uncontrolled export of works of art out of Ireland, I chose that as my theme. I put together some slides of recently-exported pictures by Irish artists which had hung in historic Irish houses from the day they were painted, mainly in the eighteenth century. From recent Sotheby's and Christie's auction catalogues, I had lots to choose from as both firms through their Irish agents – an industrious Knight of Glin in the case of Christie's – were extremely assiduous in persuading penurious Irish aristocrats to send their family treasures to London for sale. Several of my slides showed the beautiful eighteenth-century James Latham portraits of the Cosby family which had recently gone from Stradbally Hall. I later wrote a note about the proceedings for myself.

> On the afternoon in question, the Conference was honoured by the arrival of the Leader of the Opposition who was accorded a round of applause at his entrance. This was Mr Haughey who was accompanied by his henchman

– Press Secretary P.J. Mara – and possibly by Tony Cronin as well.

I had a good audience (although I had not known that Mr Haughey would be there) and I intended to make good use of it. My lecture would be trenchant. I showed my slides, identified the artists, the subjects, and the houses from which they had been exported, and as one slide after another faded from the screen, I turned directly to the audience and pronounced in each case, 'Gone!'. 'Ooh! là' muttered the French people in the audience; 'Ach so!' exclaimed the Germans; 'Wow!' came from the Americans; 'Tch tch!' from the British; and the Dutch, the Spanish, and the Italians expressed similar dismay and horror. When I had finished, an Irishman in the audience rose to his feet and, addressing the crowded lecture-hall, said 'Chairman, would the next Taoiseach....' there was cheer at that, '...would the next Taoiseach assure us that when he is back in office he will put a stop to this plunder.'

Mr Haughey stood up to an expectant hush.

'Yes,' he said, 'when I have been in office in the past, notably as Minister for Justice or Minister for Finance, I have looked into this question many times and formed a view.'

This was what the audience wanted to hear.

'I know that such regulation exists in Britain, France and elsewhere,' he went on, 'but things are not similar in Ireland. And so, with the best advice, I have always come to the conclusion that regulation would not work – or indeed be appropriate – in Ireland.'

This was not what the audience wanted to hear.

He continued for a few minutes in similar vein, outlining how Ireland was different. An unease began to permeate the audience. Then, in summing up as it were, he said, 'But if I was asked my personal opinion ...'

Now, we were going to hear the meat of the matter.

'... I would say that the more old pictures of Irish aristocrats that are exported from Ireland – and the sooner

– the better it would be.'

A chorus of dismay rose up from the audience, a prolonged 'Ohooooooooooooooo!' and even one or two muted boos. Mr Haughey had done what he very rarely did, he had made a tremendous gaffe in public. The audience was completely shocked: it was palpable, with whispered conversations breaking out here and there.

'You may well go cooooo,' he pressed on before sitting down, 'but that's my opinion.'

Here we were, with Dublin presenting itself to Grey Gowrie, Jack Lang, Dominique de Menil and the world as a cultural capital and yet the country's Taoiseach-in-Waiting was, it seemed, entrenched in an attitude of profound and abysmal ignorance.

There were journalists from all the main newspapers and from RTÉ in the theatre: they had probably been tipped-off by P.J. Mara that Mr Haughey would be attending. I awaited – with some glee, I have to say – the coverage of the intervention that would be published in Monday's papers. It was certainly newsworthy by any reckoning. But when the papers came out on Monday morning there was a report of the Conference but nothing – nothing whatever – about the dramatic moment when Mr Haughey showed his true colours. P.J. Mara, it seemed to me, had done a very good job in obliterating the gaffe from the record.

When Mr Haughey became Taoiseach for the third time, in March 1987, I decided to invite him to officiate at something in the Gallery. We had a big exhibition planned for August 1987 and this seemed an ideal opportunity. It was *Irish Women Artists from the Eighteenth Century to the Present Day* and it would open to coincide with the *Third International Interdisciplinary Congress on Women,* which was to be held in Dublin that year. A 'Congress ... on Women' I thought. What could be more alluring? If this was not an event that would appeal to Mr Haughey, nothing would. And I was right. His office replied immediately that he would be delighted to open the exhibition.

The opening was to be one of our 'black-tie, nine o'clock' affairs but, when it came to planning it, I realised that there were so many women delegates to the Congress it would not be possible to have them as well as our usual guests and so a Preview Reception was arranged for the Congress one evening and the Opening with Mr Haughey the following night. When he arrived, he looked around and could see many familiar faces. His face fell.

'Where are the women?' he asked. (Those were the exact words that he used.)

'They were here last night,' I explained. There were too many to include this evening.

'I could see that he was not at all pleased.' I had foolishly not fully appreciated that 'the women' were the principal reason he had come and I was somewhat taken aback.

This man is bats, I thought.

He made his speech and then made the best of the evening, circulating freely and being pleasant. But of all the hundreds of guests there, young and old, from all walks of Irish life, who did he seek out and spend most time talking to?: Eileen, Countess of Mount Charles. It was noticeable, to me and to other guests as well. He remained engrossed in conversation with her for much longer than any protocol demanded. I thought about it afterwards. I remembered that he did not see me – a farmer's son from County Meath, but a Protestant – as 'Irish'; and I recalled his words that the more old pictures of Irish aristocrats that are exported from Ireland – and the sooner – the better it would be. Yet, here he was, sniffing-out blue-blood, and singling out one of the relatively few titled aristocrats in the Gallery that evening and engaging her in prolonged conversation.

'Was he really bats?' I wondered. 'Perhaps not. But he was very, very complex.'

In what proved to be my final months as Director, I received a letter one day from someone I did not know. In the letter the writer proposed presenting a portrait of Mr Haughey, by an artist I had never heard of, to the Gallery. I knew immediately that I had no intention of pursuing this but, over my eight years in office, I had learned some small modicum of sense and I could perceive a trap. For me to turn down, out of hand, a portrait of Our Leader would be a mistake. I reflected on what to do. I decided to write to Mr Haughey, who was then Taoiseach, and seek his counsel.

In my letter I said that we had been offered the picture but that the artist was not generally known and I was not even sure if Mr Haughey had actually sat for the portrait, or if it had been done from a photograph. Perhaps he could enlighten me. I said that, of course, it was very much a desideratum that the Gallery would have a portrait of someone who had contributed so much to Irish life but that I knew that other well-known artists had painted him in the past. If he felt that one of those pictures would represent him better in the Irish Portrait Collection, then I would prefer to follow that route.

He telephoned me directly, and immediately, on receipt of my letter.

Yes, he said, there are other portraits which would be more appropriate. I have them out here at Abbeville. Maybe you should come out and look at them.

He suggested a morning later that week.

> It was a sunny morning when I drove out to Kinsealy and, yes, Abbeville, as it sits in the landscape, is basically a beautiful place. One half of the hall-door was open – in the grand manner of Irish country-house hospitality – when I arrived and I had no sooner got out of the car when the Taoiseach came out the door to greet me. I had not known what to expect but I need have had no fears: he was gracious in the extreme. No longer the thug who had humiliated me in the Council Room of Government Buildings some years previously, he was this morning a charming country gentleman: I was meeting 'Squire Haughey'.

'There's no one here today,' he said, 'so I'm afraid I can't offer you coffee but come in.'

Things were in a slight muddle in the hall and, when he noticed me looking at the piles of pictures stacked on the floor in a room to the right, he said, 'All of this stuff is on its way down to the Island. We are more and more down there.'

The staircase, if I am correct, rises from the hall and the Taoiseach gestured towards it.

'There are some of the portraits,' he said.

I must have been very nervous because, the thing is, I can't remember any of the pictures. He had been painted by Edward McGuire and by Robert Ballagh among others, but whether those were the portraits I saw, I don't recall. He did not press any particular portrait on me and indeed seemed to have rather lost sight of why I was there.

'Would you like to see the house?' he asked.

He led me round. Abbeville had been built in the 1770s but greatly modified and extended by the great architect of eighteenth-century Dublin, James Gandon, in the 1790s: the splendid dining-room is Gandon and so is the ballroom. But it was another space to which Mr Haughey first introduced me: I am not sure if it was in the basement. This was called the bar and it had been designed for Mr Haughey by his crony, the controversial Irish architect, Sam Stephenson. Designed it may well have been but to me it looked (and smelled) like a country pub. Mr Haughey was very proud of it but I was appalled by the place and wanted to get out of it as soon as I could. 'The plots, treacheries, and wickednesses that have been hatched here,' I thought and shuddered.

But there was worse in store. We went through the double mahogany doors that led to the ballroom. A beautiful room with a trio of bow windows at one end, delicate 'Adamesque' plasterwork on the walls into which circular canvasses said to be by Angelica Kauffmann were inserted, a handsome chimneypiece, niches, but no furniture: the room was, after all, designed by Gandon for dancing. Unlike the bar, the place seemed little-used although I am sure that it must have been the setting for *ceol-agus-rince* during Mr Haughey's time. An object, the only thing in the room, caught my attention. Down at the darker end, a heap of navy blue, scarlet, gold braid and brass was thrown on the floor. I stared at it, wondering what it was. Mr Haughey noticed.

'You are looking at that,' he said with a smile as he ushered me over.

Close up, I still could not make it out – it looked like some form of livery.

'That's the saddle for my horse that Gaddafi gave me,' he said with a chuckle.

I was stunned. Then I knew that I really was in the presence of evil.

The tour over, he showed me out through the hall door. The fountain was there. I had heard about this from Austin Dunphy, the architect who had sourced and installed it, and so I expressed interest and we went over to look. With a vaguely quatrefoil-shaped basin and a tiered central fount, it was surprisingly simple: certainly not Versailles. The curiosity was the mosaic plaque set into the ground beside it. It depicts a crest and motto and the name *Charles James Haughey* inscribed below. But, oddly, above the crest, the words *Ex Libris*. The mosaicist has obviously copied a bookplate without understanding what the Latin meant. Does Mr Haughey understand how absurd this is? I wondered.

Thanking him for his kindness, but with no mention from him of which of his portraits he would like to see in the Gallery, I made my way.

My encounters with Mr Haughey demonstrated to me that there was not just one Mr Haughey but several and I must own that, if the truth were told, I did not care for any of them. But then he did not care for me either. When I resigned from the Gallery, I wrote to inform him. This was merely a courtesy as the Governors and Guardians (my employers) had already accepted my resignation. Responsibility for the Gallery had been transferred during my time from the Department of Education to the Department of the Taoiseach so that the Taoiseach was officially my Minister. As the Minister for Education had been called upon to sanction my appointment, I deemed it correct for the Taoiseach to be informed by me of my resignation. He replied formally to 'thank me for the outstanding contribution' I had made to the Gallery and praised my 'administrative ability, intuitive insights and unceasing commitment to furthering the best interests of Gallery'. He sent me his 'best wishes for the future'.

I learned (some years later) that he took a very keen interest in the appointment of my successor.

Endnotes

1. Poet, novelist and cultural commentator and a central presence in Dublin Literary life for decades. Obituary, *Irish Times*, 28 December 2016.
2. (1924–2002). Son of a French dress-designer living in Dublin, he studied architecture at UCD (although with a pronounced interest in acting and the theatre) and had a distinguished career in the Board of Works where he worked with Raymond McGrath on several Irish embassies abroad. He was responsible for the refurbishment of Government Buildings and the Royal Hospital Kilmainham as well as the introduction of the '1 per cent for art' scheme. Obituary, *Irish Times*, 19 October 2002.

3. (1929–2002). Contemporary art guru and art critic. Married to the architect, Robin Walker.

4. Dr Rosemarie (1943–2012), an internationally recognised scholar of seventeenth-century Spanish art and lecturer in the history of art at UCD. She compiled the catalogue of the 1988 ROSC exhibition. Her husband Seán is an engineer and artist.

CHAPTER 17
UNDER THE GOYA

I first met the Beits at a dinner given by Rosie Talbot in London in 1979 and, although I did not keep a diary at the time, I jotted down an account of the evening afterwards.

Rosie, having inherited Malahide Castle from her brother, Milo, on his death in 1973, had sold it up in order to pay death duties and, although over 60 at the time, moved to the family property (also called Malahide) in Tasmania. Up to this, her experience of life had mainly centred on being a volunteer counsellor with the Samaritans in Dublin but in Tasmania she proved herself a model and able sheep-farmer on her 21,000-acre estate. Each year she returned to Europe and made the equivalent of a royal progress, staying in the great houses of her many friends in England and Ireland. In Ireland it was Dunsany, Birr, Glin, Russborough, Baronscourt and Kilruddery; in London it was with Lord Justice Roualeyn Cumming-Bruce and his wife, Lady Sarah, who lived on Mulberry Walk, off the King's Road. Rosie could not – or did not – entertain there and so she gave her parties in an odd establishment in Belgrave Square, the Anglo-Belgian Club (but sometimes in the Lansdowne Club), and each year she would include me on her guest list. I was delighted by this but many of her other guests, who were being entertained as reciprocation for having Rosie to stay, were less so: Rosie's annual visitations seemed to them to come round far too promptly from one year to the next. Rosie, who loved to be amused and was always tickled by gossip, had quite a severe and stiff reserve: she wanted to be fun and she could be witty and sharp but something always seemed to be holding her back. She presided over her guests rather than receiving them warmly but from time to time her stern expression would crack and her face would light up in a naughty smile. Her parties were carefully thought out and her guests put together with insight but the lunches or dinners had a tendency to be rather stiff; and, in that context, the Beits fitted in perfectly because they could be rather stiff too.

On first meeting, Clementine Beit seemed to me to be utterly ghastly: superior, grand and condescending. And quite out of it as far as the modern world was concerned. But, on getting to know her (as I was to in years to come) this initial impression proved to be incorrect. Her grandeur was simply a product of her upbringing and the life she had lived as the wife of an inordinately wealthy aristocrat.

I was seated on her left at Rosie's party and, before we had unfolded our napkins, Lady Beit turned to me.

'Now, do tell me,' she said, 'where do you come from?'

'County Meath,' I said.

'Oh! really. We love County Meath, we adore County Meath, we know everyone in County Meath.'

Now it was my turn to say 'really'.

'Yes. We know Sheila and Randal (the Dunsanys), the Musgraves, the Waddingtons, Eileen Mount Charles, the Langrishes, and, of course, Thomas and Valerie (the Longfords) are our great friends.'

This was a round-up of every aristocrat in the county.

'And what is the name of your place?'

'Rathcormick.'

Lady Beit turned her attention to the turtle soup which had been placed before her. She seemed to enjoy it and, as she dabbed the corners of her mouth with her napkin, she turned to me again.

'Now, do tell me,' she said, 'where did you go to school?'

'Kilkenny College,' I said.

'Oh! really. We love Kilkenny, we adore Kilkenny, we know everyone in Kilkenny. We know the McCalmonts, Hubert and Peggy Butler, we know . . .'

And on it went.

'But, you know, I never knew there was a school in Kilkenny.'

'Well, it has been there since the seventeenth century,' I said.

The fish had arrived, and then the saddle of lamb followed by a strawberry parfait and it was only over the *petits-fours* that Lady Beit addressed me again.

'I think our hostess wants the ladies to move to the drawing-room,' she said, rising from her chair and manoeuvring herself in the direction of the staircase.

I did not realise it at the time, although it dawned on me some time later, that – with Rosie as her accomplice – Lady Beit had been on a mission that night and she wanted to know about me for a particular reason.

The Beits were very friendly with James White (they 'adored' James White) and Sir Alfred was on the Board of the National Gallery. James had announced his intention to retire that year and the Beits would have been told by him that I would be a possible candidate for the Directorship. Rosie too would have been *au fait* with this possibility and Rosie would have been very much on my side. Her interest in me derived from her affection for Speer, and so she hatched her little plan – she loved hatching little plans – of producing me for the Beits' inspection.

While my family background and schooling – rather than any qualifications I might have had – were what mattered most to Clementine Beit, Sir Alfred was of a mind to dig a little deeper. He was seated to my left with Olda FitzGerald chatting away between us.

Leaning across Olda, he addressed me directly.

'How much did the National Gallery pay for the Mentmore Fragonard?' he said.

(I was an Assistant Keeper in the National Gallery at this time.)

He was referring to the painting of *Psyche Showing Her Sisters Her Gifts from Cupid*, which the gallery had recently acquired after some controversy. The painting had been incorrectly catalogued in the celebrated Mentmore Sale[1] and not recognised as a Fragonard by Sotheby's. It was bought by the dealer David Carritt – who realised what it really was – for £12,000 and was subsequently sold by him to the National Gallery for half a million.

Sir Alfred knew all about this – David Carritt was a friend of the Beits and often stayed at Russborough – but Alfred wanted to hear it, as it were, from the horse's mouth and, on this occasion, I was the horse's mouth.

'Oh!', I said, 'the Gallery never reveals how much it pays for acquisitions.'

In retrospect, I am horrified that I was so cheeky but Sir Alfred was not one to be defeated.

'Well,' he said, 'I know anyway because David Carritt offered it to us first.'

After that, Sir Alfred talked to me for quite a time and I realised that he was very pleasant and indeed quite *simpatico*.

Sir Alfred Beit was indeed most congenial. In his diary, James Lees-Milne[2] writes that he liked him 'much, for he is on the ball, interested in everything, and amused if not amusing'. He was exceedingly tall, held himself well and, although seventy-six at the time when I met him, very handsome in an exquisite and refined sort of way. He dressed immaculately and in a mode that was always calculatedly appropriate to the occasion. His father, who was not nearly as good-looking, had been painted by the society portrait painter, Giovanni Boldini, but it would have been only John Singer Sargent who could have done justice to Sir Alfred's elegant *hauteur*. The horrid portrait which the Irish painter Edward McGuire painted of the Beits in the 1970s is a travesty and serves only to demonstrate the artist's obvious detestation of them and all that they stood for.

Descended from a Hamburg Jewish family, Sir Alfred was born in London, the second son[3] of Otto Beit (later Sir Otto): Sir Alfred's mother was a Carter from New Orleans. Described by the decorator and gossip, Nicky Haslam,[4] as a 'willowy young Randlord', an aristocratic upbringing – Eton and Christ Church, Oxford – led Sir Alfred to a flirtation with politics and he was elected an MP in 1931.

His father had died the previous year. But the rough and tumble of politics was not for Sir Alfred – his real interests lay in music and the arts (he was an accomplished pianist) – and on losing his seat in the 1945 election and fearful of the new Labour Government, he and Lady Beit (he had married Clementine in 1938) moved to South Africa. There, he became fiercely anti-apartheid: 'we madly disagreed with it', Lady Beit would say. In Sir Alfred's obituary, which he wrote for *The Independent*, James Lees-Milne, who knew him from the 1930s, described him as

> cultivated and wise; informative, forthright and fun to be with. Insatiably curious, ever-seeking knowledge, yet serious conversation with him usually ended in peals of laughter, especially when the jokes were turned upon himself. Over the years his wife's teasing dispelled any Teutonic earnestness. He was a highly civilised, very good and most lovable man.[5] According to Lees-Milne, Alfred had, 'until he was 36, enjoyed a golden bachelorhood. Fair, good-looking, tall and eligible, he was much sought after. He greatly appealed to women, who found his origins romantic. These were German and Jewish.'

Sir Alfred's 'golden bachelorhood' came to an end in 1938 when, at the age of thirty-five, he married the 22-year-old Clementine Mabell Kitty Freeman-Mitford the daughter of Major Clement Bertram Freeman-Mitford by his wife, Helen Alice Ogilvy. Alfred proposed – as Lady Beit loved to recall – while standing under Goya's *Portrait of Doña Antonia Zárate*. Significantly perhaps, Doña Antonia was not an aristocrat but, as an actress and the daughter of an actor, the wife of a singer, and the mother of a poet, part of an artistic world that was perhaps closer to Alfred's heart than the quarterings, crests and coronets of the nobility. Clementine's father was killed in action at Loos in May 1915, five months before she was born: had he survived, he would have inherited – on the death of his father in 1916 – the title Baron Redesdale. Instead, it went to his younger brother, Clementine's Uncle David. David was the father of Nancy, Unity, Diana, Debo and the other Mitford sisters. Lady Beit told me – on more than one occasion – that, had she been born a man, she would have been Lord Redesdale and there would have been 'no Mitford Hons and Rebels'. (She loved saying this, but never in a boasting way, and she said it to everyone else as well.) She had been close to her Mitford cousins and in 1937 had gone to Munich with Unity who introduced her to Hitler: the Führer then took the pair of them to the Bayreuth Festival for ten days.[6] Lady Beit never mentioned this escapade, at least never to me. Nor did she ever mention that her trips to Germany at this time were not just confined to ten days at the opera in Bayreuth with Hitler. According to her cousin, Deborah Mitford (Duchess of Devonshire), Clementine also 'struck up a close friendship with an SS officer (an episode in her life that was conveniently forgotten after her marriage to Alfred Beit).'[7] Clementine Ogilvy's mother was a first cousin of Clementine Hozier who married Winston Churchill. But there was more to it than that as Lady Beit's Redesdale grandfather was widely believed, through an infidelity, to be Clementine Hozier's father. The Churchills' son, Randolph, was one of Clementine Beit's earliest *beaux*. Sir Alfred's bride, therefore, was very well anchored to the British aristocratic Establishment while he, on the other hand, would have still been considered by some – on account of his Jewishness – as an outsider and an *arriviste*. It was that element, I think, which made him different and a great deal more interesting and engaging than many British aristocrats.

Lady Beit, by the time I knew her, was a plumpish figure with a settled facial expression that bordered on the sour: when animated she was altogether more attractive. She had silken white hair swept up from her forehead and rolled at ear level: it looked as though she had found a style in the 1940s and had never seen any reason to change. One could never be entirely certain if she had ever been a great beauty: pretty, undoubtedly so; elegant, yes; but beautiful, perhaps not. She spoke in rich deep tones and her words seemed to rumble from her mouth. When she said her set piece – 'Had I been born a man,' etc. – I would often chuckle to myself as, although she was entirely feminine, it was not impossible to imagine her as actually a man. She liked to talk and could be very amusing but one's amusement derived more often from the way she said things rather than her actual words. James Lees-Milne found her rather tedious: she 'buttonholes one with long, unpointful stories'.[8] She told Lees-Milne that 'she read Proust over and over again.

He was the greatest novelist in the world and George Pointer's biography the greatest biography ever written of a novelist.' She never shared this *aperçu* with me: had she done so, I would have told her that I had never been able to get to grips with Proust. She did, however, once startle me by asking me if I was Catholic. An Irish person meeting me could never had made such a misattribution. In speaking to Sir Alfred, whom she treated with great affection, she would become a winsome wee girl: 'Alfred, do tell Homan your story …' or 'Alfred, can I tell Homan your story?'

One of her favourite topics, after Russborough was opened to visitors in the 1970s, was 'the public' and, from the way that Lady Beit told things, it really seemed that, although Sir Alfred had been an MP, Lady Beit had never been aware of the public before this time.

'On Sunday afternoons, when we are here, of course,' she would enunciate, 'we go to the tea-room and we take our trays and select our scones and cakes, and move with the queue. Just like everyone else.'

The sourness would disappear from her expression as she said this and she would light up.

' . . . and we pay,' she would add. 'Alfred brings money and when we get to the till, we pay. And, you know, we love seeing everyone enjoying their day out and knowing that Russborough is no longer just for us.'

In writing to thank me for giving him lunch in the Gallery, the architectural historian, Gervase Jackson-Stops, recorded his astonishment at seeing this and wrote (30 June 1982): 'We got to Russborough just in time to find the Beits queueing up with a tray at their own self-serve tea counter.'

Even on my first encounter with Alfred Beit under the watchful countenance of The Hon Rose Talbot, I found him to be very human, open, and lively company. He was, it goes without saying, inordinately wealthy and his collection of Old Master paintings was one of the very finest in existence. His wealth came from South African diamonds; his collection originated with his Uncle Alfred who died in 1906 and it had descended to Sir Alfred by way of his father, Otto, who died in 1930.

The first Alfred Beit had joined the Hamburg office of a firm of South African merchants, Lippert & Co, in the 1870s and in 1874 he spent a year in Amsterdam where he learned the diamond business. In 1875, he sailed for Capetown and became one of Lippert's representatives at Kimberley, returning to Hamburg in 1878. He had spotted that Cape diamonds, far from being the inferior products they were assumed to be, were as good as any in the world; and, borrowing £2000 from his father, he returned to Kimberley and set up his own diamond company dealing with diamonds, diamond shares and gold. In 1888, he made London his headquarters. Apart from diamonds, Beit's fortune also derived from gold mining in the Transvaal. When he died at the age of fifty-three in 1906, he left over £2m to charities in England, Germany and South Africa.

From 1888, with the advice of the distinguished Director of the Kaiser-Friedrich-Museum in Berlin, Dr Wilhelm Bode, Beit formed his art collection; and in 1895 moved the collection to the house he built at 26 Park Lane, London. Many of his purchases, such as the series by Murillo, the Hobbema, the pair by Metsu, the van Ruisdael and the Jan Steen came from English country-house collections and were acquired through established London dealers such as Agnew and Colnaghi but others were purchased elsewhere. The Vermeer first surfaced (in modern times) in 1881 when it was with the Paris dealer, Sedelmeyer, and it was bought by Alfred Beit from another dealer in Paris (Kleinberger) in about 1900.

On inheriting the pictures, Beit's brother, Otto, augmented the collection further with masterpieces by Goya, Velázquez (possibly bought from Hugh Lane), Gainsborough, Raeburn and Frans Hals and at this time the paintings hung at his home, 49 Belgrave Square. It was still there when Sir Alfred inherited but was soon moved by him to the mansion which he purchased on Kensington Palace Gardens. Sir Alfred in his time sold some paintings, but nothing of great import, and when he did so (as he explained) he always replaced them with other works:

> 'A sterling rule to observe when selling works of art', he wrote,[9] 'if you do not actually need the money for living purposes, is to replace immediately by buying other works of art more to your own taste'.

By this means, the large Oudry in the hall at Russborough today was purchased by Sir Alfred after he and Lady Beit came to live in Ireland.

After my initial meeting with the Beits at Rosie Talbot's dinner, I was not to meet them again until I came to Dublin as director of the gallery.

In my first months, while I met the Beits at numerous social events, I was never invited to Russborough. And then, in about October (I had taken up office in June), Lady Beit rang me one day at the Gallery, quite out of the blue. After a very few preliminary remarks, she came to the point.

'Homan, Alfred and I have been conferring and we would both adore it if you would come and stay with us at Russborough for Christmas. We do so much hope you will come. There will be other guests as well.'

I was more than surprised by the call. I didn't feel I really knew the Beits, they had never entertained me up to this, and an invitation to stay, and for Christmas, left me more in shock than in awe. Coming from anyone else, I would have looked upon the summons as rather forward. Lady Beit knew nothing of my family situation, but she would have known that Christmas was a family time and that I was likely to be committed to a family Christmas. As it happened I wasn't: my mother, who had lots of other family, had for many years excused my absence at Christmas which I was accustomed to spending in Rome staying with Speer. As it was only October, I had not given any particular thought to my Christmas plans that year but I knew that I would be staying privately in London and that there was no question of my making any other arrangement. And so, I thanked Lady Beit for her kindness and said no.[10]

I did not know that it is unacceptable to turn down an invitation from royalty and, while the Beits were not royalty, they may have considered themselves – in the absence of many other challengers for the role – royalty in Ireland. By saying 'no' to Lady Beit's invitation, therefore, I committed the most tremendous *faux-pas*. And I was not forgiven. They were always very friendly to me but it was not until my final weeks in the Gallery eight years later that I was ever bidden socially to Russborough. I may not have missed very much. When Cecil Beaton dined with the Beits in London (in August 1968), he wrote:[11]

> Never has a more boring evening been endured by ten
> elderly people. I could think of nothing interesting to ask

anyone throughout the wasteful evening. The twenty eggs, the chicken and tarragon, and raspberries had been cooked in vain. The bills for decor might as well not have been incurred. Poor Alfred, he is so kind and nice, Clem too, but ouch! the emptiness.

When I was, at last, invited to Russborough it was to a small informal dinner. It was given in my honour – as Lady Beit said in a little speech – to thank me for what I had done for them. It was eight years after my Christmas tactlessness: had I been forgiven? Or, had I really done something for which the Beits felt they owed me some thanks?

When I worked, in a very junior capacity, in the Dublin Gallery in the years 1971–73, the Beit pictures were brought into the Gallery each winter and hung there for the several months of the Beits' annual absence in South Africa. There was very little fuss made about the pictures and no particular precautions taken in respect of security, either on their transport to and from Russborough or while they were in the Gallery. It didn't seem relevant. Some few lectures would be given about the paintings, by myself as well as others; and as Russborough was not at that stage open to the public, those Gallery visitors who were interested (and informed) enough to appreciate such magnificent treasures took advantage of the opportunity afforded by the Gallery showing. But hordes of visitors to see the Beit Pictures there certainly were not; and indeed I would surmise that the vast majority of the Irish public had neither heard of the Beits or their Pictures, and nor did they care.

All of that changed – and changed dramatically – on 27 April 1974. That night, a young woman speaking with a French accent knocked on the door of Russborough and, speaking through the door, requested assistance with her broken-down car. When the door was opened, three masked men armed with AK-47 rifles stormed in and ordered the butler's son to guide them to the library where Alfred and Clementine were quietly listening to music. The intruders tied them up with stockings, dragged Lady Beit down to the basement, and shouted at the 71-year-old Sir Alfred that he was 'a capitalist pig'. Thereafter, Lady Beit's reminiscence that the Goya was 'special to her for a particular reason' – Sir Alfred's marriage proposal – had to be amended: it was 'special to her for two reasons'. As she was bundled down the stairs, she glanced back at Alfred, bound and gagged and crouched under the Goya; and she believed at that moment that it was the last time she would ever see him.

'I was convinced that, like the unfortunate Romanovs, I was to be shot in the cellar,' she would say.

Within minutes, nineteen paintings had been selected by the young woman – a British upper-class heiress, Bridget Rose Dugdale, who had joined the IRA – removed from their frames, and taken away in the back of a Ford Cortina. A ransom demand was subsequently received from the IRA. The paintings were found, in a cottage rented by Dugdale in County Cork, a week later. The theft, one of the greatest art robberies of all time, attracted worldwide headlines; Bridget Rose Dugdale's name became known to everyone, and has remained so. The Beits' ordeal at the hands of the thieves elicited a sympathy for them among the Irish public that their privileged lives would otherwise have denied them; and the Beit Pictures achieved a renown – and a following – that their annual display in the National Gallery of Ireland had never managed to engender, not even remotely. The Beits themselves revelled in their new-found notoriety and talked willingly about the robbery to anyone who would listen. It became Lady Beit's party piece, perfected by being told so often, and very entertaining. 'I said to the Garda...' (pronounced as Gaw-r-daw) '... such a very nice Gaw-r-daw'. As celebrities, the couple were even interviewed on national television by Gay Byrne.

As to Bridget Rose Dugdale, she was convicted, sentenced to nine years, and sent to Limerick Jail where she gave birth to a son, the child of her lover and accomplice in the Beit raid, Eddie Gallagher (whom she later married, also in Limerick Jail). The writer, Ferdinand Mount, knew Rose Dugdale both as a child and as a debutante and was 'fond of her'. He said as much to the Beits when he ran into them subsequent to the robbery.[12]

'Oh dear,' Sir Alfred replied, 'that's what everyone says. You must forgive me if I cannot entirely share your opinion.'

As a coda to the story of the Dugdale raid, I have a personal recollection. One day when I was director of the gallery (11 July 1982 to be precise) I popped into the gallery shop.

Today, being a Saturday, I worked in the Gallery as usual. Talking to the men behind the counter, I thought I saw Bridget Rose Dugdale with her son. As she was standing at the counter, an American woman came up and asked the assistant if the Vermeer, of which there was a print for sale in the shop, was on show. Embarrassedly (for he too had recognised Dugdale), he said no and that it was in a private collection. Which collection? The Beit Collection. Where is that? Near Dublin. Is it possible to get in to see it? Yes. Where exactly is it? And so on . . . All the time Miss Dugdale was listening and the poor assistant, Matt Crowe, acutely discomfited. Dugdale then bought a Gallery catalogue, surveyed the collection of Beit prints that were for sale, and left.

It might have been expected that the Beits would have become disenchanted with Ireland following their trauma and frightened to remain in the beautiful, but isolated, home which experience had shown them to be very vulnerable. But neither rancour nor fear were part of the Beits vocabulary and, instead of moving back to London (where they had a home), they stayed on. More than that, they made plans to open Russborough to the public and established (in 1976) the Alfred Beit Foundation as a means of achieving that aim.

Liz Shannon, the wife of the American Ambassador in Dublin at the time, Bill Shannon, recorded in her diary.[13]

> August 4, 1978. We drove out to Blessington this evening to Russborough House, the home of Sir Alfred and Lady Beit. Tonight the Beits gave Russborough and its contents to the Irish Nation. In a very moving ceremony which took place on a small, makeshift platform in the hall, Sir Alfred, tall, distinguished and handsome, stood next to his wife, whose white hair framed her strikingly beautiful face and deep blue eyes. Each of them made a short and eloquent speech about the house, its contents, and their plans for opening it up to the public. Then Sir Alfred handed the Taoiseach, Mr Lynch,

a white envelope which presumably had in it the official document containing the legalities of the gift.

I do not know what could have been in the white envelope which Sir Alfred gave to Jack Lynch that evening but it was certainly not a deed gifting Russborough and its contents to the Nation. Liz Shannon, like many people in Ireland, even to this day, was mistaken. The Beits gifted Russborough to the Alfred Beit Foundation which is an independent body with no official ties to the Irish State. It has a board of Trustees but no Government official sits *ex-officio* on that board which is made up of representatives of the National Gallery, the RDS, the universities, the Irish Georgian Society, An Taisce and other bodies. As to the contents, relatively few (if any) were transferred to the Foundation at that time and certainly none of the more important pictures. This is not to deny the Beits' generosity: making Russborough over to an independent foundation as a means of opening the house to the public was a very generous act but it was not a gift to the Nation. And *The Beit Pictures* – the cream of the collection – remained firmly the property of Sir Alfred.

It is very unlikely that the Beits ever considered making Russborough over to the State. They were old friends of Derek Hill, who had long planned to present his home in Donegal and its interesting (but very modest by Beit standards) collection to the nation. By 1974 when, following the robbery, the Beits would have been thinking about the future of Russborough, Sir Alfred wrote to Derek after the latter had been staying at Russborough:[14]

> I was amazed to learn that [your] proposed gift to the Government has been on the go for eleven years. In my opinion this means that they can no longer be taken seriously – especially as we now have a different Government. I would abandon the idea myself...and sell St Columb's'.

Clementine told Derek more bluntly that the Government had no money and that he might go on for another eleven years 'with them playing blind man's buff with you – no matter who you see & talk to, be it a minister or the Holy Ghost'. The Beits were not the sort of people to wait around for anyone for eleven years and so they planned their Foundation independent of any government involvement.

I do not believe that the Beits deliberately conveyed the impression that Russborough was a gift to the Nation: guile and mendacity were not in their nature. It was simply a misunderstanding that took root in the public imagination.

When I was an assistant keeper at the London National Gallery in the 1970s, I was privy to certain confidential documents. One of these, which would be taken out and discussed and possibly amended at curatorial meetings from time-to-time was called *The Desiderata List*. This was a schedule, relatively short, of old master paintings in historic British collections which the gallery deemed desirable in the event of their ever being sold; and the director would periodically write to the owners expressing the gallery's interest and outlining the tax advantages for an owner selling directly to the gallery. The list was divided into 'Category A' – essential – and 'Category B' – worthy and hoped-for. Prominent under 'Category A' were a number of pictures from the Beit Collection: the Vermeer and the two by Metsu for a start, also the Goya, the Velázquez, the Steen and the Ruisdael, and others as well. When I scrutinised this list I had no doubt where my loyalties lay, although I never voiced my view. I thought it was a damn cheek – and dangerous to Ireland's interests – for the London National Gallery to list any Beit pictures as *desiderata*. The Beit pictures were, as far as I was concerned, Ireland's pictures.

There was another complication of which I also became aware. It was believed in certain Establishment art circles in Britain that, when the Beits moved to South Africa in 1946 or 1947 taking the pictures with them, they had not necessarily complied with the appropriate export regulations. Michael Levey told me this on more than one occasion, both when I was in London and after I became director in Dublin.

Knowing all this, I was determined when I came to the Dublin gallery that, even if I achieved nothing else, I would secure the Beit Pictures permanently for Ireland and that the only definitive way of achieving this – Beit Foundation and Russborough notwithstanding – would be to have them donated to the National Gallery.

I was surprised to find, over my first year or so in Dublin, that nobody seemed to know precisely what Sir Alfred's intentions were with regard to the pictures. Was he going to bequeath them to the Foundation, to the National Gallery of Ireland, to London, or even to South Africa? Did he even personally own them or were they already tied up in some trust? James White told me that there was a list in the drawer of the director's desk, and so there was. But it was just a list, possibly in Sir Alfred's hand, with no indication as to why the list had been compiled or what it meant. Eventually, I came to the conclusion that nothing had been decided about the future of the pictures and that the way was open for me to act. And the only way to act was to ask the Beits directly what their intentions were. But how?

Russborough had been built by Joseph Leeson, First Earl of Milltown, in the 1740s and lived in by his descendants until the early-twentieth century. It had housed the collections – paintings, furnishings and artefacts – which Leeson, and subsequently his son, had acquired, mainly in Italy, on the Grand Tour. In 1902, the last Countess of Milltown presented the contents of the house, including the picture collection, to the National Gallery of Ireland. I thought it would be a wonderful idea for the Gallery to re-hang Russborough as it had been in the eighteenth century. This could have been readily done as the Gallery had all the Milltown pictures and much of the furniture. More to the point it would free up the Beit Collection which, as a fair exchange, could then come to the Gallery. I thought of putting this proposal to the Beits. But, when I mulled it over, I realised that the Beits would not at all care for the idea of their house, their love-affair, becoming – once again – a Milltown house and that I was unlikely to succeed in persuading them otherwise. I needed to think again.

I decided to sound out Bill Finlay. When the Beit Foundation was set up, James White as director of the gallery was asked to sit ex-officio on the board. When he announced his retirement as director (and before I took up office), his place on the Beit board was taken by Bill Finlay. I did not mind about this in the least. I hated sitting on committees and the opportunity to develop a closer rapport and friendship with the Beits mattered a great deal more to Bill than it did to me. One day, I said to Bill, 'You know, it seems to me that nobody has any idea as to what is to become of the Beit Pictures. Do you know anything?'

He admitted he didn't but that he 'was now taking a great interest in the Beit Foundation'.

I then said that it had crossed my mind to actually ask the Beits outright.

Bill became alarmed.

'Don't attempt to do any such thing,' he said, 'Alfred might be very offended. Let me turn it over in my mind. I might take soundings.'

I could see that Bill's reasoning was sound but, in spite of that, I had no intention of paying the slightest heed to it.

I decided instead to speak to Terence de Vere White. As I had got to know Terence more, I found him to be sensitive and sensible, kind, fey, warm (in spite of a shy reserve) and he and his wife, the biographer Victoria Glendinning, had gone out of their way to show friendship towards me. They would invite me to their home when I was in London and I found that I was (to an extent) able to open my heart to them. Terence, who knew about art and had been a collector all his life, was astute and wise and he had the ability to give the sort of advice one did not always want to hear, but without causing offence. Furthermore, being a novelist, he had a developed understanding of human nature.

And so, I took the subject of the Beit Pictures to Terence. At that stage, I was still of a mind to propose to the Beits the Milltown exchange plan. Terence, without a moment's hesitation, thought it a marvellous idea. He said to me that 'from his experience in life, an idea put to old people by someone young like you could immediately appeal to them'. He added that I should take the bull by the horns and ask the Beits directly. This was what I wanted to hear.

On reflection, I felt I needed to address the subject with the Beits when they were on home ground, informal and relaxed, as it were, with little fear of distraction and to that end I had to plan to go to Russborough. One day after a board meeting, I mentioned to Sir Alfred that I was interested in augmenting the gallery's library and that if he had any old Sotheby's or Christie's auction catalogues or back issues of art magazines, they would be very welcome if he wanted to part with them. He was immediately receptive and suggested that I come down to Russborough one day when he was there and select what I wanted. On 5 August 1982, in the afternoon, I drove down. As this was an encounter which I knew I would want to remember, even if it resulted in my being thrown out the door, I wrote an account of it afterwards for myself.

> I arrived and Lady Beit (as though she was ushering a small boy back to the nursery) said to Alfred, 'Now, Alfred you go and sort the catalogues with Homan and then come back and we'll all have tea.'
>
> Alfred and I worked through the catalogues on the library floor and then came back.
>
> 'Alfred, do you think I can put my theory to Homan about the Velázquez?' said Lady Beit.
>
> I was taken to the Velázquez and told, yet again, about it being cleaned and the scene of the *Supper at Emmaus* being uncovered in the top left corner.
>
> Then Lady Beit's theory.
>
> 'You see, if you look closely, the apostle on the left can only been seen by his right hand,' she said. 'Now why would Velázquez not have put him in complete? I feel that the frame may conceal part of him. But how can we find out?'
>
> I suggested that one might take the picture out of its frame.
>
> 'But could we do that? Would it be safe? Of course, Rose Dugdale took all the pictures out of their frames, but could we?'
>
> I explained to her how the frame was placed on the picture. She didn't listen and we came back to Sir Alfred and she told him, and me, again about her theory without wanting to hear how the riddle might be solved.
>
> At tea, I felt nervous but I was also calm. I understood perfectly that if I asked for the pictures they could both take great offence and I would be finished. I led round to the subject and eventually got Sir Alfred to volunteer that, after their deaths, the pictures were left to the Foundation. Step one completed. I now knew what I believed no one else had found out. Step two. I raised the subject of the special association between the gallery and the Foundation based on the personal contacts and affection that existed

towards the Beits in the gallery. But I warned that, when they are dead and gone and the gallery is in different hands, such an association might not prevail. I mentioned that it was so important that the Foundation would always be able to call on the expertise of the gallery in conservation and other matters and, eventually, I ventured that perhaps the association might be given some more solid basis. They were now gripped and wanted to hear more. It was going well. I then veered off this line and moved in the direction of the uncertainty of people's wills being carried out the way they had intended. Alfred jumped in with a story demonstrating how true this was. I nodded my head in agreement. Lady Beit began to go silent. I then spoke of the future of the Foundation and the cost, in the very distant future, of supporting it. Alfred volunteered 'indeed yes. Even already it was costing much more than they had envisaged – the re-wiring had to be done, etc.' I said it would be dreadful if in future any of the pictures had to be sold to pay for the wiring and the roof.[15] I then painted a worse case scenario: in a hundred years' time, I conjectured, all the pictures sold, no funds to support the Foundation, its being disbanded, and the name Beit commemorated no more. An air of deep thought and alarm spread across Lady Beit's serene face.

We moved to the drawing room and I then made as though the conversation was ended and asked their forgiveness for my impertinence in raising such a very private matter with them. But, like hounds on the scent, their appetites were whetted, they wanted more and pressed me to talk on. I couldn't believe how well it was going. I sat down.

'What can we do?' they chorused.

Now was my moment. And I said straight out that if the pictures were bequeathed to the gallery (with the provision that the gallery could exhibit them at Russborough, I added as a sop), they could never be sold as they would be protected by the Act of Parliament by which the gallery was established. There was no other way to ensure that the Beit Collection would be, for ever and ever, the Beit Collection.

Lady Beit did not talk again for some time and I began to wonder if I had overstepped the mark. But Sir Alfred was taken by the idea and we talked on. Eventually, Lady Beit was aroused from her thoughts.

'But Alfred, should we not make the whole Foundation over to the gallery?'

My stratagems, cruel though they might have been, had led to more than I wanted. To introduce the Foundation into the equation would mean discussion with the Foundation trustees, possible argument, and as a result my goal might never be achieved. So I told them firmly that the gallery would not be legally entitled to take over the Foundation. Next, Lady Beit said, 'Do you think we should talk with Bill (Finlay)?'

'Oh! dear no,' I said to myself.

I knew that Bill's involvement at this stage could muddy the waters while he took time 'to turn things over in his mind and take soundings'. I wanted discussions to remain for the moment between the Beits and me. But I had to think quickly.

'At this stage,' I said, 'I feel it is a purely a matter for your professional advisers, your solicitors and accountants. It's for them to assure you that such a gift (I used the word 'gift' for the first time) or bequest could be made. Bill is a trustee of the Foundation and also a governor of the gallery. He might perceive a conflict of interest. To be involved would make him uncomfortable, I feel sure.'

'Homan is right,' said Sir Alfred. 'We'll take it to London and work it out.'

They then thanked me profusely, begged that they might discuss it further with me, and I left the house two hours after arriving, well pleased.

Reading this account now, for the first time in more than thirty years, I am not entirely sure that I feel completely proud of myself. Yes, I frightened the Beits, but that is what I had been intent on doing. But Lady Beit, at least, must have been happy with the discussion and she must have told people in later years that it was I who suggested the gift to the Gallery. Her obituary in the *Daily Telegraph* mentions that I 'tactfully suggested that ... the handover to the nation should take place.'[16]

The official history of the Gallery[17] records that 'for a long time the Beits hesitated'. They didn't. Sir Alfred telephoned me a few days later to say that they were very taken by the idea but could I just confirm that the gallery had the power to exhibit pictures, indefinitely, in a location other than the gallery.

'Of course,' I said, 'the 1963 National Gallery of Ireland Act permits us to do so. We have pictures on indefinite loan to Irish embassies the world over. There would be no problem with Russborough.'

Sir Alfred made a list of the paintings he intended to give, seventeen in all. The cream of the Collection including the Vermeer and the two by Metsu, Lady Beit's favourite Goya and her problematic Velázquez, the magnificent *Castle of Bentheim* by Jacob van Ruisdael, Hobbema's *Wooded Landscape* and *The Marriage Feast at Cana* by Jan Steen. Only one picture, the Frans Hals *Lute Player*, had a small question mark hang over its attribution: it is thought by some to be by Judith Leyster. Gainsborough's *Cottage Girl*, a Raeburn, and Murillo's rare series telling the story of 'The Prodigal Son' topped off the list.

My Diary records that I met with the Beits again three weeks later (25 August 1982) when Sir Alfred told me that, as there were a number of considerations to be taken into account as to how the gift would be made vis-à-vis his own affairs, his solicitors and accountants had advised him that the formalities were likely to take some time. And some time they did take: years, to be precise. But all was not plain sailing. In my diary for 23 May 1983, I noted:

> I hear from Alfred Beit that he cannot gift his pictures to the gallery. He would be liable for tax in the UK and in Ireland. The pictures must remain forever the property of his estate.
>
> I am bitterly disappointed.

It was not until two years later that I heard more. On 1 November 1984, I met the Beits together with their solicitor, Paul Guinness, and it was presumably at that meeting that I was told of the trusts that would need to be created in order to facilitate the gift. I consulted the gallery solicitor, William Earley of Mc Cann Fitzgerald (9 November 1984), and reported back to Paul Guinness on 13 November.

It would have been at this time that I first informed Bill Finlay of what was to take place, the magnificent gift that was to come to the Gallery, and the arrangements that were being proposed. Thereafter, Bill was fully involved (as he had to be) and in late-1985 he and I met several times (15 October and 12 December 1985) with William Earley to plan the trust which the Gallery would be required to set up.

Admired and liked by the Beits, and as Chairman of the Governors and Guardians and on the board of the Beit Foundation, Bill's involvement reassured them that they had made a wise decision. I also needed Bill's participation because, as director, I did not have the authority to accept the proposed arrangements. These involved the setting up (by the Beits) of an English charitable foundation to which the Beits first gave the pictures; and it is my recollection that this foundation was required to hold the paintings for some time before donating them to an Irish trust, the Argus Trust, the trustees of which were the Director and Chairman of the National Gallery of Ireland and (at that time) Sir Alfred. The purpose of the Argus Trust, which was formally established in May 1986, is

> to provide for the acquisition of works of art for public exhibition in Ireland and exhibit these works in the National Gallery of Ireland or elsewhere in Ireland as may be agreed between the Trustees and the Governors and Guardians.

Initially, and as a test to ensure that the trust arrangements which the Beits' advisors had put in place would be accepted by the tax authorities, only one painting, Jan Steen's *Marriage Feast at Cana*, was transferred to the Argus Trust. That was in May 1986 and then, in November that year the further sixteen paintings which were destined for the gallery were transferred. Under the terms of the Argus Trust, its trustees (myself, Bill and Sir Alfred) had to formally apply to the Governors and Guardians to procure the exhibition of the paintings in the Gallery and the governors and guardians had to formally accept them for exhibition. It was in this convoluted way, when the Argus trustees petitioned the governors and guardians at their meeting in December 1987, that the governors and guardians were first made aware that, in essence, the Beit paintings – the cream of the collection – were being presented to the Gallery.

It had, as far as I was concerned, been a long road but I could not have known at the time that there would be further obstacles to overcome.

Endnotes

1. Mentmore in Buckinghamshire was built in the 1850s for Baron Mayer de Rothschild to house his fabulous art collections and descended on his death to the Earls of Roseberry. In one of the greatest art auctions of the late-twentieth century, the contents were auctioned over several days by Sotheby's in 1977. The sale attracted enormous international interest and was viewed by museum and art trade experts from all over the world; but it was only the dealer David Carritt who recognised that the painting of *Psyche*, catalogued as Carl van Loo, was by Fragonard. The episode goes some way to explaining how I could have failed to recognise the Dublin Caravaggio.
2. James Lees-Milne, *Deep Romantic Chasm: Diaries 1979–1981* (2000).
3. Sir Alfred's elder brother committed suicide, aged 18, in 1917. John Mulcahy, 'The Enigmatic Alfred Beit', *Irish Arts Review*, vol 32, no 3 (2015). Referring to William Laffan & Kevin V. Mulligan, *Russborough, A Great Irish House, its Families and Collections* (2014).
4. Nicholas Haslam, *Redeeming Features: a Memoir* (2009).
5. *The Independent*, 14 May 1994.
6. Mary S. Lovell, *The Mitford Girls* (2001).
7. Deborah Devonshire, *Wait for Me! Memoirs of the Youngest Mitford Sister* (2010).
8. Lees-Milne, *Deep Romantic Chasm* (2000).
9. Foreword to the Exhibition Catalogue, *National Gallery of Ireland Acquisitions 1986–1988* (1988).
10. It seems that other invitees might also have said 'no' as the Russborough *Visitors' Book* records no guests at Russborough that Christmas. Thanks to Robert O'Byrne who consulted the Russborough Visitors' Book for me.
11. *Beaton in the Sixties: the Cecil Beaton Diaries* (2003).
12. Ferdinand Mount, *Cold Cream: my early life and other mistakes* (2008).

13. Elizabeth Shannon, *Up in the Park: The Diary of the Wife of the American Ambassador to Ireland, 1977–81* (1983).

14. B. Arnold, *Derek Hill* (2010).

15. My words, uttered and written down by me in 1982, proved to be prophetic and my warning was justified. In December 2006 sixty-two bronzes which had been gifted to the Foundation were sold at Christie's for £3.8 million; and in November 2013 twenty items of porcelain were sold at Sotheby's for £1.2 million. As I write (in June 2015) eight Old Master paintings, the property of the Foundation have been sent for sale to Christie's.

16. *Daily Telegraph*, 1 September 2005.

17. Peter Somerville-Large, *1854–2004: The Story of the National Gallery of Ireland*, (2004).

CHAPTER 18
MIDNIGHT NEAR MOONE

Sir Alfred Beit was 79 at the time that I asked him to present his Collection to the Gallery. During the time it took for him and his advisers to make the necessary arrangements to effect the gift, I feared, with the advancing years, that all could be lost. The Grim Reaper was lurking in the shadows. As it happened, he wasn't the only one. Martin Cahill, Dublin's most notorious criminal, went to Russborough in the early hours of Thursday 22 May 1986 and stole eighteen of the pictures. The haul included the Vermeer, the two paintings by Gabriel Metsu and the Goya, all four of which were to be included in the gift to the gallery.

Lord Kilbracken was given to writing pithy letters to *The Irish Times* in these years and he penned his response to the second Russborough robbery. 'To paraphrase Oscar,' he wrote, 'to lose a Vermeer may be regarded as a misfortune; to lose it twice seems like carelessness.'

And there was an element of carelessness to this second robbery. Cahill had paid several visits to Russborough as a paying member of the public in the preceding weeks: did he – one wonders – queue, and pay, for tea and scones alongside the Beits? On the night in question, he approached the house with his gang across the fields from the north side. He cut a small piece out of a pane of glass in the French doors, which allowed him to force open the shutters on the inside. He stepped inside, activated the alarm, and promptly stepped out again. The alarm was connected to the local Garda station. By coincidence, a Garda car was no more than a mile from Russborough at the time and, within minutes, they were at the house where they were met by the administrator, Colonel O'Shea. O'Shea (alone) went and checked the room where the alarm had been activated, said he saw nothing and, on the assumption that the alarm was faulty, turned it off. The Gardaí left and O'Shea went back to bed. Cahill, who can only have been just outside, came back into the house and within six minutes had taken his haul. Later that night he dumped seven of the paintings near Blessington Lake: the remaining eleven he placed in an underground bunker which he had constructed during the preceding weeks in the woods not far from the house. There the majority of them remained for seven years, although one Metsu found its way to Turkey, the Vermeer and the Goya to an attic in the Dublin suburb of Tallaght. In June 1993 Cahill moved all the pictures through London (where two were stolen from him) to Antwerp and on to a bank vault in Luxembourg. All were recovered by police in Antwerp in September 1993.

Cahill, who was familiarly referred to as 'The General', was not just notorious: his appearance was widely known to the Irish public because, in an 'only-in-Ireland' episode, he had been interviewed by a reporter, Brendan O'Brien, on prime-time television. Wearing a distinctive hooded green anorak as disguise, he was stopped on the street by O'Brien and, knowing that he was on camera, he responded – albeit evasively – to the reporter's questions. It was truly bizarre. The painter Tom Ryan satirised the incident in a witty cartoon which he kindly gave me. Captioned *The Chairman of the Board of Governors and Guardians introducing an important military visitor to the Director of the National Gallery of Ireland circa 1988*, it showed me with 'the General' (in his signature anorak) and some few Beit paintings in the background. Above them a notice pinned to the wall: 'Beit Collection: What's Left'.

The story of the recovery of the Beit Paintings is not my story.[1] I had retired as director, and left the gallery and Ireland, two years after the paintings were stolen. But, among the several false trails pursued over the years by police in Ireland and internationally, in their attempts to find the paintings, I had my adventures too and, for the most part, I wrote notes.

> Wednesday 23 July 1986. Royal Wedding Day. (It was Andrew & Sarah Ferguson this time). The gallery was somewhat disrupted as someone had brought in a TV and most of the staff (with my approval) were watching the

events in London. I had to record a programme for RTÉ in the morning. Janet Drew (my secretary) had taken the day off so my mail remained unopened all day. At about five in the afternoon, finding myself with nothing else to do, I opened one or two letters. The third letter I came to was addressed in childish capital letters and looked like the sort of letter we receive when someone is looking for a job as a gallery attendant. I opened it and started to read. Before I had read very far, I realised it was a ransom demand for the Beit pictures. This fact took a moment to sink in. I immediately dropped the letter onto the desk for fear of adding my fingerprints to the paper. After I had read the letter, I re-read it. 'To Mr Potterton, Director': they got my name right. The demand was for £25,000 in return for which Goya's *Portrait of Doña Antonia Zárate* would be returned. I was to deposit the money the following night at twelve midnight in a barrel which was placed in the hedge beside an auction sign (J.P. McDonagh and Sons) on the side of the road six miles beyond Kilcullen, County Kildare. The letter threatened that I was not to inform the Gardaí or my life would be in danger and that I was dealing with a professional gang who were armed.

My first reaction was to ring Bill Finlay. He was on the point of leaving Dublin for his fishing retreat in Mayo. I told him that it was my instinct that I should contact the Gardaí and did he agree? He said yes. I then rang the Inspector (Moore) in charge of the Beit robbery and told him that I needed to see him. He said he would not be in his office tomorrow but I stressed that I needed to see him immediately but did not want to come to his office and neither did I want him to come to me. We arranged to meet at six that evening in the Aisling Hotel, near the Phoenix Park. I asked the Assistant Director, Raymond Keaveney, to come to my office and I showed him the letter: he was as shocked as I. I placed the letter and the envelope in a cellophane folder so that they could be read without being touched and I xeroxed them. I set off for the Aisling, but with a wary eye in case I was being watched and followed.

TO MR. POTTERTON.
      DIRECTOR,
WE WILL RETURN ONE
OF THE BEIT PAINTINGS
IN RETURN FOR CASH
PAYMENT, THE PAINTING
WE WILL RETURN IS
DONA ANTONIA ZARATE
BY GOYA, FOR £25,000,
IN CASH. WHEN WE
GET THE MONEY YOU
WILL BE TOLD BY
LETTER WHERE YOU
WILL GET THE PAINTING
ON THE MAIN ROAD
BETWEEN KILCULLEN
AND CARLOW YOU WILL
SEE AN AUCTION SIGN

ON THE LEFT HAND
SIDE OF THE ROAD,
ABOUT 4 MILES BEYOND
KILCULLEN. THE MONEY
SHOULD BE PLACED IN
A RUSTY DRUM AT THAT
SPOT. IT IS A RED
AUCTION SIGN BY J.
P. MC DONAGH, AND SONS.
THE MONEY MUST NOT
BE MARKED OR
RECORDED.

AND ON NO ACCOUNT MUST
THE GARDA OR SECURITY
BE INFORMED. IF ANY
ATTEMPT IS MADE WE WILL
KNOW. AND YOUR LIFE
AND THE LIVES OF OTHERS
WILL BE IN DANGER.
YOU ARE DEALING WITH
PROFESSIONALS, AND WE HAVE
THE MANPOWER, AND EQUIPMENT
TO DEAL WITH ALL OCCASIONS.
THE MONEY SHOULD BE PLACED
AT SAID SPOT ON THURSDAY
NIGHT 24TH JULY, AT 12.00
MIDNIGHT. THIS IS TO LET
YOU SEE WE HAVE THE
PAINTINGS SAFE AND IN
GOOD CONDITION.

MR. H. POTTERTON
NATIONAL GALLERY,
MERRION SQUARE,
      W. 2.
      DUBLIN

I met Moore and his assistant, Phil Sheridan, and handed them a magazine in which I had concealed the folder: he immediately started to take it out of the folder until I stopped him. His initial reaction was that the letter was genuine. He then told me that they knew who had stolen the Beit paintings but that they did not know where the paintings were and that there was no point in making an arrest as then they would never find the pictures. I said that my reaction to the letter was that I should not deposit the £25,000 but that I had to reply and ask for some proof that the sender had possession of the pictures. Agreeing with me, they said they would have a conference the next morning and come back to me.

That evening, I had supper, alone, with a close friend, Desiree Shortt. I told her, without saying what, that I was in a state about something and that if the occasion arose, would she be prepared to let me meet with some people in her house without her asking me what it was about? I had in mind any future meetings with Moore and Sheridan. She did not hesitate for a moment. 'Of course,' she said, and asked no more.

Desiree Shortt was an exotic bloom in the garden that was Dublin Society. (I write in the past tense as my story is in the past tense but she is still very much in the present.) About a decade or so older than me she had in the six years or so that I had known her, become a close, and always entertaining, friend. Her daily life was, as a rule, peppered with incident; and drama was second nature to her. She could be challengingly indiscreet and sharp in her observations but, as a contradiction – one of many – she was very loyal and, if asked to keep a confidence, could be relied upon to do so. A fall from her horse on the hunting-field had led her to pursue the profession of china-restorer, in which she had achieved renown; but her passion was the enormous eighteenth-century house in the inner city which she had purchased on a whim many years previously. It had once been the home of the Provost of Trinity College, John Pentland Mahaffy, but had suffered over the ensuing decades the indignity of becoming a tenement. When

Desiree purchased it, twenty-seven souls lived there in quarters partitioned out of the noble upstairs rooms and sharing between them a single lavatory. Desiree, as chatelaine, was obliged to live in the basement. But very soon she managed to engage with most of her upstairs neighbours and many of them became her friends. She related to people from all walks of life. 'A Joan Collins in a Sean O'Casey world' is how one of her friends described her. Over the years the tenants gradually moved out and, as they did so, style and comfort began to seep up from Desiree's basement lair and rooms were restored to their original magnificence.

The ground floor rooms – a huge dining room and a *petit salon* to the front – were treated first. The latter was painted in a shade of Kerrygold and there, as a friend and at her request, I had hung in cascading patterns between dado-rail and ceiling, Desiree's collection of blue-and-white plates. The result was delightful, charming and, above all, opulent. A pair of wing-back armchairs flanking an Adam-esque chimneypiece indicated that the room was for living in and it was here that Desiree 'received'.

The following morning the Inspector telephoned me and said they would have to see me and I arranged to meet them at Desiree's at noon. They said that at their conference they had decided that the letter should be replied to in the way I suggested. Tentatively, they then asked me if I would be prepared to drop off the reply in the manner requested in the letter. I said I certainly was not keen on driving down into Kildare at midnight but that I would consider going at about eight when it would still be daylight.

Various possibilities were proposed such as my having a Garda concealed in the back of my car and general Garda cover. They asked for my fingerprints to be taken to distinguish them from other prints on the letter. They said they would confer and meet me back at Desiree's at four.

I now felt that I was being unfair to Desiree and that I should confide in her as to what I was involved in. Besides, as Bill Finlay was still in Mayo and more or less out of contact, I needed to talk to a friend even though I was able to discuss every step with Raymond, who is very sane and balanced. Desiree was horrified when I told her: horrified and very alarmed. She said that I would be mad to go anywhere near Kildare – that I would be walking straight into a kidnap situation – and that I should give the Gardaí my car and tell them to go and deliver the reply themselves. When I came back to the gallery, I consulted Raymond. Janet also knew about events by now as the Gardaí had placed a bug on my private gallery telephone line as a preliminary to my giving the number to the criminals. On reflection, I decided that I would agree to drive down to Kildare, but not in my own car, and that I would do so about six o'clock in the evening, during the rush hour. I went back to Desiree's at four and met the Inspector who said that they wanted me to go at midnight and that they would give me police cover from Kilcullen. I pointed out that I could easily be pulled out of my car before Kilcullen and that I wanted cover all the way and, additionally, some means of signalling if I was in danger. This was agreed. It was also agreed that I would leave from my own flat at 10.45 and that a Garda would come to the flat at 10.00 to wire me up with radio contact. I went home from Desiree's about 8.00.

I lived in a second-floor flat to the front of number 78 Merrion Square,[2] a house that was no more than 100 yards from the Gallery. A doctor and a dentist occupied the lower floors during the day, two young architects lived on the top floor, and an elderly man, Humphrey Langan, had a room on the same floor as me. At nights, the place was very quiet. A long overgrown garden stretched out to the rear leading to a dilapidated and unused mewshouse, which opened to a lane. There was a simple Yale lock – no more – on the hall door to Merrion Square, the same on the door to the garden, and the same again on the decaying door that led from the mews to the lane.

By arrangement I went out through the garden to the laneway beyond the mews at 10.00. The Garda was to be carrying a newspaper and a brown holdall and was to show me his identity. When he appeared, he was certainly not like any Garda I had ever seen: young and slight, with tangled curly black hair, a cheerful grinning face and dressed in an open-necked shirt with faded blue jeans, and white plimsolls. If this was a Garda undercover, undercover he certainly was. He told me during our subsequent conversation that even his girlfriend did not know how he was employed. I was not surprised. I brought him through the garden and up to my flat: I had earlier drawn the curtains. He told me that I was to have radio contact and he fitted it into my jacket: there was a radio receiver in my pocket and a microphone pinned to the inside. Then a wire came down through the sleeve to a button, which I was to keep in the palm of my hand and press before speaking. I had a receiver concealed in my ear. My code was Red 22 and his was to be 216. He then briefed me that I was to make contact at Newland's Cross, Naas and again in Kilcullen and that I was not to leave Kilcullen until precisely 11.45: if I was there before that, I was to wait. He told me that I would be followed all the way and that, in the event of there being any car at the assigned spot, I was to drive on. In case of an emergency, I was to come in on the radio with the code. I was to radio when I was leaving the flat. The young Garda left by the way he had come, through the garden, and I waited. When I left the flat at 10.45, I radioed and heard in return others radioing, 'he's off'.

I had been given an assigned route, along the canal and out the Naas road. I noticed some cars passing me and following me but it was difficult to be certain if they were the police or the criminals. The drivers never looked at me. As I made my way, some cars became familiar as they passed me more than once; and one, with only one headlight, was recognisable as was a Ford Fiesta driven by a woman with very long tousled hair and a man in the passenger seat. There was a great variety of cars: old and new. I gave the signals at Newland's Corner and Naas and arrived in Kilcullen at 11.35: it was further than I thought. I pulled in to wait, as instructed, till 11.45. When I pulled in, I noticed a lorry parked in front of me. After a few moments a man came along and went to the lorry. He opened the back of the lorry in a way that I could see in and I wondered if he was one of the criminals, and was I about to be given a glimpse of the paintings? He took a piece of paper out of the back of the lorry and walked towards me. I thought, is this it? Is this the letter that will tell me where the paintings are? He walked past my car and went into a telephone kiosk behind me. An innocent lorry driver making a late night phone call to his wife or girlfriend: no more.

At 11.45 precisely, I moved off and heard a voice in my ear say that I was now moving. The Gardaí had told me that the barrel and the auction sign were precisely 6.1 miles from Kilcullen so I set the milometre to zero. I took a deep breath and drove at about 45 miles per hour. I drove along and spotted the sign, drove past it per my instructions and then stopped and turned the car by backing into a laneway. I was fairly nervous by this stage and I then turned the car so that I was facing back towards Dublin, with the barrel on the opposite side of the road. A car came towards me and another from behind: I think both of these may have been garda cars, but they could have been the criminals. I fastened my jacket, took the panic button in my palm, and got out of the car with the letter when both cars had passed. I turned on the blinkers and left the headlights on, but dipped. I had instructions that I was to look in the barrel and see if there was a letter. I walked across the road quickly and looked in the barrel by tilting it towards my headlights: there was nothing in it. I left my letter, came back to the car, locked my door from the inside, and moved off ... at speed. In Naas a message came into my ear that I was to slow down: '216 to Red 22, come in.'

'Red 22 to 216, come in,' I replied.

'216 to Red 22, slow down.'

'Red 22 to 216, roger.'

I drove back to Dublin and on this drive only started to recognise the police cars as the same cars kept appearing but in the most unobvious way. I then realised for the first time the extent of the Garda cover. It was planned that I would come back to Desiree's where the Garda who had wired me up would de-wire me. As I drove down North Great George Street, Desiree's door opened and she was there. The Garda was already inside and had told her that I had arrived.

When the young Garda, in his blue jeans and plimsolls, arrived some twenty minutes before me, he was shown into Desiree's *petit salon*, ushered to one of the wing-backs, offered a whiskey (which he refused), and engaged in conversation by Desiree. He was soon captivated, and so was she by him. Without a moment's thought, she had shaken off her familiar mantle of Georgian conservationist and had espoused with enthusiasm the Freddie Forsyth world of *The Day of the Jackal*. The Garda told her that there had been eight Gardaí cars with me all the way. According to Desiree, he was very nervous and revealed that he had been involved in the Don Tidey kidnap shootout.[3]

As I arrived at Desiree's, further and unexpected dangers awaited me.

Opposite Desiree lived a gentlemen couple, Harold Clarke and Iain McLachlann, also friends of mine and rivals to Desiree in the cause of Georgian rehabilitation. Their house had been restored sumptuously. Harold was a bridge player and on the night in question his 'four' comprised more of my friends, Ann Fuller, Brian Coyle and Marcella Senior. Marcella was given to chatter and laughter; a more restrained ebullience – but an ebullience nonetheless – was the hallmark of Ann and Brian. That night, hours of conventions, rubbers and slams, several bottles of Jacob's Creek, and a superb dinner prepared by Iain had done little to exhaust the liveliness of all three as they exited Harold's at the very moment I was parking my car.

I saw what looked like several thugs loitering in the street but I was able by this time to conclude that they were part of the Task Force. It was one in the morning. I saw Marcella Senior come out and get into her car and, as I was parking mine, she pulled alongside for a chat. I could have killed her. Having given her short shrift, I got out and walked across the street to Desiree's. Harold followed me with Ann and Brian trailing him. I was terrified that the Gardaí, believing that the trio was a danger to me, would close in on them. I was also terrified that the three would embrace me, as would have been normal, and trigger the alarm concealed in my jacket. They wouldn't go away.

'What are you doing visiting Desiree at this hour of the morning?' they asked.

Eventually I got rid of them and Desiree let me in. The young Garda looked relieved when I came in and was generous enough to say that I had been a very brave man. He removed my radio, microphone and panic button and after a couple of moments went his way. I told Desiree all about the whole drive, she hung on every word and then, with all her instincts in the right place, made me ham sandwiches and gave me a whiskey. As I hadn't wanted to go back to my own flat, I had arranged with Desiree to stay with her. I suddenly felt very tired – apart from anything else, the drive down and back had been long – and asked to go to bed. I slept well.

The Inspector subsequently told me that the criminals had watched from a slope in a neighbouring field as I left the letter in the barrel and that they had picked it up immediately afterwards. It was a local gang, he said, centred on the village of Moone and known to the Gardaí and nothing to do with Martin Cahill.[4]

The letter I deposited in the barrel that night stated that I needed to see evidence that the recipients had the Beit pictures and to that end they should let me have a photograph of the paintings, which included the front page of a current newspaper. I also said that I wanted all nine paintings and to know the sum required for that. I suggested a drop-off point for future communications in the gardens of Merrion Square and I gave them my private Gallery telephone number with the instruction that, if they called, they should introduce themselves as 'Bernard MacNamara'. They replied some days later by sending me a photograph of a hand-painted pathetic daub, intended as the Goya, with the front page of the *Sunday Independent* included. It was immediately clear that I was dealing with idiots: they had not even had the sense to buy a print of the picture from the Gallery shop and attempt to fool me with that. I was, again, to reply by depositing £25,000 in the barrel at midnight on Friday 1 August.

As the trail was so manifestly false, the negotiation, as far as I was concerned, was now concluded and I had no need to involve myself further. In spite of that, the Inspector asked me to make a further drop-off in reply. This, I refused to do but offered to lend my car (and my jacket if necessary) to the Gardaí so that they could pursue things themselves. They borrowed the car on 1 August. I never enquired as to what was the outcome but some few days later 'Bernard MacNamara' called me.

'You informed the Gardaí,' he said, 'and you were warned not to do that. There will be consequences.'

And the phone went dead.

I suppose I was anxious in the weeks following this drama but I did not keep any notes of how I felt or of anything else that took place. I was certainly vulnerable. My flat fronted Merrion Square, which was largely deserted at night and it was easy for anyone to observe if I was at home. It would also have been simple to gain access to the house, which was also largely deserted. When I would return late at night, I would look about me before getting out of my car. By communicating with the criminals, I had placed myself in danger. (Jennifer Guinness, the wife of a wealthy Guinness banker, had been kidnapped by armed criminals in Dublin three months previously; and in 1983 one of the Task Force and a soldier had been killed in the shootout that occurred in the rescue of the kidnap victim Don Tidey.) But, dispirited that the Beit paintings were still missing, I got on with things in the Gallery and resolved to put my midnight adventure out of my mind.

But I did wonder, what had things come to? I was the director of Ireland's National Gallery and yet I was reduced to careering around the Irish countryside in the middle of the night in pursuit of petty, fifth-rate armed criminals. What had happened to my lovely career as a museum professional? Where was the civilised and privileged existence I had had in London? Something had gone wrong with my life. I was sure of that.

Subsequent to my adventure in and around Moone, I was involved in one further attempt to recover the Beit paintings. The scenario this time was altogether less dangerous, or at least it seemed so, and the pursuit moved across the Atlantic to New York. Unfortunately I did not, at the time, write an account of what happened (I was rather fed up and despairing of the whole Beit saga by this stage) and I have only the vaguest recollection of the incident; but my memory is jogged by an article in *Spy*[5] magazine.

Paul Quatrochi is a New York art dealer and agent who would have only been in his late-twenties at the time I had dealings, directly or indirectly, with him. In some of the deals he made at this time he was joined by a friend, an attorney in his fifties, Tom Andrews, who had an office in a brownstone off Madison Avenue (Number 1015 to be precise) on the Upper East Side of Manhattan. Andrews is described in *Spy* as 'about five foot ten and thin (with) a florid face ... and never without a cigarette. According to one friend, he carries a gun.' According to *Spy*:

> somehow, Paul Quatrochi became the intermediary for
> someone who wanted to ransom the Beit paintings and,
> impressed at how Andrews handled another job (involving
> the sale of a dubious Modigliani sculpture) they called on

him for this job. Tom Andrews contacted a leading British lawyer and asked him to approach the Irish Government on his behalf. The price for the return of the works was one million British pounds. Andrews and Quatrochi denied and still deny that they were to receive any of this money. At a meeting at Andrews's office in New York, Homan Potterton, then director of the National Gallery of Ireland, offered to pay about $350,000 to bring the paintings back to Ireland: Quatrochi and Andrews rejected that figure. Potterton then asked that a special agent of the FBI's anti-terrorist unit in New York become involved. Quatrochi and Andrews both say they were about to be locked up but avoided this fate by identifying an Irish national as the person they had been representing. The Irishman was subsequently incarcerated in federal prison on drug charges. This time Quatrochi and Andrews failed.

My memory revived by this article, I recall that the 'leading British lawyer' contacted by Andrews was no less a person than Lord Goodman.[6] His name (even though he was not at all involved) meant that this ransom demand was taken very seriously when it was passed to the Irish police. I was approached by the Gardaí, and asked to act.

As I was not anxious to become involved in another silly (and potentially dangerous) goose-chase in respect of the paintings, I asked that Andrews send me up-to-date photographs of the paintings, which would establish that he was acting on behalf of the real thieves. This he did, sending me on 15 January 1988 nine photographs (followed by a tenth) of the paintings out of their frames. 'I look forward to receiving your comments,' he wrote, 'and my client is prepared to work directly with you should you wish to proceed further with the matter.' I was satisfied that the photographs were genuine: the pictures had never been photographed, as far as I knew, by anyone else out of their frames and so I arranged to meet with Andrews in New York (on 24 February 1988). Through the Gardaí (Inspector Moore) I did, however, ask that I would be accompanied by some form of police presence and that is how an undercover FBI agent was with me.

At the meeting, I would have offered – with the approval of Bill

Finlay – to pay a ransom on behalf of the Gallery, the Government, or the Beits, (as I had done in the case of the Kildare criminals): it was necessary to do so in order to keep any negotiation alive. But it was an open question, in my book at least, as to whether any such ransom would ever be paid.

If the *Spy* article is to be trusted, subsequent to my meeting with him, Andrews – alarmed by the involvement of the FBI – backed off. Certainly I do not recall any further contact with him.

The Beits were in London at the time of the Cahill robbery. Interviewed by the press, Sir Alfred declared: 'I cannot think other than that one of these sort of revolutionary movements are behind the theft and they are seeking a ransom which they won't get. It is not me that has been robbed this time – it is the Irish people, since the collection is now in trust for the State.'

The significance of his words – 'the collection is now in trust for the State' – and the exact meaning of them, was ignored by the public and the press. It was deemed not to be news. It had for long been widely believed that, in establishing the Alfred Beit Foundation ten years previously and subsequently opening Russborough to the public, the pictures had already been given to the State. But, as far as I was concerned, Sir Alfred had used his words carelessly. By 'in trust for the State' he meant held by The Argus Trust for the National Gallery; but it was to be another six months (from May 1986) before the paintings were transferred to the Argus Trust and at this stage even the governors and guardians of the National Gallery knew nothing about the proposed gift and nor did the Irish public.

One morning Bill and I went down to Russborough to talk things over with the Beits. We arrived at eleven. I expected (and longed for) coffee. Instead a tray with a decanter of port and four glasses was brought in and we sipped that. I remarked on it to Bill in the car coming home and said that I had not come across port at eleven before. He assured me that it was completely normal and that he was always offered port (never coffee) when he went shooting.

The Cahill robbery did not shake the Beits in their resolve to proceed with the gift to the gallery and, furthermore, the gift would include the four missing paintings: the Vermeer, the two by Metsu, and the Goya. But it was not until the December 1987 meeting of the Board of

Governors and Guardians that the actual presentation was made. I am not sure if all the members of the board fully comprehended the momentousness of the moment: they too may have been confused, believing that the paintings had long since been gifted to the State. I asked the gallery photographer, Michael Olohan to be on hand after the meeting and he took a photograph of the Beits with Bill Finlay and myself in front of the Gainsborough. I would have liked the photograph to have been in front of the Goya so that *Doña Antonia Zárate*, on a third count, would have been special to Lady Beit. But, in order to have achieved that, we would have had to make our way to an attic in Tallaght.

I never met the Beits again after I retired from the gallery in June 1988 and had no further contact with them. I treasured the memory of the small dinner they gave for me and Lady Beit's 'few words'. But I was despondent that their magnificent generosity in presenting the pictures to the gallery was diminished by the fact that four of the paintings were missing: their loss detracted greatly from the triumph of the occasion as far as I was concerned. In the gallery, we catalogued all seventeen paintings and they were exhibited as part of an exhibition of *Acquisitions 1986–1988* in June 1988. In the preface to the catalogue, I wrote:

> The simple title *Acquisitions 1986–1988* is so understated as to be almost comic; and it rather implies that it is the policy and practice of the Gallery to acquire on an annual basis world-famous masterpieces by such artists as Vermeer, Velázquez, Murillo, and Goya. That is not to mention a few sundry items such as Gainsborough's *Cottage Girl*, a major Jacob van Ruisdael, and a Hobbema masterpiece. In no single year since the foundation of the Gallery in 1854 has it acquired such an array of masterpieces and indeed one would be so bold as to claim that few galleries anywhere, or at any time, can ever have had such acquisitions within such a short space of time. These extraordinary circumstances have arisen, not through some astonishing act of irresponsible generosity on the part of the Irish Government, but through the munificence of Sir Alfred and Lady Beit.

James Lees-Milne has written about a curious conversation which he had with the Duke of Beaufort in 1989.[7] The Duke told him that 'Alfred Beit wanted a mistress but could not afford one.' At this time, Sir Alfred was 86 and surely beyond such longings but the Duke may have been recalling some earlier confession on Sir Alfred's part. Next, the Duke asked Lees-Milne if 'Alfred was really rich at all.' This comes as something of a surprise. Could it be that the Beits at the end of their lives were not wealthy any more? Might their great fortune have been dissipated by decades of living an extravagant life of leisure without gainful employment, maintaining homes in London, South Africa and Ireland, their trust funds managed (or mismanaged) by solicitors and accountants? To the best of my knowledge, Sir Alfred did not provide the Alfred Beit Foundation with the endowment needed to maintain Russborough in perpetuity. Perhaps, no more than a mistress, he could not afford it.

Sir Alfred died, aged 91, on 12 May 1994. Probate taken out in London shows that his estate was valued at £403,315. Lady Beit survived him by more than ten years: she died, aged 89, on 17 August 2005. Her estate came to more than £7 million. For supposedly wealthy people, these were relatively small amounts. True, their real wealth may have been hidden in trust funds, foreign companies and the like; but nevertheless there may have been something in what the Duke of Beaufort said and the Beits may have been 'in reduced circumstances' at the end of their days.

Both Beits are buried, near Russborough, in St Mary's Churchyard, Blessington.

In 1994, Martin Cahill was shot and killed, probably by the IRA, in broad daylight, while seated in his car near his home in Ranelagh, south Dublin.

Rose Dugdale is still alive.

I have avoided any further contact with the criminal world.

And the Beit Pictures, all seventeen of them, are on display in the National Gallery of Ireland.

Endnotes

1. It has been well researched and written, together with an account of the robberies, by Matthew Hart, *The Irish Game: a True Story of Crime and Art* (2004).

2. My flat, really only a room, was photographed by Walter Pfeiffer and published in a book by Marianne Heron, *In the Houses of Ireland* (1988).

3. In 1983 Don Tidey, the Chief Executive of Associated British Foods, was kidnapped in Dublin and held for twenty-two days. He was rescued following a shootout between a Garda taskforce and the kidnappers.

4. In his book, *The General: Godfather of Crime* (2013), Paul Williams, without mentioning me, refers to this operation and states that the gang was connected to Cahill. But he also states that the ransom demand was £100,000 and that 'a bunch of old papers' was deposited in the barrel. Not by me, they weren't.

5. John Connolly with Nick Rosen, 'Scumbag Descending a Staircase', *Spy*, October 1992.

6. Arnold Goodman (1913–95), a lawyer and, for decades, at the very heart of the British Establishment. One-time chairman of the Arts Council, deputy chairman of the British Council, chairman, English National Opera and Master of University College, Oxford.

7. James Lees-Milne (ed.), Michael Bloch, *Careless Turmoil: Diaries 1983–92* (2004).

CHAPTER 19
My Knitting in the Fire

When I was a very small boy, I developed an enthusiasm for knitting. Not complicated knitting – I never learned to turn the heel of a sock or manage a Raglan sleeve – but simple 'one plain, one purl', which used up the remnants in my mother's knitting-basket and resulted in long, very long, multicoloured scarves.

As a very large family, and before the days when television dominated family life, we would all sit around the fire in the evenings, my mother darning socks, my big sister Alice reading, my other sister, Rosina, sitting quietly, my older brothers playing Monopoly or cards, my father working in his office adjacent; and me, knitting. On one such evening – and I do not remember this but my mother never forgot it – when the peace of the room was only interrupted by occasional shouts from the direction of the Monopoly table, I suddenly jumped up from where I had been sitting on the sofa and threw my knitting, needles and all, into the fire. There was a huge whoosh, an alarming crackling as the needles curled in the heat, and flames leapt out of the fire-grate towards the hearthrug. In an instant, Alice – her book hurriedly discarded – was on her knees with the tongs attempting to salvage the charred remains of my labours and, more anxiously, prevent the chimney going on fire.

'For goodness sake Homan!' my mother exclaimed, 'what is it now? What on earth has possessed you?'

'I hate knitting,' I blubbed.

My brothers got up from the games table and crowded round the sofa laughing.

'Is that what the pattern book says you are to do,' one of them jeered.

'The scarf looks better to me now that it's a bit singed,' said another.

Alice had retrieved it by then and it lay, a molten ball of black, on the tiles of the hearth.

'You are the very limit,' my mother said, 'typical. You might have set the house on fire.'

But for all her life she remembered the incident with laughter.

'I can still see Alice crouched down on the floor trying to fish the knitting out of the fire,' she would say. 'But you know, that is what you were like. You would fly off the handle for no reason at all. Of course, it didn't help that the others always teased you.'

What had happened was that I had dropped one stitch too many and the holes in the scarf were beginning to make it look like crochet. I became dissatisfied, I was fed up with trying to get it right, it was no use. In an instant, I decided that I was finished with knitting.

The episode, in a way, became a metaphor for my life and there have been other times over the decades when I have, so to speak, thrown my knitting in the fire. And eight years on from becoming Director of Ireland's National Gallery – with all the frustrations that attended that role – was one of those times.

I had become terrified that some major disaster in the Gallery was looming: a conflagration caused by the out-of-date electrical wiring or, more dramatically, a spectacular criminal raid and daylight robbery of the gallery. There had, a year or so previously, been a raid during opening hours at the Hugh Lane Gallery in Dublin. I had been unsettled – and considerably unnerved – by my Beit escapade in County Kildare at midnight. The dilapidated and dangerous state of the building, constant union negotiations, staff dissatisfaction, government cuts and more cuts, my salary taxed at 67 per cent, the impossibility of it all became the 'dropped plain-and-purl' of my existence: there were, for my liking, too many holes in the scarf I had been trying to knit and it was time to throw it in the fire.

And that is what I did. Not so precipitously as I had done as a small boy – life had taught me to have some patience – but in the fire nonetheless.

My frustration (not to mention the shame it caused me personally) at not being able to get the Gallery made safe or even clean-looking – much less completely refurbished – is well-documented in the Minutes of the Board. As early as February 1981, I brought to the Board's attention that the electrical wiring was outdated and dangerous and that the Office of Public Works, at my request, were examining it; and in April 1981 I reported that 'environmental conditions are unsatisfactory and do not even approach accepted standards for a museum environment. I have approached the Board of Works in the matter and they have expressed their concern.' 'Concern', and little more, was all that the Office of Public Works expressed and continued to express over the years that followed (documented consistently in the Board Minutes). By October 1986 the Governors and Guardians 'expressed their deep concern that the necessary plans for the refurbishment of the Gallery being prepared by the Office of Public Works would not be ready to go to tender until mid-1987 and that work could not commence on the scheme until September 1987'. December 1986: 'The Board expressed concern over the possible further postponement of the date of commencement of the refurbishment and proposed that a letter be drafted to the Taoiseach outlining their concern over the situation.' Then in May 1987 'the Director informed the Board that new discussions were in hand based on a smaller-scale scheme which would, in the light of the response from the Departments of the Taoiseach and Finance, be more-realistically viable.' In October 1987 the Director reported through the Chairman that 'the recent Government Estimates do not provide for the refurbishment. However, the Secretary of the Department of the Taoiseach has given an assurance that when National Lottery proceeds would be allocated, some funds would be designated for the refurbishment scheme.'

By this stage, however, I had come to the conclusion that no refurbishment would take place in the foreseeable future, that it was merely a Civil Service merry-go-round, and that I was wasting my time – and my life. In a calm and reasoned (to myself) way, I decided to resign.

I told Bill Finlay a year ahead of the date I planned to leave and said I would give the Board nine months' notice. Bill said very little. He no doubt wanted to 'turn things over in his mind'. He was not someone who liked the *status quo* to be disturbed, he had found that I worked well with him, and he was (I knew) proud of being Chairman of the Gallery as it functioned under my Directorship. On a personal level, he was not someone who cared for emotional involvement so that, although I am sure he liked me, it was not at all in his nature to have any deep discussion with me concerning my frustrations. He knew, because I told him, that it was the postponed refurbishment plans that were the straw that had broken the camel's back; and that was it as far as he was concerned. He did ask me to defer my decision and then, when the time came, he asked me to defer it again; and that I refused to do. I wrote to him (17 November 1987) to emphasise that I would be leaving:

> Today you have asked me to postpone my decision again ... but I really think to give the Board less than six months' notice would be seen, both by the Board and by the general public, as very shabby of me and, as I am decided to go in June, I must tell the Board at the December meeting. If Lottery Funds are made available for the refurbishment scheme, it is most important that a new Director would be in office from the beginning to oversee the work. I certainly would not be saying publicly that I was leaving because of frustration with the Board of Works; but the Taoiseach's Office would know it. If anything, my leaving might be a further persuasive factor in seeing to it that the money would be allocated.

Having finalised the matter with Bill, I arranged to have lunch in London with Terence de Vere White in order to tell him. But Bill may already have apprised Terence of the fact as, when I said to Terence, 'there is something I want to share with you and I hope you will not be too disappointed in me', he immediately interrupted me: 'You are going to resign,' he said.

We had some small amount of discussion but he did not try to dissuade me. He did know, after all, from my letters to him before I was ever appointed, that the Directorship might never be what 'I asked of life' as he had put it. And he left it at that.

I did not discuss my decision with any of my friends. I told my mother one evening when visiting her. 'That's a big step,' she said, 'are you sure? You've always made your own decisions but I've seen for myself that you are always worried and it's not right for a young man to have such worries as you have.' But I had made up my mind and I did not want to be dissuaded. It was, I was convinced, the right thing for me to do. It was also my intention that I would 'go quietly'. I would not barter. I would not issue any ultimatums: 'either the Gallery refurbishment is put in hand immediately or I resign'. That, I knew, would be very foolish. I had done my best, and I had failed. It was for someone else to try instead. 'In the circumstances, I feel that I have done all for the Gallery that I can do,' was the line I took and that was what I said to the Board in announcing to them that I was resigning. My announcement left them nonplussed. For the most part, they said nothing. Only the painter, Tom Ryan, spoke up.

'Chairman, there is something about this that we are not being told,' he said in his forthright manner.

He was quite angry.

'There must be reasons behind this. The Director can't just sit here and tell us that he has done all that he can for the Gallery, and that he is leaving. Chairman, we need an explanation.'

'It's the Director's decision,' was all that Bill would say.

Sixteen years later, Peter Somerville-Large was reduced to writing that 'the reasons for my leaving were obscure'.

Following the Board Meeting, I asked the staff to come to my office and I told them. Then too there was silence but Raymond Keaveney (who would succeed me as Director) wrote me a very generous letter afterwards (14 December 1987).

> Your announcement last Friday took us all somewhat by surprise and left us each a little speechless, as you no doubt noticed. I myself, although aware that you were unhappy with the lack of progress and cooperation on a number of important projects, never thought that you would resign, since you always managed in the past to devise some ingenious strategy to circumvent the apathy and bureaucratic maze which bedraggles even the most minor of undertakings in the Gallery. In some ways your resignation could be seen both as a good career decision and as an act of self-sacrifice, as there is no doubt that the list of achievements you have accomplished over the short

eight years you have been here would look impressive on any C.V., while there can be little doubt that the powers that be will have to seriously reconsider their attitude to Gallery matters in the light of your decision to resign and the reasons which provoked that decision. Regardless of what is said to you over the next six months, or so, before your departure, I for my part wish to let you know that the past eight years have unquestionably been the most fruitful and satisfying of my life, and I must thank you for allowing me to achieve all that I did during your time as Director. Yet it is not simply what I have personally achieved under your directorship that I must be thankful for, but also for the benefit of watching you yourself operate and run the Gallery, your pursuit of its welfare and your constant struggle and vigilance with Government departments and other bodies to protect its interests, regardless of the personal consequences.

Michael Wynne also set pen to paper (11 December 1987):

You set an example in scholarship and positively encouraged it among those who could possibly add to it. In this area I have tried to do my best. Never have I felt such support than since you took over the Directorship. For this I shall always be grateful.

Although I was careful not to state publicly that it was the shocking condition of the Gallery that had occasioned my resignation, word somehow leaked out that that was the case and that the Gallery was, in fact, a scandal. The journalist, John Armstrong, informed himself very thoroughly on the issue and wrote an article in *The Irish Times*[1] and RTÉ made a half-hour documentary which was shown at prime time. Dramatic footage showed holes in the roof which allowed rain through to the galleries below, paintings that had warped or flaked through ineffective air-conditioning, filthy and decades-old wall-coverings in almost every gallery, and other horrors. I was interviewed for the programme but took care not to appear intemperate. Senator Katherine

Bulbulia brought the matter up in the Seanad.[2] She spoke eloquently, setting out the situation in no uncertain terms, and her contribution – being a detailed record – is worth quoting.

> I am very disturbed indeed by recent reports that paintings in the Gallery are deteriorating. They are flaking, cracking and warping because of failures in what has now become an obsolete air-conditioning system. This system breaks down frequently and, because there is no refrigeration plant, the rapid change and fluctuations in temperature levels and humidity cause the wood or canvas backings of some paintings to crack and warp. Homan Potterton, who I am sorry to say has announced his forthcoming retirement, has gone on record and described conditions in the National Gallery as a national disgrace. Homan Potterton is not an alarmist, He is not given to exaggeration and he is not a self-seeking publicist. He does care very deeply about the Gallery and about its contents and he has done a tremendous job in his time in promoting the Gallery and attracting people to it. Homan Potterton, in speaking on the Gallery and the Collection therein described the condition of some pictures, due to damp, as extremely distressing. I was distressed to read this and I think it is important to draw the attention of the Minister to the situation. I know funds are short and we have certain agreed parameters of expenditure but still it is important that Ministers should know what is going on, where the difficulties lie, and the costs involved. There will be no point when some of these pictures are damaged beyond repair in involving ourselves in a great hand-wringing exercise. That would be too late . . . I understand that recently the Government postponed indefinitely a major £5 million refurbishment plan for the Gallery which was to include the installation of a new air-conditioning system. We have all been overjoyed with the recent munificent Beit Gift, it is currently hanging in Room 28 on the ground floor, next to Room 30 where some of the

largest humidity fluctuations have been recorded. I have taken pains to deal at some length with the problems [in the Gallery] . . . and the effect . . . on the paintings which are the treasure of the Nation, which belong to all of us, and which have been entrusted to the Government to maintain, care and house in appropriate and fitting circumstances. I would ask the Minister to take it to heart.

At the December 1987 meeting of the Governors and Guardians, I announced that the Beit Collection was being presented to the Gallery. It was at the same meeting that I gave six months' notice that I was resigning. Then at my penultimate Board Meeting, in April 1988, I announced that the Minister for State at the Department of Finance (Noel Treacy) had visited the Gallery and had been shown the deplorable condition of the building for himself. However, at my last Board Meeting, in June 1988, I left it to Bill Finlay to make the announcements, and this he did.

The Department of Finance had allocated £5.6 million for the first phase of a Gallery refurbishment.

It appeared that my resignation (one way or another) had produced the result, which eight years of lobbying on my part had failed to do. But it was too late for me. I no longer cared. Like the knitting of my childhood, I was burnt out. I only knew that I wanted to walk away.

In my last weeks, many friends gave wonderful leaving parties for me – it became almost a Season – and I was made aware of the warm friendships I had established in Ireland during my eight years. I was reminded of the marvellous, and very privileged, life that I had led there and how lucky I had been. James and Aggie White were invited to most of these parties but James could hardly bring himself to speak to me, such was his disappointment in me. It was noticeable and made me feel disappointed for his sake too. The Governors and Guardians gave a dinner for me in No 90 Merrion Square, the house which I had persuaded them to buy with Shaw Funds and which I had had renovated. Wives were invited and I think that this may have been the first occasion that Victoria Glendinning appeared officially in Dublin as Mrs de Vere White. I brought out the showy Milltown silver and had it polished by Weir's: tureens, candelabra, flagons, fruit dishes, platters were used to decorate the tables. Bill Finlay or Terence de Vere White made a speech and presented me with a silver salver. It was a generous gift that I appreciated, although I did not care for the modern design and the kind inscription had been engraved askew. Victoria noticed my reaction.

'You didn't like the salver,' she whispered to me afterwards.

With the eye of a writer, she also noticed that I had not particularly enjoyed the evening, that in my mind I was already far away. She said it to me and she was right. The affection in which I had once held the Gallery had evaporated.

A few days later, emptying my office, and packing my bags, I put my eight eventful Dublin years behind me and left Ireland for other shores.

Endnotes

1. 15 January 1988.
2. Seanad Report, vol. 118, 20 January 1988.

APPENDIX

Books

1975 *Irish Church Monuments, 1570–1880* (Ulster Architectural Heritage Society).

1976 *A Guide to the National Gallery* (National Gallery, London Publications).

1976 *Reynolds and Gainsborough: Themes and Painters in the National Gallery* (National Gallery, London Publications).

1977 *The National Gallery, London* (Thames & Hudson).

1978 *Pageant and Panorama: The Elegant World of Canaletto* (Phaidon Press).

1978 Conjoint author (with Peter Harbison and Jeanne Sheehy), *Irish Art and Architecture: from Prehistory to the Present Day* (Thames & Hudson).

1979 *Grandes Museos del Mundo: National Gallery, London* (Ediciones Danae, Barcelona).

1981 Conjoint author (with Raymond Keaveney, Adrian Le Harivel and Anne Millar), *National Gallery of Ireland: 50 Pictures* (National Gallery of Ireland Publications).

1981 Edited with an Introduction, *National Gallery of Ireland, Illustrated Summary Catalogue of Paintings* (National Gallery of Ireland Publications).

1983 Edited with an Introduction, *National Gallery of Ireland, Illustrated Summary Catalogue of Drawings, Watercolours and Miniatures* (National Gallery of Ireland Publications).

1986 *Dutch Seventeenth and Eighteenth Century Paintings in the*

National Gallery of Ireland: a Complete Catalogue (National Gallery of Ireland Publications).

2001 *Rathcormick:A Childhood Recalled* (New Island).

2006 *Potterton People and Places: Three Centuries of an Irish Family* (Choice Publishing).

Exhibition Catalogues and Pamphlets

1973 'The O'Connell Monument' (Gifford & Craven, Dublin).

1974 'Andrew O'Connor, Sculptor' (Catalogue of an exhibition, Trinity College, Dublin).

1975 'Caravaggio's Supper at Emmaus' (Painting in Focus exhibition, The National Gallery, London).

1976 'Pictures from Eighteenth Century Venice' (Catalogue of an exhibition for the Arts Council of Great Britain shown at Bristol, Wolverhampton and Norwich).

1977 'Meisterwerke Venezianischer Malerei' (Catalogue of a loan exhibition from the National Gallery, London shown at the Wallraf-Richartz Museum, Cologne).

1979 'Venetian Seventeenth Century Painting' (Catalogue of a loan exhibition at the National Gallery, London).

1987 'Dutch Paintings of the Golden Age from the Collection of the National Gallery of Ireland' (Catalogue of an exhibition for the Smithsonian Institution Traveling Exhibition Service shown at seven venues in the US).

1988 'The Beit Pictures' (in National Gallery of Ireland: Recent Acquisitions) (National Gallery of Ireland exhibition catalogue).

Articles in Periodicals

1972 'A New Classical Decorative Scheme: G.B. Cipriani at Lansdowne House', *Apollo* (October 1972).

'A new pupil of Edward Pierce', *Burlington Magazine* (December 1972).

'A little-known Irish memorial', *Country Life* (28 December 1972). 'William Kidwell, sculptor, and some contemporary mason-sculptors in Ireland', *Irish Georgian Society Quarterly Bulletin* (July–Dec. 1972).

1973   'An American sculpture at the Dublin Exhibition of 1865: Harriet Hosmer's Sleeping Faun', The Arts in Ireland (Autumn 1973).

1974   'The Monuments of Andrew O'Connor', *Country Life* (3 January 1974).

'Garrick as Roscius', *Country Life* (7 February 1974).

'The Sculpture Collection (in the National Gallery of Ireland)', *Apollo* (February 1974).

'Sir Frederick Burton at the National Gallery', *Country Life* (9 May 1974).

'Dublin's Vanishing Monuments', *Country Life* (23 May 1974).

'American Sculptures in the National Gallery of Ireland', *The Arts in Ireland* (Autumn 1974).

'A commonplace practitioner in etching and engraving: Charles Exshaw', *The Connoisseur* (December 1974).

1976   'Reynolds's portrait of Capt Robert Orme in the National Gallery', *Burlington Magazine* (February 1976).

1978   'Canaletto's views of S Geremia and the entrance to the Cannaregio', *Burlington Magazine* (July 1978).

1979   'A Saraceni for the National Gallery', *Burlington Magazine* (January 1979).

Aspects of Venetian seicento painting', *Apollo* (November 1979).

1982   'Recently-cleaned Dutch pictures in the National Gallery of Ireland', *Apollo* (February 1982).

1984   'New acquisitions at the National Gallery of Ireland', *Irish Arts Review*, vol. 1 (1984).

1989   'Museum News: New York, New York', *Apollo* (April 1989).

'Drawings from a Queen's collection', *Apollo* (May 1989).

'Fracas at the Frick', *Apollo* (June 1989).

'Inigo Jones in SoHo', *Apollo* (July 1989).

'The very model of a modern art museum: the Kimbell Art Museum', *Apollo* (October 1989).

'Corporate Wrights', *Apollo* (December 1989).

1990   'Canaletto at the Metropolitan Museum' exhibition review, *Burlington Magazine* (January 1990).

1991 'Friedrich versus Bierstadt', *Apollo* (April 1991).

'The Fauve Landscape: from London to the Cote d'Azur', *Apollo* (June 1991).

'Corot to Monet', *Apollo* (July 1991).

'From Nolde to Manet: an unprejudiced collection', *Apollo* (September 1991).

'Northern European Paintings in the Philadelphia Museum' and 'Peintres Hollandaises au Musée de Bordeaux', *Burlington Magazine* (September 1991).

'The Morgan Library Expands', *Apollo* (November 1991).

'Nathaniel Hone and John Quinn: A correspondence' *in Art is my Life: A tribute to James White* (Dublin 1991).

1992 Fra Bartolommeo Drawings' exhibition review, *Apollo* (April 1992).

1993 'Jack B. Yeats and John Quinn', *Irish Arts Review*, vol. 9 (1993).

1994 'Letters from St Louis: Ireland's exhibit at the St Louis World's Fair 1904', *Irish Arts Review*, vol. 10 (1994).

1996 'Aloysius O'Kelly in America', *Irish Arts Review*, vol. 12 (1996).

2002 'Suggestions of Concavity: William Trevor as Sculptor', *Irish Arts Review*, vol. 18 (2002).

2003 Obituary, James White (1913–2003), *Burlington Magazine* (September 2003).

2011 'Tutor to the Edgeworths: Rev. Frederic Potterton (1826–1912)' *Teathbha: Journal of the County Longford Historical Society*, vol. 3, no. 4.

2013 'In Lunacy of Potterton', James Joyce Online Notes, No. 5 (September 2013). The same article published as 'In Lunacy of Potterton: a County Meath link to Joyce's Ulysses', *Ríocht na Midhe, Records of Meath Archaeological and Historical Society*, vol. 25 (2014).

INDEX OF PERSONS